The Saving Truth

Kurt E. Marquart

TRUTH, SALVATORY AND CHURCHLY
Works of Kurt E. Marquart

Ken Schurb, Editor
Robert Paul, Assistant Editor

I

The Saving Truth

Doctrine for Laypeople

Luther Academy

ISBN: 978-1-935035-15-2

Printed in the United States of America
Lulu.com

"Truth for the Formula of Concord is salvatory and churchly. This means that it is neither a matter of individual, virtuoso brilliance nor one of social accommodation, academic nicety or bureaucratic formality. The truth is God's, and the church is God's, and he creates and cultivates his church by means of his truth. The church and the truth belong inseparably together."

$\sim$ Kurt E. Marquart

from his essay
"The Contemporary Significance of the Formula of Concord"

CONTENTS

FOREWORD

By The Rev. Matthew C. Harrison, D.D., LL.D.
Assistant Pastor, Village Lutheran Church, Ladue, Missouri
President, The Lutheran Church—Missouri Synod

The editor of this volume has requested that I provide a foreword, first wearing my "former Kurt Marquart student hat," then shifting to my "synod president hat."

Kurt Marquart, more than anyone else, put the fire in my belly for the Lutheran confession. I had arrived on the Fort Wayne seminary campus in the fall of 1985 knowing less than nothing. I was immediately thrown into a first-year dogmatics (doctrine) course with "Dr., I mean, Professor Marquart." (I only called him "Kurt" some twenty years later, well into my tenure as Executive for World Relief and Human Care.)

His method in that course was quite simple. In preparation for each class period, he assigned us to read about 10–20 pages of Franz Pieper's *Christian Dogmatics*. Before the period began he would emerge from his office in the "tunnel" underground between the two classroom buildings, but he usually got to class just a minute or two late because students had cornered him enroute to ask questions about this or that theological conundrum. He always seemed to be followed by several students who wanted answers to questions. Kurt had a theological clarity that transfixed his students, most of whom were struggling out of experiences of poor catechesis and worse pietistic practice.

We'd be waiting when he entered the classroom, always wearing a black shirt (usually a bit faded), round collar and black suit. Thin, head jutting forward (which made him look as though always leaning into an issue), he would proceed to the lectern and place on it one of the green volumes of

Pieper's *Dogmatics*. Grasping the lectern with both hands, he'd clear his throat and bring the full class to attention. "Gentlemen . . . gentlemen. Right . . . Please prepare for a quiz." If this period came before morning chapel, he'd often slip in some remark about the ungodly early hour, for he very much preferred class times later in the day. Then would follow ten questions. Always ten, and often tricky. Always true or false, designed to make sure we had read the material. He would ask the final question, pause a few seconds, and say, "Right, then." We'd have our neighbors grade our quizzes as the class proceeded to go through the answers to the quiz questions one by one. Professor Marquart would use this opportunity for instruction. The papers would be handed in so they could be figured into our grades along with our class participation and exam scores.

I recall one occasion when a student was having difficulty grasping a particular but very significant point of Lutheran theology. The student apologized for taking the class's time. Marquart responded: "No need to apologize, dear brother. This is why we are here. You will be asked to swear unconditionally to the Lutheran confession. Now is the time for questions." We knew the confession was serious—more serious, in fact, than anything else.

Classes sometimes included stories from Kurt's pastorate in Toowoomba, Australia. Yet, much like Norman Nagel, he spoke little of himself. It wasn't until years later that I came to know that Kurt had been born in Estonia, fled communism as a boy and lived in a refugee camp in England. He studied in Bronxville, then at Concordia Seminary, St. Louis, before his first call to Texas. From there, he went to Toowoomba. All this produced an accent as intriguing and mesmerizing as the depth of his theology.

He had read Wilhelm Oesch particularly during his student years in the '50s, when seriously liberal winds had been blowing on the St. Louis campus. He was galvanized by Oesch especially on issues of biblical inerrancy and authority. Hermann Sasse influenced him deeply on matters sacramental and on issues of church fellowship. From Springfield, he once wrote J. A. O. Preus that he had learned "Biblical/Lutheran ecclesiology" from "Walther, Oesch, and Sasse (in that order)."[*] He had met Sasse at the 1959 LCMS Convention, and after a rocky start of a relationship with Sasse in Australia during the '60s, he came to be treasured by Sasse as a true colleague. When I was a student, Norman Nagel had just translated

* Kurt Marquart to J. A. O. Preus, 14 April 1976, Typescript, Walther Library, Concordia Theological Seminary, Fort Wayne.

the "We Confess" series of Sasse documents, and Kurt put us on to all of them and more. Kurt believed that C. F. W. Walther faithfully represented the ecclesiology of the New Testament, Luther, and the Lutheran Confessions. He taught us the dogmatic connections to the liturgy: *lex credendi, lex orandi* and vice-versa. He was fluent in Latin, German, and Russian. Where an insight from Eastern Orthodoxy—usually an historical quip from history—illuminated the sacramental truth of the New Testament and Lutheranism, he gladly shared it. We encountered all of this and much more in his classes.

After class he would exit, usually with a half dozen inquirers in tow, politely trying to answer as many questions as possible, making his way to the door and down the hall, down the stairs to his tunnel office, which was barren. No art. No pictures on the wall. Cold tile floor. Cinder block walls. Metal desk piled with books and papers. Metal file cabinet. Two chairs. Totally utilitarian. He preferred to do his work at home in the late hours.

After graduation with a Master of Divinity degree, I stayed on at Fort Wayne for Master of Sacred Theology (S.T.M.) studies. I became graduate assistant for the Systematics Department. It was 1989, just at the time of the ouster of my S.T.M. advisor, Dr. Robert Preus, from the seminary presidency. In the swirl of controversy, or as Kurt said it, con-TROV-ersy, Kurt was loyal to Robert. (So was I.) At the same time Kurt was also completely politically inept, or so I thought. His testimony was powerful, I later understood, in part due to his deep piety. I don't recall him ever saying a seriously negative word about anyone. This piety resulted in his only rarely spouting off about political/theological squabbles in the church. His heart beat for the theology of "the Gospel and all its articles." Amid the rise of the church growth inventories for pastoral skills, Kurt would ask, "But does he pray?"

Kurt's humor was unconquerable. In fact the genius of the Fort Wayne seminary, an ethos shaped by Dr. Preus, was raucous humor. It was a humor directed squarely at ourselves and most other sacred cows of the LCMS, and that got one or more of us in trouble from time to time. At the quarterly "Q" parties, students would incessantly make fun of their professors, bad theology and practice, political nonsense in the church, etc. Kurt participated fully, although on occasion eschewing excesses. Great theological discussion combined with self-deprecating humor was an ingenious and spontaneous mixture which produced an ethos on campus and loyalty to the school. As a former resident of Australia, Kurt also celebrated Guy Fawkes Day every year. The would-be destroyer of the English Parliament hung in effigy from a tree in the Marquart yard, scarecrow-like, and filled with fireworks. Moments before lighting the figure, Kurt said, "In case there is any unclarity, this is not Norb." (Dr. Norb Mueller had taken Dr. Preus's position as interim.) Kurt's sense of humor did not, however, extend to rock 'n roll. He forbade his children to listen to it, which they all proceeded to ignore (albeit on the sly). He loved bagpipes, and I beheld his delight when on a birthday his friends and family had arranged a whole bagpiping corps to come bellowing and marching up his driveway. He was patient and generous to a fault with foreign students, almost always siding with them no matter the cause.

One of the last times I recall seeing my venerable teacher was in the Lutheran Church—Missouri Synod International Center, some years before I was elected President. ALS was deeply affecting him. His dress had gone from clerical black to parachute pants and gold chains, and his eyes were darkening. He was increasingly frustrated by theological dilettantes wanting to import Eastern Orthodox or other categories into the LCMS. He was miffed at those who gave our own fathers short shrift, made the liturgy its own goal, and who rejected the clear, classic categories of Lutheran Orthodoxy. These things perturbed him because they obscure the Gospel.

As the president of the Synod, I am indebted to Kurt for all these things. And the future of the LCMS as a faithful church proclaiming Christ is dependent upon us happily appropriating the past with gusto (Walther's *Law and Gospel, Church and The Office of the Ministry,* Luther, Pieper, etc.), recognizing that all doctrine, all liturgy, all life in the church serves to proclaim the Gospel of free forgiveness in Christ, as Kurt loved to say, "achieved two thousand years ago, eight thousand miles away," and delivered here and now in Word and Sacrament.

I count myself eternally grateful to have known Kurt and to have been his student. Our Synod and the church around the world have been blessed to have known and heard him as well. May his legacy long endure, for it is the true legacy of the Gospel and the genius of the Lutheran confession!

EDITORIAL INTRODUCTION

"We're the practical sem."

I have lost track of the number of times I heard that sentence from the lips of Dr. Robert Preus while he served as President of Concordia Theological Seminary, Fort Wayne, Indiana. He used to say it as he recruited prospective students. So far as I know, never did he try to evade or avoid this well-worn nickname for the Springfield seminary. Even after the institution moved back to its original site of Fort Wayne under his direction, Preus continued to embrace the old nickname.

In so doing he redefined it somewhat, after the fashion of the classic Lutheran theologians he knew and loved. They insisted, in an amalgam Latin-and-Greek phase, that theology is a "habitus practicus theosdotos." "Practical" hardly amounted to "second-rate" where Robert Preus was concerned. On the contrary, the practical seminary thrived on the best instruction in biblical, doctrinal, and historical theology, all to inform pastoral practice.

Therefore Preus wanted men like Kurt Marquart to teach at Springfield–Fort Wayne. For no one agreed more strongly with Preus than Marquart. I can't count how many times I heard Marquart say that Christian doctrine is basically simple.

As Marquart taught the required seminary doctrine courses—in many ways, his favorites—he seemed determined to avoid unduly complicating matters. Forays into esoteric thought most often came only because some student had asked a question. Even then, though, Marquart soon reverted to what he called the "essentials." His own presentations turned out to be long on context, calling attention to the ways in which any particular doctrinal point was embedded in the great themes of God's revelation in Christ such as the Incarnation and the Trinity, Law and Gospel, justification by grace through faith, the means of grace, and the theology of the cross. Marquart understood very well that what he was teaching was God's own saving evangelical truth, the Gospel, in due distinction from the Law. One of his doctrine classes immediately before or after chapel doubled his students' devotional delight. "That's morning devotion right there," one said while leaving the day's class.

Nobody questioned the professor's erudition or his preparation, which showed themselves in his every verbal expression and via his practice of lecturing with few, if any, notes. Yet Marquart wore his learning lightly in the basic doctrine courses. His daily routine in the classroom was calculated to teach and reach each student before him. Those who sought greater depth could take electives. Or they could engage in more extensive theological reading, as Marquart routinely urged students to do. In the required classes, though, an experienced pastor was giving future pastors a demonstration of the way shepherding is done: simply and humbly, soberly but with good humor, holding forth in such a way as to be understood by everyone, making incisive application to contemporary circumstances and events, and above all, constantly riveting on the incarnate Savior and the marks of the church.

Not surprisingly, the prospect of a lay-level doctrine book by Professor Marquart was greeted warmly by many pastors and pastors-to-be. We were hearing about it already when I was a seminary student during the early 1980s. Despite some of the rumors, however, the book had not yet been written. It was never fully completed, although Marquart did finish drafting seven of his nine projected chapters by the time the project was scrubbed in the late 1980s. In this volume we are most pleased to publish these seven chapters, in an edited version, for the first time anywhere. They make up the lion's share of this book, all the chapters but two and three.

Ironically, the two never-written chapters were to have been on topics from seminary courses that Marquart had taught the most over the years. The projected titles for those chapters were "The Holy Trinity and Creation" and "The Person and Work of Jesus Christ." While it was tempting to try and fill in these gaps with what Marquart *might* have written on these topics for this doctrine book, we have not engaged in any such guessing games. In partial (and it is only partial) replacement for these two chapters, the present volume contains pieces on these subjects that had been composed for other purposes.

- Specifically regarding Christ, we have included a brief article that Marquart wrote called "The Incarnation of God." It is chapter three.

⁘ Regarding the doctrine of God, we have been so bold as to pull in a contribution by Marquart's mentor, friend, and former colleague and seminary president, Robert Preus. "The Living God" originated as a more scholarly paper, Preus's keynote presentation for an International Council on Biblical Inerrancy conference on "Applying the Scriptures." (Marquart spoke at this meeting too. His paper on "War" is in our volume three.) The Preus essay appears in edited form as chapter two. It is included here by the kind permission of the Alliance of Confessing Evangelicals.

In his manuscript Marquart most often quoted the Bible from the New International Version. These days it is no longer possible to obtain permission to print quotes from any edition of the NIV prior to the 2011 version, which of course Marquart never saw. In most cases this makes no significant difference, since the 2011 wording is either unaltered from the previous or the changes are slight. However, there are a handful of instances in which the present publication has quoted another translation. Biblical quotations from translations other than the NIV are marked as such in the text.

A word about style: Kurt Marquart spoke and wrote "the King's English" in more ways than one. One of these ways involves spelling. There has been no attempt to make Marquart's deployment of letters conform to contemporary American usage or, for that matter, to regularize his own spellings of certain words.

Volumes two and three of this set will offer various writings in which Marquart addressed himself to pastors and scholars. You can "take an elective" with those volumes and do more extensive reading in them. Start, however, with Marquart's profoundly well-considered presentation of doctrinal basics. It will benefit laypeople. Pastors too!

Ken Schurb

ABBREVIATIONS

AC	Augsburg Confession
AE	*Luther's Works* American Edition. 75 vols. Jaroslav Pelikan, Helmut T. Lehmann, and Christopher Boyd Brown, gen. editors. St. Louis: Concordia; Philadelphia: Fortress Press, 1955.
Ap	Apology of the Augsburg Confession
ASV	American Standard Version
The Church	Preus, Robert D., editor, and John R. Stephenson, assistant editor. *Confessional Lutheran Dogmatics*. Vol. IX, *The Church and Her Fellowship, Ministry, and Governance*, by Kurt E. Marquart. Fort Wayne, IN: The International Foundation for Lutheran Confessional Research, 1990.
Ep	Epitome (of the Formula of Concord)
Examination I	Chemnitz, Martin. *Examination of the Council of Trent* Part I. Translated by Fred Kramer. St. Louis: Concordia Publishing House, 1971.
Examination II	Chemnitz, Martin. *Examination of the Council of Trent* Part II. Translated by Fred Kramer. St. Louis: Concordia Publishing House, 1978.
FC	Formula of Concord
KJV	King James Version
LSB	Commission on Worship of The Lutheran Church—Missouri Synod. *Lutheran Service Book*. St. Louis: Concordia Publishing House, 2006.
LC	Large Catechism
NIV	New International Version
RSV	Revised Standard Version
SA	Smalcald Articles
SD	Solid Declaration (of the Formula of Concord)
Small Catechism	This refers to the 1986 translation of Martin Luther's Small Catechism in *LSB* and in: *Luther's Small Catechism with Explanation*. St. Louis: Concordia Publishing House, 1991.
SC	Small Catechism
St.L.	*Dr. Martin Luthers Saemmtliche Schriften*. 23 vols. Edited by Johann Georg Walch. St. Louis: Concordia Publishing House, 1881-1910.
Tappert	Tappert, Theodore G., translator and editor in collaboration with Jaroslav Pelikan, Robert H. Fischer, and Arthur C. Piepkorn. *The Book of Concord: The Confessions of the Evangelical Lutheran Church*. Philadelphia: Fortress Press, 1959.
Tr	Treatise on the Power and Primacy of the Pope
Triglot	*Concordia Triglotta*. St. Louis: Concordia Publishing House, 1921.
TLH	*The Lutheran Hymnal*. St. Louis: Concordia Publishing House, 1941.
WA	*D. Martin Luthers Werke. Kritische Gesamtausgabe*. Weimar, 1883.

The Saving Truth

Doctrine for Laypeople

Chapter One

HOLY SCRIPTURE

Book of Christ

Editor's note: We have not managed to locate pages 1 and 23 of Marquart's original typescript for this chapter. The chapter below begins with the first full paragraph as found on page 2 of the typescript. No attempt has been made to reconstruct the contents of page 1 except for the first section title below, which is an editorial contribution. The absence of typescript page 23 will be noted at the appropriate place below, not far into the chapter's second section.

THE INSPIRED SCRIPTURE
AND ITS THEME

Jesus Christ did not enter human history haphazardly. He came at the end of a long line of divine revelations, as the glorious Goal and Culmination of that line. For God had spoken "to our ancestors through the prophets at many times and in various ways, but in these last days he has spoken to us by his Son" (Heb. 1:1–2).

This finality of God's speaking by His Son means much more than a mere up-to-date-ness, the way a later news bulletin supersedes an earlier one. In His Son, God shows and gives Himself with a radical directness and intimacy, so that in the Son we see and hear what prophets and kings of old had longed to see and hear, but did not (Luke 10:24). God's ancient spokesmen, the prophets, were but sinful creatures who did not know the divine mysteries at first hand and even found them puzzling (1 Pet. 1:10–12). They simply repeated faithfully what God told them. It is very different with the Son, Who does not merely pass on words at second hand. He is Himself God, the eternal Word (John 1:1). Unlike mere prophets, He has the Spirit "without limit" (John 3:34). He speaks from personal knowledge and with absolute authority, for He alone "came from heaven" (John 3:13).

What the Son has come to impart to us, however, does not consist of lessons in cosmic engineering, a sort of theosophy stripped of its mumbo-jumbo. His knowledge of course embraces the ultimate secrets of our created universe's innermost recesses. Yet all this pales into insignificance before something infinitely more sublime: Jesus makes known to us the God whom no one else has seen, but with whom He shares Godhood (John 1:18; 6:46). The word for "making known" or "explaining" used in St. John 1:18 is the one from which we get our English words *exegete* and *exegesis*. Jesus, the God-Man, is the authentic Exegete of God on earth, attested at His transfiguration not only by Moses and Elijah, the representatives of the Law and the Prophets, but also by God the Father's own command: "Listen to him!" (Matt. 17:5).

Jesus therefore is not simply one topic among others in the Bible. As the Way, the Truth, and the Life (John 14:6), He is in fact the Theme and Content of this holy book from beginning to end. "All the prophets testify about him" (Acts 10:43). The Holy Scriptures testify to Jesus (John 5:39), and are therefore able to make us "wise for salvation through faith in Christ Jesus" (2 Tim. 3:15). This is why St. Paul "resolved to know nothing" in his missionary labour "except Jesus Christ and him crucified" (1 Cor. 2:2). Paul's faithful pupil Martin Luther echoed this sentiment fifteen hundred years later: "Take Christ out of the Scriptures, and what will you find left in them?"[1]

As Scripture's real Theme, Jesus also becomes the Key for its proper understanding and interpretation: "And beginning with Moses and all the Prophets, he explained to them what was said in all the Scriptures concerning himself" (Luke 24:27). The word for "explained" here has the same root as our word *hermeneutics*, the art and science of interpretation.

"Christians" (Acts 11:26; see 1 Pet. 4:16) do not bear that sacred name in vain. They belong to the Christ, through Whom came "grace and truth" (John 1:17), and Whose life-giving word and teaching makes them spiritually free (John 8:31–32). Their mother is the spiritual Jerusalem, who is free, unlike her counterpart under the Law (Gal. 4:26). Christ alone is the Head of His Bride, the church, and He is, in the strict sense of the word, her one authentic Teacher: "you have one Instructor, the Messiah" (Matt. 23:10). Life and liberty come from the Voice of the Good Shepherd alone. Bearers of other teachings are "ferocious wolves" (Matt. 7:15), "thieves and robbers" (John 10:8).

Christ Himself wrote down nothing. He left that to His *apostles*. (The word means "sent out," and was used of ambassadors with full power to act in the name of their king.) These men were not sent into the world to report their own personal views and impressions. They were equipped rather with Christ's own authentic message and teaching authority.

---

1. AE 33, 26.

Nothing was left to chance. After three years of intensive training in the Saviour's own "roving seminary," these men were promised the Holy Spirit. He would guide them into all truth (John 16:13). Their public testimony would not depend on their own, possibly faulty, reconstructions. The Spirit, Jesus said, "will teach you all things and will remind you of everything I have said to you" (John 14:26). Others would, until the end of time, come to faith "through their message" (John 17:20). Those who would keep the Saviour's teaching would keep the apostles' too (John 15:20), for these are not two teachings, but one and the same (John 16:15; 17:8–14). Together with St. Paul (Gal. 2:8), these apostles were to attest the truth about Jesus and His work of salvation, culminating in His triumphant resurrexion from the grave (Acts 1:21–22). Therefore the Christian church is built on the "foundation of the apostles and prophets, with Christ Jesus himself as the chief cornerstone" (Eph. 2:20). The holy church is *apostolic* (Nicene Creed). Whatever is not apostolic fails to be Christian (Gal. 1:8–9).

The apostles, and the "prophets" associated with them, wrote down their teaching so that all future generations of believers might "know the certainty of the things" being taught as the Good News of Christ (Luke 1:4). The documentary record of the New Testament is authenticated by the Lord's actual companions (1 Jn. 1:1–4). Their God-given proclamation (1 Cor. 2:13), now set down in writing, stands for all time as the objective source and standard for Christian teaching. For "these are written that you may believe that Jesus is the Messiah, the Son of God, and that by believing you may have life in his name" (John 20:31). Scripture, then, is the place where Christ teaches Christ most purely (Luther).[2]

Once the Bible has been properly located within the divine economy of salvation, it must be allowed to describe itself in more detail. It should be noted here that when the New Testament speaks of the "Scripture" or the "Scriptures," the reference is usually to what we now call the Old Testament. Yet already the later books of the New Testament itself apply these terms also to the earlier books of the New Testament (2 Pet. 3:16; also compare 1 Tim. 5:18 with Luke 10:7). Christ and His apostles always treated the Scriptures as the very Voice and Word of God Himself. The sacred text had for them ultimate, divine authority, beyond which there could be no appeal.

---

2. *Editor's note:* "Holy Scripture, especially the New Testament, always inculcates faith in Christ and magnificently proclaims Him" (AE 26, 146).

Christ Himself repeatedly cites all three of the customary subdivisions of the Old Testament: "The Law" (or "Moses"), "the Prophets," and "the Psalms," including the other poetical books. (See Luke 24:44.) In the case of the Pentateuch, Christ not only cites from it direct divine pronouncements (Matt. 15:4; 22:31–32), but also attributes the words of Moses to the Creator Himself (Matt. 19:4–5). Indeed, our Lord teaches that "It is easier for heaven and earth to disappear than for the least stroke of a pen to drop out of the Law" (Luke 16:17). Christ's own majestic "But I tell you" is aimed not against the written Law as such, but against false and superficial applications of it (Matt. 5:21 ff.; note that the addition "and hate your enemy" in St. Matthew 5:43 is found nowhere in the Old Testament). The Prophets, too, are always cited as authentic and authoritative, whether individually (Matt. 12:39; 24:15) or collectively (Luke 11:50–51; 16:29–31). The consistent claim of our Lord that He is "fulfilling" their prophecies necessarily includes truth-claims for these prophecies as genuine revelations of God's own will and purpose. (See Matt. 26:54–56; Luke 4:21; 18:31; 22:37.) The same is true, finally, of "the Psalms." Quoting the opening verse of Psalm 110, the Lord attributes it to "David, speaking by the Spirit" (Matt. 22:43). Quite revealing is the Saviour's treatment of Psalm 82:6. He argues from the exact wording here, in fact from the use of the word "gods," crediting God Himself with this choice of words. Jesus then rules out any possibility of dissent by invoking as self-evident the principle: "the scripture cannot be broken" (John 10:34–35 KJV).

The New Testament writers, of course, express exactly the same attitude toward the sacred Scriptures as did their divine Teacher. Their oft-repeated formula "It is written" takes for granted that what follows carries the full weight of God's own authority. The Saviour, it will be remembered, had used that same expression, a single word in Greek, to ward off the Tempter's interpretive wiles, which had worked so well in the case of the First Adam (Matt. 4:1–11; compare Gen. 3:1–6). The references to fulfilled prophecy in the Gospels and in Acts are simply too numerous to mention. St. Paul solemnly confesses that he believes "everything that is in accordance with the Law and that is written in the Prophets" (Acts 24:14). The Scriptures are the "oracles" (KJV) or the "very words" of God (Rom. 3:2). So closely is the sacred text identified with God Himself, that "Scripture" can simply stand for "God," as in Romans 9:17 ("Scripture says to Pharaoh") and in Galatians 3:8 ("Scripture foresaw").

Finally, there is the classic proof-passage, 2 Timothy 3:16, which really does not go in any way beyond what we have already seen to be the uniform approach to the sacred text: "All Scripture is God-breathed [or:

God-Spirited] and is useful for teaching, rebuking, correcting and train-ing in righteousness." From this text we get our English words *inspired* and *inspiration*. We have quite the same teaching in 2 Peter 1:21, that "prophecy never had its origin in the human will." Rather, it was as they were carried or borne along by the Holy Spirit that men spoke from God. It should be self-evident by now that if this "God-spiration" applies to the writings of the Old Testament, then all the more to that apostolic proclamation, "whether by word of mouth or by letter" (2 Thes. 2:15), which flows out of the very fullness of Pentecost itself! This Gospel about His Son God had "promised beforehand through his prophets in the Holy Scriptures" (Rom. 1:2). What those prophets foresaw for the future has "now been told you by those who have preached the gospel to you by the Holy Spirit sent from heaven" (1 Pet. 1:12).

According to Holy Scripture's testimony to itself, it is God's own very word, teaching, message, and truth. Scripture does not merely "contain" the divine Word. Nor does it "become" that Word when conditions are favorable. It *is* itself God's Word. Therefore Scripture never amounts to a mere museum exhibit of God's past speaking: it remains His living voice today.

The present writer vividly remembers a lecture on this subject given some years ago in Brisbane by a liberal theologian. The paper had two parts. In the first part the lecturer showed, from the sort of texts quoted above, that for Jesus and His apostles the Old Testament Scriptures were without exception or qualification the inspired, authoritative, infallible written Word of God. That much was certain. Then in part two came the question: Do we today have to agree with this judgment of Jesus and the apostles? This the lecturer proceeded to deny, on the grounds that we, with so much more modern information at our disposal, could not be ex-pected to accept antique ideas! Those who disavow Jesus' view of the Bible are rarely that honest to say so. They talk instead about "re-interpreting" the texts according to what their authors "really" meant. This predictably leads to rather tricky uses of language, to say the least.

The word *inspiration* itself has been a frequent victim of verbal abuse. Someone may say that Scripture is "inspired" and mean simply that it is "inspiring," like a Shakespeare sonnet perhaps.

Or one might affirm what Thomas Huxley ridiculed as "inspiration with limited liability." This enables one to run with the hares while hunt-ing with the hounds. One flashes the "inspiration" passport whenever one's orthodoxy is challenged, but keeps the notion vague enough to al-low for exceptions and exemptions at every turn. Is some scholar alleging errors in a biblical text? Very well, then; those bits are not inspired. To counter this tactic the church had to coin terms like "plenary inspiration" or "verbal inspiration." The first means that inspiration is full or comprehensive, and the second that it embraces the very words of the text. Neither term goes one whit beyond 2 Timothy 3:16, which says that all Scripture is God-inspired. If all Scripture is inspired, then inspiration is "plenary." Since all Scripture consists of words, inspiration is necessarily "verbal." If Holy Scripture is not inspired plenarily and verbally, then it is not inspired at all. To call it "inspired" nevertheless is then to exploit the hallowed emotional *connotations* of the word *inspiration*, while shirking all intellectual responsibility for its semantic face value or *denotation*.

Sometimes one hears the objection that the words *verbal* and *plenary* violate the mystery of inspiration by seeking to explain how it occurred. On the contrary, the terms *verbal* and *plenary* safeguard not the "how" but the "what" of God-inspiredness according to 2 Timothy 3:16 and all parallels. If inspiration in that sense is denied, then there is simply no inspiration at all. Hence, no mystery! The "what" of inspiration is that the sacred text, all of it as originally given in Hebrew and Greek, is God's Word in human language. How this came about we must, as in the case of other articles of faith, leave to God. Verbal, plenary inspiration does not imply a mechanical dictation or any other "theory." The human writers were not automata. Their cultural and other individual characteristics came to full expression. (The Greek of the Letter to the Hebrews, for instance, is much more refined than that of St. Mark's Gospel.) Yet the outcome, the concrete text, is without qualification the Word of God. That and nothing else is the meaning of inspiration, verbal and plenary, confessed already in the Nicene Creed: "Who spoke by the prophets."

The argument about inspiration often starts all over again when words like *inerrancy* and *infallibility* are introduced. The first term means "without error," and the second, "unable to deceive." The Latin roots of both words occur in this clear-cut confession from the Large Catechism: "My neighbor and I—in short, all men—may err and deceive, but God's Word cannot err."[3]

It should be clear that inspiration and inerrancy go together. If the Bible is inspired, then it is God's Word. If it is God's Word, then it must correct us, and not we it. To say, "Yes, God says so, but on this point I respectfully disagree," is even logically absurd. Theologically, it is nothing less than a "kind of impenitence," as the Anglican scholar James Packer

---

3. LC IV 57 (Tappert, 444).

has put it.[4] An "inspiration" divorced from inerrancy is as incoherent a notion as "bread" without nourishment or "money" without value. It is a play-inspiration, made up by a play-theology which has as much to do with the real thing as a Monopoly game has with the Federal Reserve Bank.

The objection that inerrancy is not taught in the Bible really amounts to the quibble that the word "inerrancy" is not found there. Neither, of course, is the word "Trinity." Yet what both words stand for certainly is taught in the Bible. *Inerrant* is simply a technical-sounding word chosen to keep the words *true* and *truthful* honest. The sacred Scriptures everywhere take it for granted that God's Word is the absolute truth (Ps. 12:6; 119:160; John 17:17), and so the opposite of all error, falsehood, and deceit (Matt. 22:29; John 8:44; 2 Thes. 2:9–15; 1 Jn. 2:21). Recall that the Lord Himself, in an argument turning on the use of one word, treats the exact wording of Ps. 82:6 as beyond criticism and appeal, on the grounds that "the scripture cannot be broken" (John 10:35 KJV). The word for "broken" here can mean being broken up or torn down, as for example in the destruction of buildings.

It is true that absolute submission to biblical authority implies much more than belief in the Bible's inerrancy. After all, properly printed multiplication tables are "inerrant." They contain no error.

Yet it must be added that full submission to biblical authority certainly implies nothing less than Scripture's inerrancy. St. Paul echoed the Saviour perfectly with the confession, "I believe everything [literally: all things] that is in accordance with the Law and that is written in the Prophets" (Acts 24:14). Such language becomes nonsensical the moment *any* parts of Holy Scripture are declared open to debunking as erroneous or mistaken.

Much opposition to inerrancy really rests on misunderstanding. Take the notion that St. Matthew's and St. Luke's versions of Pilate's spiteful sign on the cross cannot both be correct since some words and the word-order differ. Literally translated, the first reads, "This [One] is Jesus, the King of the Jews" (Matt. 27:37) and the second, "The King of the Jews [is] This [One]" (Luke 23:38). But the sign was written in three languages, and no doubt without any pedantic concern for linguistic invariance.

More importantly, however, confusing inerrancy with uniformity of wording mixes apples and oranges. It is what philosophers call a "category mistake." Inerrancy is concerned with the truth-value of sentences and

---

4. J. I. Packer, *"Fundamentalism" and the Word of God* (Grand Rapids, MI: Eerdmans, 1958), 21.

hence with their semantic content, not their mere grammatical form. What St. Matthew and St. Luke and the others were reporting quite truthfully was not the assertion that "the word 'This' was the first word on Pilate's sign," but rather what the sign said: "This is Jesus, the King of the Jews." The sign's message can be clothed in any number of different sentence forms, including indirect quotation and summary. By way of illustration, "He said he'd be gone for the evening" can be a perfectly correct, indeed preferable, version of a tedious recital such as: "At lunch the evening's activities were discussed. First, John thought he would go to the library. This led to a lively discussion of literary classics all during soup. . . . But by the end of the veal cutlets, and having nearly choked on one of them, John had decided to go to a concert instead, with pizza afterwards, etc., etc." Infinitely more embellishments are always possible.

Lawyers and judges are well aware that good witnesses often tell markedly different stories, and that those who agree too closely have probably been coached. Human existence is complex, and different perspectives on it may reveal very different aspects of a situation. However, these do not contradict but supplement each other. To focus and pounce on literary discords as evidences of falsehood or contradiction is to betray a bookish inexperience of life and of the world. Such pettifogging about words sees truth as a tidy assemblage of shallow little transparencies, whereas the real world is often turbulent, opaque, and not at all plausible. When dealing with ancient texts, it also constitutes arrogance to assume errors and contradictions rather than modestly blaming the limitations of one's own knowledge and understanding of the exact circumstances and background. It was about this conceit of having mastered the sacred text that Luther was thinking at the very end of his life in this world: "Let nobody suppose that he has tasted the Holy Scriptures sufficiently unless he has ruled over the churches with the prophets for a hundred years. Therefore there is something wonderful, first, about John the Baptist; second, about Christ; third, about the apostles. 'Lay not your hand on this divine Aeneid, but bow before it, adore its every trace.' We are beggars, that is true."[5]

The same kind of point applies in principle also to the question of the *canonicity* of certain New Testament books. The issue of the *canon* is too complex to be pursued here in detail.[6] It will suffice for present purposes to point out that a small number of books (Hebrews, 2 Peter, Jude, James,

---

5. AE 54, 476.
6. Interested readers are referred to the classic treatment by Martin Chemnitz. See *Examination* I, 168–195.

2 and 3 John, and Revelation) are called *antilegomena* ("spoken against"), because some in the most ancient Church doubted or denied their apostolic authorship and genuineness. It is well known that, like some of the ancients, Luther was less than complimentary about James, which he did not regard as authentic. It is not honest therefore to cite Luther's comments about James to claim that the Reformer harbored a loose view concerning divine inspiration, when Luther himself did not have in mind an inspired writing at all. What must be borne in mind is that all the articles of faith rest squarely on the undoubted books of the New Testament, called *homologoumena* ("confessed" by all). These include all four Gospels, Acts, all the letters of St. Paul, 1 Peter, and 1 John. Given the Bible's "redundancy" (to borrow a term from modern information theory), there is more than enough support for every article of faith in the *homologoumena*. Not a single article depends on any of the *antilegomena*. It is the church's practice to read the *antilegomena* under the sure guidance of the *homologoumena*, and never to bind anyone's conscience without clear warrant in the latter.

As with inspiration, so with inerrancy: it applies either completely or not at all. A partial inerrancy is no inerrancy. It is an illusion to think, for instance, that one may grant errors of fact in Scripture so long as one excludes errors of theology. The central Christian mystery of the Incarnation (1 Tim. 3:16) will not allow such a scheme. If God truly became flesh and dwelt among us (John 1:14), then the historical and geographical particulars (Luke 1:1–4; Acts 1:1–3; 1 Jn. 1:1–3) cannot in principle be dismissed as somehow falling beneath the dignity of "theological" status. The miracle of God-made-Man means that divinity and humanity, faith and facts, theology and history, are inextricably intertwined and cannot be divorced without rending asunder what God has joined together. Faith and theology are closely tied to facts and history (in the sense of what actually happened in space and time), but not simply in the way a banana grows within its peel. With the banana, one can pull away the peel and enjoy the real thing all the more. However, if one were to peel away all the historical facts from Christianity, no faith and theology would remain. For the faith and theology of the incarnate, crucified, and risen Son of God are *all about* the facts of the matter. The space-time realities do not merely run alongside the theology. Nothing would be left of the Apostles' Creed or of the Bible if all the "facts" were extracted.

Even what seem to us "minor" facts can have a surprising significance. The anointing of Jesus with precious perfume a week before His death certainly does not seem as important as some of the other events recorded by the evangelists. Yet the Saviour Himself says of this "minor" incident that "wherever this gospel is preached throughout the world, what she has done will also be told, in memory of her" (Matt. 26:13).

Modern theologians are forever trying to find plausible ways of complimenting Jesus on His good intentions while discounting what He actually said. For example, it has been suggested that in much the same way as a leading expert on Homer is not discredited as regards his classical knowledge if he proves mistaken about local train traffic, so one's belief in Jesus as Lord would not be troubled in the least if He had been wrong about this and that.[7] What this admittedly "very imperfect analogy" overlooks is that while absent-mindedness amounts to an amusing foible in professors, it turns out to be a fatal absurdity in God. God is not a Specialist with His own "field," accustomed to deferring to other specialists in theirs. Faith confesses Christ not as an authority over a cozy little nook called "religion," but as Maker and Ruler of the universe. The world is full of experts, professors, and authorities of all kinds (compare 1 Cor. 8:5), but it has only one Redeemer. "I have spoken to you of earthly things," He says, "and you do not believe; how then will you believe if I speak of heavenly things?" (John 3:12).

The apostle Peter understood this point from the outset. Told by the Lord to "put out into deep water, and let down the nets for a catch," Peter begins to object: "Master, we've worked hard all night and haven't caught anything." Had he been a modern theologian he would have continued: "Look, I truly value Your advice in matters of religion. But please leave the fishing to me; I do know something about that." Instead, tired and irritated though he is, Peter checks himself and answers: "But because you say so, I will let down the nets" (Luke 5:4–5).

If to err is *human*, though, does not insistence on inerrancy belittle or even deny the full humanity of Christ and of the Bible? In a word, no. As God did not become a sinner when He became man, He is not so helpless that He cannot keep His Word pure and truthful even when He gives it through sinners, in human language! Nowhere does Scripture discount its own or Christ's authority on the grounds of its or His humanity as such.

Here we encounter a profound truth. The divine-human mystery of the Bible is of a piece with *the* mystery of Jesus the God-Man. The inerrancy of Scripture follows as necessarily from its divine inspiration as the sinlessness of Jesus follows from His divinity. Both are equally articles of faith. That is, one does not conduct "research" on the life of Christ in

---

7. John Huxtable, *The Bible Says* (London: SCM Press, 1962), 70.

order to determine whether He perhaps lost His temper in the Temple-cleansing episode, or His hope and courage in Gethsemane or on the cross! Christians accept Jesus as God in human flesh, yet without stain of sin, simply because He has revealed Himself as such in His Word. There is no other basis for this Christian belief. It would be absurd to make such a truth depend on whether His life's record had so far satisfactorily withstood the moral scrutiny of His followers. It is just so with the holy book about Him. Christian faith honors the Bible as God's own Word and therefore inerrant, not because that quality stands out as self-evident or can be "proved" to common sense, but simply because it is Scripture's own self-testimony, as we have seen. All articles of faith rest on the Word of God itself, now written down in Scripture, not on human conjectures about these things based on appearances. The divinity of Christ's Word lies just as hidden to human wisdom as His sacramental presence is inaccessible to chemical analysis. One does not poke about the burning bush with Geiger counters!

Finally, "just as it is with Christ in the world, as He is viewed and dealt with, so it is also with the written Word of God. It is a worm and no book, compared to other books" (Luther on Ps. 22).[8] It is typical of God's ways with us that His Word does not come into the world as a stylish encyclopaedia of cosmic erudition, wit, and charm. The Bible is a blunt and honest book, which does not endear it to our vanities and ambitions (John 5:44). Besides, it seems full of offensive difficulties: logical, factual, moral, religious. It is even "fuzzy at the edges" (*antilegomena*!). In a topsy-turvy world divine truth must seem a lie. As Christ was mocked and insulted (Matt. 27:28 ff.; John 6:42), so also His inspired witnesses must be "genuine, yet regarded as impostors" (2 Cor. 6:8). A worm and no book indeed! All this is the written Word's lowly "servant form," which delights humble faith but thwarts all religious pretensions (1 Cor. 1–2). Our Lord said, "whoever is ashamed of me and of my words in this adulterous and sinful generation, of him will the Son of man also be ashamed, when he comes in the glory of his Father with the holy angels" (Mark 8:38 RSV).

> I beg and really caution every pious Christian not to be offended by the simplicity of the language and stories frequently encountered there, but fully realize that, however simple they may seem, these are the very words, works, judgments and deeds of the majesty, power, and wisdom of the

---

8.   WA 48, 31.

most high God. For these are the Scriptures which make fools of all the wise and understanding, and are open only to the small and simple, as Christ says in Matthew 11[:25]. Therefore dismiss your own opinions and feelings, and think of the Scriptures as the loftiest and noblest of holy things, as the richest of mines which can never be sufficiently explored, in order that you may find that divine wisdom which God here lays before you in such simple guise as to quench all pride. Here you will find the swaddling clothes and the manger in which Christ lies, and to which the angel points the shepherds [Luke 2:12]. Simple and lowly are these swaddling clothes, but dear is the treasure, Christ, who lies in them.[9]

"And blessed is the one who is not offended by me" (Matt. 11:6 ESV).

SCRIPTURE AND TRADITION

On June 25, 1530, the "Lutheran" party formally presented its confession of faith to Emperor Charles V and the estates of the Holy Roman Empire assembled in Augsburg. The impact of this confession, even on its opponents, was enormous. What had been expected was a fanatical tirade against all established order and tradition, sacred and secular. Instead the assembly heard calm, respectful explanations of basic Christian truths, evangelical and biblical in content and tone, and spiked with appeals to great theologians of the past like Sts. Ambrose, Augustine, and John Chrysostom. Prince William of Bavaria turned to Dr. John Eck, Luther's leading academic critic, and complained that Eck had misrepresented the Lutheran doctrine to him. Then William asked whether Eck could refute the confession they had just heard. When Eck replied that he could do so from the church fathers but not from the Scriptures, the prince made his famous comment: "Then the Lutherans, I understand, sit in the Scriptures and we of the Pope's Church beside the Scriptures!"[10]

It was clear that a number of notions and practices which had become customary by Luther's time had no support at all in the Bible. Among them were prayers to the saints, prayers for the dead, purgatory, indulgences, the "sacrifice of the mass," and the like. Those who wished nevertheless to defend such things, had to do so on other grounds, . . .[11]

---

9. AE 35, 236.
10. Quoted in F. Bente, *Historical Introductions to the Book of Concord* (St. Louis, MO: Concordia Publishing House), 1965 (reprint), 19. *Editor's note:* Compare AE 13, 352.
11. *Editor's note:* The last word on page 22 of the typescript is "grounds." On the missing page 23, Marquart presumably gave historical background on the

The following notion of "tradition" was devised for this purpose.[12] St. John himself said that he did not write down everything Jesus had said and done (John 20:30; 21:25). These unwritten things are passed down from generation to generation, as by an underground stream, and surface here and there in statements by this or that theologian, pope, or council.

Such a scheme becomes of course a Pandora's Box. From it the weirdest fantasies can be conjured up at will, and have been. What is overlooked here is the import of the evangelist's comment, "But these are written that you may believe . . . " ([John] 20:31). Whatever is not so written, then, on apostolic authority, is not worthy of belief. When ancient heretics appealed to a "secret doctrine" on the basis of St. John 16:12 ("I have much more to say to you"), St. Augustine replied: "Since the evangelists kept silence, who among us can say that it was this or that, or, if he dares to say it, how will he prove it? Who is so boastful and rash as to affirm, without divine testimony, . . . what are the things which the Holy Spirit did not want to write through the evangelists?"[13]

The Reformation's "Scripture alone" principle rejected tradition no more than "faith alone" opposed good works, that is, in the proper place. The whole argument was not about whether tradition should be respected, but about how the genuine Christian tradition could be recognized and distinguished from false and fraudulent tradition. This problem already plagued the apostolic church (2 Thes. 2:2). The Reformation's answer was that the Bible alone is the God-given touchstone by which to test all Christian truth-claims. In giving this answer the Reformation was in fact remaining faithful to the best tradition of the church, as represented by some of her greatest fathers.

The New Testament word from which we get our word *tradition* (via the Latin) means simply "passing on" or "handing over." It is used, for example, of surrendering, turning over, even betraying people (Mark 1:14; 3:19), of committing or commending oneself to God (Acts 14:26; 15:26), or of giving up one's soul in death (John 19:30). In the Gospels the noun form of the word for "tradition" is used only in a bad sense, that is, as human customs in opposition to God's Word (Mark 7:3, 5, 8, 9, 13). This the Saviour rebukes, citing the prophet Isaiah: "They worship me in vain; their teachings are merely human rules" (Matt. 15:9).

---

idea of unwritten tradition, which was still the topic under discussion as the text continues above, with page 24 of the typescript.

12. *Editor's note:* This sentence is the first few words on page 24 of the typescript.

13. Quoted in *Examination* I, 94–95.

In the verb form, however, the word is used also in a good sense, as in St. Matthew 11:27 ("All things *have been committed* to me by my Father" [italics added]) or St. Luke 1:1–2: "Many have undertaken to draw up an account of the things that have been fulfilled among us, just as they *were handed down* to us by those who from the first were eyewitnesses and servants of the word" (italics added). Here we have tradition at its best: God-given truth, handed on unchanged, certified as such by apostolic-prophetic authority. It is in this sense that St. Paul insists on the exclusive sway of "the teachings we passed on to you" (2 Thes. 2:15) or "the teaching you received from us" (2 Thes. 3:6). The Corinthians are praised for "holding to the traditions just as I passed them on to you" (1 Cor. 11:2). These traditions are not a secret lore about fancy obscurities. They are the publicly proclaimed Law and Gospel of God. What Paul received and in turn passed on unchanged is core content like the Holy Supper (1 Cor. 11:23) and the saving death and resurrexion of Jesus (1 Cor. 15:3–4).

Beside this bedrock of God-given, apostolic doctrine, Scripture also documents apostolic customs or practices, such as observing Sunday as the day of the Lord's resurrexion (John 20; Acts 20:7; Rev. 1:10), or the rite of laying on hands when ordaining men into the public ministry of the Gospel (1 Tim. 4:14; 5:22). Here, too, is tradition, but without divine mandate. Then there are the churchly customs of later times, gradually shaping the liturgy, including the church year. All this the Reformation kept, except for those elements, like prayers to the saints, which clearly ran contrary to apostolic doctrine. Ceremonies, argues Luther in his wide-ranging *On the Councils and the Church*, belong not in great church councils, which must deal with more important matters, but in local parishes and schools. When the schoolchildren learn to "doff their little hats or bend their knees whenever the name of Jesus Christ is mentioned," or to kneel when the schoolmaster signals with his cane at the words "And was made man" in the Nicene Creed, then the rest of the people will soon follow suit.[14]

"Tradition," then, can mean many things. Some are good, some bad; some weighty, some not. Chemnitz distinguishes no fewer than eight classes of tradition in his masterful discussion answering the Roman Catholic Council of Trent.[15] The point is that for what we believe and teach as God's truth we must have His own warrant in His written Word. Beyond that we gladly follow the good example of past ages, provided that

---

14. AE 41, 136–137.
15. *Examination* I, 217–307.

free Christian consciences are not enslaved by what God has neither commanded nor forbidden.

We modern Christians in particular have good reason to cherish the old churchly ways. Western culture has been uprooted and denuded by more than two centuries of relentless secularisation. To the extent to which we see, with T. S. Eliot,[16] the intimate and intricate connexions between cult (religion) and culture, we shall not naively undervalue historic Christian customs as worthless "cultural" bric-a-brac from bygone ages. We shall see them rather as expressive of a certain churchly spirit and outlook, and wear them gladly as badges of our humble continuity with the church of all ages.

Tradition, said G. K. Chesterton, is the democracy of the dead. He was right, of course. Yet this way of putting the matter also suggests clear limits for tradition. The church, after all, is not a democracy but a monarchy, ruled graciously by Christ. His divine Kingship sets the bounds which custom and precedent, however hallowed and venerable, may not transgress. Had he considered this side of things, the witty Mr. Chesterton would never have complained that the Reformation selectively snatched the Scriptures from tradition's grand procession and then pitted this single feature against other, equally authentic, features of that same procession.[17] Had he looked more closely at the great procession of historic Christendom, he would have seen "Scripture alone" as an affirmation, not a denial, of genuine Christian tradition.

Chemnitz, the diligent student of Christian antiquity, was able to fill many pages with citations from the church fathers. For example:

+ *St. Basil (d. 379):* "We do not think that it is right to make what is custom among them into a law and rule of the right doctrine. Therefore let the divinely inspired Scripture be made the judge by us, and on the side of those whose doctrines are found in agreement with the divine words the vote of truth is cast."[18]
+ *St. Jerome (d. c. 420):* "Whatever has not its authority from the Scriptures, is despised as easily as it is approved."[19]

---

16. T. S. Eliot, excerpt from "Notes toward the Definition of Culture," in Frank Kermode, ed., *Selected Prose of T. S. Eliot* (New York: Harcourt Brace Jovanovich, 1975), 292–305.
17. G. K. Chesterton, *The Catholic Church and Conversion* (London: Burnes and Oates, 1960), 24–25.
18. Quoted in *Examination* I, 153.
19. Quoted in *Examination* I, 155.

+ *St. Augustine (d. 430):* "Let those things be removed from our midst which we quote against each other not from divine canonical books but from elsewhere. Someone may perhaps ask: Why do you want to remove these things from the midst? Because I do not want the holy church proved by human documents but by divine oracles."[20]
+ *Augustine again (citing Gal. 1:8):* "If an angel from heaven should preach to you anything besides what you have received in the Scriptures of the Law and of the Gospel, let him be anathema."[21]
+ *St. John Chrysostom (d. 407):* "Let us not hold the opinions of the crowd, but let us inquire into the matters themselves. For it is foolish that we who do not believe others in money matters but count and reckon ourselves, should in matters of far greater importance simply follow the opinion of others, especially when we have the most exact scale, indicator, and rule, the assertion of the divine laws. Therefore I beg you all that you give up what appeals to this one or to that one and that you address all these questions concerning these things to the Scriptures."[22]

The "Scripture alone" principle necessarily implies both the *sufficiency* and the *clarity* of the Bible. Sufficiency means that Scripture contains and teaches all the articles of the Christian faith and is therefore able to make us "wise for salvation through faith in Christ Jesus" (2 Tim. 3:15). The Bible's clarity, in turn, means not that there are no unclear texts in it, but that all the articles of faith are set out in clear language: "Your word is a lamp for my feet, a light on my path" (Ps. 119:105). A lamp needing light from somewhere else wouldn't amount to much of a lamp!

In recent times discussion has focused more on the clarity of Scripture than on its sufficiency. The Second Vatican Council (1962–1965) moderated the language of Rome's tradition-principle while advancing its claims in subtler form. The Council rejected the document prepared by the Vatican's theological commission, which would have reasserted the old pattern of Scripture and tradition as "two sources of revelation," running side by side, as it were. Instead, the Council stressed tradition as the ongoing interpretation of the one biblical text by the church's teaching office, culminating of course in the papacy.[23] This approach appeals to common sense ("How

20. Quoted in *Examination* I, 157.
21. Quoted in *Examination* I, 152.
22. Quoted in *Examination* I, 157.
23. See Walter M. Abbott, gen. ed., *The Documents of Vatican II* (New York: America Press, 1966), 107 ff.

would we interpret the Constitution if there were no Supreme Court?"). It also appeals to liberal Protestants, whose biblical interpretation has gone to pieces on account of historical criticism. (See page 22 ff.)

The case was memorably put to the present writer by an Italian lawyer, during the days of Vatican II. This lawyer had doctorates in law, economics, and medicine. He was travelling from Rome to Finland to adjudicate a border dispute with the Soviet Union on behalf of the United Nations organisation. He claimed that once he had made his findings, the matter would be settled since he was the world expert on the particular point at issue. Now, reasoned the lawyer, just as others had to accept his expertise, so he in turn had to accept theirs concerning the fields in which he himself was not an expert—for instance religion. In this field, the lawyer thought, only the Vatican had credibility. "Do you realise," he asked, "that there are priests in Rome who have spent their lives studying Marxism, and who know more about it than any Marxist? The same is true of other vital branches of knowledge. When the Pope therefore decides something on this sort of advice, who am I to question the world's top expertise in religion?"

A mental experiment will help to answer this question. Casting our minds back two thousand years, to ancient Palestine, we imagine that we are trying to resolve for ourselves the puzzle of Jesus of Nazareth: is He genuine, or is He a fraud? Naturally, not being experts in religion, we consult with those are. We ask the Temple authorities in Jerusalem. Would we have discovered the truth in this way? Hardly! Christ is, after all, "The stone the builders rejected" (Matt. 21:42). Experts, as Chesterton pointed out, are very useful in technical matters. Yet when it is a question of life or death, we ask twelve ordinary men and women to decide. The experts must convince a jury of ordinary people. If they can't, they lose their case. The great issues of life and death are fundamentally simple, and must be faced by every human being. How much more in matters of spiritual life! Conscience cannot be delegated. "I praise you, Father, Lord of heaven and earth," said the Savior, "because you have hidden these things from the wise and learned, and revealed them to little children" (Matt. 11:25).

The issue is clear and simple. Christ says: "Watch out for false prophets" (Matt. 7:15). What does this involve?

> You see, here Christ does not give the judgment to prophets and teachers but to pupils or sheep. For how could one beware of false prophets if one did not consider and judge their teaching?[24]

---

24. AE 39, 307.

If the sheep were not supposed to flee from the wolves until the wolves, through their Christian council and public verdict, commanded them to flee, then the sheepfold would soon be empty, and the shepherd would within one day find neither milk, nor cheese, butter, wool, meat, nor even a hoof. . . . Not only the whole flock of sheep but also every single sheep by itself has the right and power to flee from the wolves as best it can, as also it does, St. John. 10:5: "they will run away from him."[25]

If every sheep is entitled to its own opinion, though, will there not be total chaos? And why bother with shepherds if the sheep themselves decide everything? Here one must distinguish sharply between two soundalikes. One is *private judgment*, and the other, *private interpretation*.

There is no right of private interpretation. No one has the right to make Scripture mean whatever he wishes (2 Pet. 1:20). Nor has anyone the right—whether in the name of pope, clergy, scholars, or majority opinion—to impose on the church his own private interpretation, that is, an understanding of Scripture which cannot be proved from the sacred text itself.

Private judgment is something completely different. It is a must. Christians have the right and duty to make sure, and be convinced in their own conscience, that what they are being taught is really God's Word.

So these two sound-alikes contrast like night and day. Private interpretation means personal, subjective whim. Private judgment is bound strictly to the clear, sufficient, and objective norm of Holy Scripture: " . . . they received the message with great eagerness and examined the Scriptures every day to see if what Paul said was true" (Acts 17:11).

It is fitting to conclude this section with an admonition, based on St. Matthew 24, attributed to that great preacher of ancient Antioch and then Constantinople, St. John Chrysostom ("Gold-mouth"):

When you shall see the wicked heresy, which is the army of Antichrist, standing in the holy places of the church, then let those who are in Judea head for the mountains, that is, those who are Christians should head for the Scriptures. For the true Judea is Christendom, and the mountains are the Scriptures of the prophets and apostles, as it is written: "Her foundations are in the holy mountains." . . . The Lord, therefore, knowing that there would be such a great confusion of things in the last days, commands that Christians who . . . want to gain steadfastness in the true

---

25. St.L. 17, cols. 102–103.

faith should take refuge in nothing else but the Scriptures. Otherwise, if they look to other things, they will be offended and will perish, because they will not know which is the true church, and as a result they will fall into the abomination of desolation which stands in the holy places of the church.[26]

SCRIPTURE, REASON, AND EXPERIENCE

In Reformation times the term "Scripture alone" asserted the sole sway of divine authority in the church, against human pretensions in the name of "tradition." Two centuries later the main rival to Scripture was not tradition but reason, followed soon by experience. "Scripture alone" had now to be maintained along this new front. As in the case of tradition, what had to be rejected was not reason itself, or religious experience, but a wrong understanding and use of them.

Today, when we take the tricks of technology for granted, it is hard to imagine the sense of wonder and exhilaration which attended the rise of modern science. Sir Isaac Newton (1642–1727) came to be held in awe as the very embodiment of scientific genius:

> Nature and nature's laws lay hid in night.
> God said, Let Newton be, and all was light.

Alexander Pope's famous lines celebrate the cult of reason, of scientific rationality. The eighteenth century saw itself as the Age of Enlightenment. The searchlight of scientific, mathematical reasoning was wresting from nature one after another of her secrets. Could not this light be turned with equal profit on the age-old questions of philosophy and religion? Mankind, it was thought, had come of age, and needed a form of religion more in keeping with the dignity of these new riches of the mind. The past had been filled with superstition and mystery, of bowing and scraping before a celestial Autocrat. It was time now for a religion in the spirit of science and common sense.

What came of this was Deism and moralism. There is a God, the soul is immortal, and a happy hereafter comes by way of a decent and respectable life here and now. The emptiness of this "reasonable" religion was only poorly disguised with the bogus mysteries and ritual of Freemasonry, which arose at that time and gained immense popularity. As this "reasonable" religiosity trickled down from the universities, where the clergy were trained, to the parishes, the result for church life was progressive collapse.

---

26. Quoted in *Examination* I, 156.

Mystery, sacrament, and liturgy all had to yield to common sense, and churches became lecture-halls featuring "practical" talks. Two examples from that time will illustrate the spirit of the thing. One is a Christmas sermon, based on the traditional Gospel about the Christ Child in the manger. The preacher sang the praises of stall feeding, in the interests of scientific dairying! Another sermon, on Good Friday, expounded the desirability of making one's last will and testament in writing, and this on the basis of Pontius Pilate's words "What I have written, I have written"![27] Offered stones for bread, the people left the European (largely "Lutheran") state churches by the millions. They have not returned to this day, as tourists easily discover.

In the course of time a reaction set in to the excesses of "rationalism," the worship of reason. However, fashionable theology had by then developed a strong distaste for the authority of divine revelation, and tried to solve its problems with human ingenuity. The enormous influence of F. Schleiermacher (1768–1834) brought about a massive shift from reason to emotion. Schleiermacher defined religion as an absolute "feeling of dependence." In this way he thought he could set theology and the church free from the tyranny of rigid reason. Not surprisingly, however, the imagined liberation from the frying pan of rationalism put theology into the fire of emotionalism. Modern fever-swamps of shapeless religiosity and occultism suggest that the cure turned out to be worse than the disease, the last state worse than the first.

A major part of the Enlightenment's sea-change in culture and religion was a radically new approach to the Bible. No longer did theologians assume Scripture to be true in every particular, and on those terms no longer could it be the supreme authority. Now it was considered subject to the same critical investigations as other literature. Like other historical documents, it had henceforth to be carefully tested for bias, error, and outright fabrication. The instrument with which all this was to be done has become known as "the historical-critical method."

As this intricate subject cannot be pursued here at length, interested readers are referred to other sources for more detailed discussions.[28] It

---

27. Ralph Dornfeld Owen, *The Old Lutherans Come*, reprinted from *Concordia Historical Institute Quarterly*, April 1947, 5.

28. See Edgar Krentz, *The Historical-Critical Method* (Philadelphia, PA: Fortress, 1975); Ernst and Marie-Louis Keller, *Miracles in Dispute* (Philadelphia: Fortress, 1969); John Reumann, Samuel H. Nafzger, Harold H. Ditmanson, eds., *Studies in Lutheran Hermeneutics* (Philadelphia: Fortress, 1979); Thomas Sheehan, *The First Coming* (New York: Random House, 1986).

will be enough for the purposes of this chapter to note two major features of historical criticism, as applied to Scripture. The first has to do with the very nature of this criticism, and the second with its consequences.

It is true that historical criticism is often combined with an anti-supernatural bias which rules out all miracles in advance. This is the heirloom of an old-fashioned scientism. Yet the real point of the historical-critical principle is something else. It is often claimed that historical criticism is simply a neutral set of scholarly tools or procedures, allegedly necessary for the understanding and interpretation of any text. Actually, it is just this "neutrality" which is the problem when Holy Scripture is in view.

In the case of other documents, it is of course perfectly in order, indeed necessary, to approach them with a critical frame of mind. This involves not prejudging questions of fact until all the relevant evidence has been properly sorted out. For judges, impartiality clearly stands out as the highest virtue. In the context of judging historical documents, this would mean that no one source or witness may be given preferential treatment or be allowed any privileged standing. Any version of an event may be called into question on the basis of a different account in another plausible source.

Yet this is precisely what Christian theology cannot grant when it comes to the Bible, which faith recognizes as the very Word of God. When Scripture speaks, God speaks, and the matter is settled. No human authority is or can be on a par with the divine standing of Holy Scripture: "Let God be true, and every human being a liar" (Rom. 3:4)! Attempting to "correct" Scripture, whether with Aristotle, Josephus, or Einstein, is as absurd in theology as it would be in law to appeal from the Supreme Court to a local traffic court.

Nor may theology strike a pose of neutrality or impartiality between Holy Scripture and other documents. That would fly in the face of Christ's words: "Whoever who is not with me is against me, and whoever does not gather with me scatters" (Matt. 12:30).

It is necessary to introduce here the old distinction between reason as master and reason as servant. To understand any statement at all, it is necessary to use reason in the form of grammar, logic, and the like. This so-called "servant use" of reason is indispensable also in the case of Holy Scripture (Matt. 13:19; Acts 8:30; 1 Cor. 14:19). Indeed, since we are to love God also with our minds (Matt. 22:37), we can never lavish too much intellectual effort on His inspired Word. Ministers of that Word must naturally also acquire a working knowledge of Greek and Hebrew, so that they may study the sacred text in the original languages.

Totally different from this is the "master use" of reason. That use seeks not simply to understand, but to judge the truth of what has been understood. It is this "master use" of reason which is the essence of historical criticism.

Critic or *criticism* comes from the Greek word for "judge." Now, clearly God's Word is to judge us, not we it. Subjecting Scripture to historical criticism amounts to a grotesque reversal of roles: the sinner fancies himself on the bench and God's Word in the defendant's dock! A theology so conducted resembles Edgar Allan Poe's nightmare about an insane asylum taken over and run by the patients.

Sound theology bases itself squarely on Holy Scripture as "the only true norm according to which all teachers and teachings are to be judged and evaluated."[29] This is the Reformation's "Scripture alone" principle, as reasserted by the Formula of Concord. If Scripture is indeed "the only judge,"[30] then human reason cannot also be judge, under whatever pretext.

By definition, however, historical criticism claims the role of judge, for it insists on the scholar's right and duty to subject all historical claims and documents, without exception, to systematic doubt, cross-examination, and possible falsification. Only one conclusion is possible: "Scripture alone" and the subjection of Scripture to the historical-critical method are mutually exclusive. One must choose between them. And behind the Reformation's "Scripture alone" stands the majesty of God Himself, in His chosen messengers: "We demolish arguments and every pretension that sets itself up against the knowledge of God, and we take captive every thought to make it obedient to God" (II Cor. 10:5).

Finally, having sketched the nature of historical criticism, it is only fair to point out its major results in theology. After all, "By their fruit you will recognize them" (Matt. 7:16). The fact is that the gradual acceptance of historical criticism by the churches in our time has radically altered the whole theological landscape. One newspaper religion writer put it like this in 1977:

True or false?
—Jesus did not regard himself as God made flesh and probably did not call himself the Messiah.
—Jesus did not rise bodily from the dead.

---

29. FC SD Rule and Norm 3 (Tappert, 504).
30. FC Ep Rule and Norm 7 (Tappert, 465).

If you said "false," you are in step with popular understanding of the New Testament but out of step with the prevailing views of most prominent biblical scholars.

This conclusion comes from interviews with U.S. scholars who reflect the teaching at all but the more conservative universities and theological schools.

The interviews also revealed the width of an enormous gap between contemporary New Testament studies and the assumptions of the general public, even most churchgoers. . . .

"Maybe it's time we levelled with the public," one scholar said.[31]

An example from a textbook on "form criticism" leaves no doubt about what is at stake and why. St. Peter's great confession in St. Mark 8:27 and following is turned, by means of editorial surgery, into this blasphemous account of what "really happened": Peter confessed, "You are the Messiah" [v. 29], and Jesus replied, "Get thee behind me, Satan" [v. 33 KJV], for according to a prominent critic, "Jesus rejects messiahship as 'a merely human and even diabolical temptation'"![32]

Wherever such tenets are embraced, total devastation must follow. What this has meant for nominal world "Lutheranism" becomes terribly clear in the sad observation of Hans Asmussen, former president of the chancery of the Evangelical [Lutheran, Reformed, and United] Church of Germany:

> This is in fact the picture of wide sectors of our Lutheran Church today: clergymen read aloud the Christmas story, which they consider a fairytale. They read aloud the Easter story, to which they find access only after several reinterpretations. At the grave, they witness to the resurrection of the dead, which they consider a myth.[33]

Historical criticism is of course no respecter of confessional boundaries. A leading U.S. Roman Catholic theologian has written of his own church:

> In Roman Catholic seminaries . . . it is now common teaching that Jesus of Nazareth did not assert any of the messianic claims that the Gospels

---

31. John Dart, *Los Angeles Times*, 5 September 1977.
32. Edgar V. McKnight, *What Is Form Criticism?* (Philadelphia, PA: Fortress, 1969), 73.
33. Hans Asmussen, "The Dogma of the Holy Scriptures," *Lutheran World* 13 (1966):186.

attribute to him and that he died without believing that he was Christ or the Son of God, not to mention the founder of a new religion.

One would be hard pressed to find a [Roman] Catholic biblical scholar who maintains that Jesus thought he was the divine Son of God who pre-existed from all eternity as the second person of the Trinity before he be-came a human being.[34]

Christ and His Word stand and fall together. The mystery of God-made-Man is bound up indissolubly with the mystery of His own Word about Himself, given through His chosen human vessels. Like the seam-less robe of Christ, Holy Scripture will be treasured whole or gambled away whole. More than two millennia of clever and not-so-clever attempts to dissect and profane the sacred text serve only to highlight its "sacra-mental" integrity and grandeur.

SCRIPTURE AND CREEDS

Non-committal religious chatter is one thing. Confession is quite another (Matt. 10:32). It was not enough for the twelve simply to report what vari-ous people were saying about Jesus. They themselves had to take a stand. Jesus asked them point-blank: "Who do you say I am?" Then Peter con-fessed, in the name of all: "You are the Messiah, the Son of the living God" (Matt. 16:15–16).

All our great creeds and confessions have as their embryo, as it were, the New Testament's "JESUS IS LORD." At first sight it may seem far-fetched to trace the Nicene Creed, let alone the Formula of Concord, to that simple New Testament slogan. Yet even though an oak tree also does not look much like an acorn, it *is* the acorn at a later stage of development. Similarly, compressed beneath the surface simplicity of "Jesus is Lord" lies the full trinitarian dynamic of God's saving self-revelation. Christian truth is both simple and complex (Matt. 11:25). Three words confess it all, yet not all the books in the world can exhaust it! Someone has said that Holy Scripture is like a river in which lambs may safely wade and elephants swim.

Today many deplore what seems to them a tendency to needless elab-oration and complication. They grow impatient with "theological hair-splitting" and would have us abandon all this "scholasticism" in favor of a return to the "simple Bible." This impulse amounts to simplistic nos-talgia, though.

---

34. Thomas Sheehan, *New York Review of Books*, 14 June 1984.

It is true of course that not all theological development has been healthy. A great deal of it has in fact been mistaken and even perverse. Just as an embryo can suffer genetic damage and grow hideously misshapen, so also theology, when its internal controls are disturbed. Yet this is just why creeds and confessions are necessary: there must be readily applicable "clinical tests" to tell the healthy from the pathological.

The ever-churning tides of culture and language require that the message of Holy Scripture be constantly interpreted and applied anew. As this happens, counterfeit interpretations arise as well as genuine ones. In economics it is said that bad money drives out the good. In theology, too, care must be taken to screen out attractive falsehoods, lest they swamp the unflattering truth. Then would arise a sludge of fickle opinions, presenting the unwary with the illusion of "freedom of choice" among equally good options.

The moment one takes a particular stand, one has a creed. (*Credo* is Latin for "I believe.") Orthodox ("right-teaching") creeds and confessions safeguard the genuine sense of Scripture against distortions. When conflicting teachings compete for the loyalty of Christians in the name of Scripture, one cannot simply "stick with the Bible itself" and ignore all these pesky "interpretations." The whole point is to recognize what is the *correct* understanding of the Bible, and to assert it against counter-claims. Failure to do so gives equal rights to all views and effectively robs Scripture of any and all sense and meaning.

Decisions about the correct understanding of Scripture are embodied in creeds and confessions, and thus have been preserved through the centuries. (Creedal hymns like Philippians 2:6–11 and 1 Timothy 3:16 document the practice of framing short summaries of the faith already in New Testament times.) Without such creedal decisions nothing is ever settled. One would have to reinvent the wheel every time a difference arises. "No creed but Christ" is itself a creed, and a self-contradictory one!

Since the church is not an occult society, its worship contrasts deeply with all mythological mumbo-jumbo. Note the pointed contrast between myth and truth in 2 Timothy 4:4; Titus 1:14; and 2 Peter 1:16. Not epic fancies or mind-numbing frenzies (1 Cor. 12:2!) shape Christian worship, but the very being of God Himself in all the awesomeness of His mercy (John 4:21–24; 1 Pet. 2:9). The church was well aware from the beginning that if the resurrexion of Jesus was not utterly factual, the whole thing was worse than useless (1 Cor. 15:14–19). A "symbolic" or otherwise imaginary resurrexion is no resurrexion at all. "But Christ has indeed been raised from the dead" (1 Cor. 15:20). The solemn attestation of 1 Corinthians 15:4, "that he was raised on the third day according to the Scriptures," is regarded even by leading critical scholars as a creedal formula cited by St. Paul from earlier, eye-witness sources.[35] The Nicene Creed took up this language almost verbatim.

The Nicene Creed further forms a very good example of how new language sometimes becomes necessary precisely to maintain the old truths unchanged. The old truth was that Jesus is God. This Arius and his followers denied, although their language grew more weaselly as time went on. When the Arians said "Jesus is Lord," this was the old language of the Bible being used to cover up the new falsehood that Jesus was not really God. To smoke out the denials and evasions, the Nicene Creed (really the Creed of the Councils of Nicaea, 325, and Constantinople, 381) framed "new" language: "God of God, Light of Light, very God of very God, begotten, not made," and especially: "being of one substance with the Father." This last expression, *homoousion* in Greek, was especially hated by the Arians. They opposed it as new-fangled. Yet just this "new-fangled" language preserved the old truth while the old language was used to conceal new error. When "bad things happen to good words," it is probably time for a creed to set matters right.

The classic creeds and confessions all arose in times of great ferment in the church. There have been two such creed-forming ages. The first settled the great battles about Christ as both God and Man, which occupied the church's attention in the early centuries. Some thousand years later came the great upheavals of the Reformation age. The debate at that time turned on the nature of the salvation gained by Christ and the terms on which it is offered to sinners.

Over the last two centuries, since the Enlightenment, Christianity has experienced probably the deepest crisis of all in the systematic subversion of its biblical foundations.[36] Some churches have understood and responded to this crisis better than others, but so far no creed or confession has crystallised out of this conflict which could command general assent as a proper settlement. Why? For one thing, perhaps such general settlements are no longer feasible after the confessional splintering of Christendom which followed the Reformation.

Yet there is a deeper reason, which makes it difficult even for smaller portions of Christendom to take a stand and make it stick. That reason is

35. See Gary R. Habermas and Antony G. N. Flew, *Did Jesus Rise from the Dead?: The Resurrection Debate*, Terry L. Miethe, ed (San Francisco: Harper and Row, 1987) 23, 52 ff., 68 ff., 128, passim.
36. *Editor's note*: Recall that Marquart wrote these words during the 1980s.

likely to be found in the skeptical spirit of the times, which shapes public opinion in the industrialised world, and seeps, along with carcinogenic pollutants, into our very bones. In this murky light all creeds are suspect, and no truth can be final. Doubt rears its head.

For convenience's sake we may distinguish between "Advanced Doubt" and "Beginners' Doubt." Advanced Doubt considers all religions equally questionable. Beginners' Doubt holds that Christianity is generically true, but that no one particular church's version of it can be right while the others are wrong.

Doubt often hides itself behind the Christian virtue of humility, yet it stands fundamentally at odds with the Christian outlook. It rather comports more with the spirit of the Hindu story about the elephant and the blind men. As the men touched different parts of the animal, they said, "An elephant is like a rope," or, "No, an elephant is like a pillar" and so on. The point made by the story, of course, is that our grasp of reality is much too limited to warrant making sweeping statements about the whole of it. This point is fair enough, in appropriate places and times. However, it leaves utterly out of account direct divine revelation.

Since God knows the Big Picture exhaustively, whatever He says about anything must be the ultimate truth on that subject. This does not mean that theology offers an encyclopaedic account of the cosmos, any more than it implies that the biblical writers were omniscient. It means only that, however narrow the scope of the biblical revelation, it is absolutely true so far as it goes. A statement can be true without being the whole truth about everything! Now, the biblical revelation is totally true even though it is piecemeal and selective. It resembles a strip-map, which shows nothing beyond ten or twenty miles on either side of the main highway. In this sense, "we know in part" (1 Cor. 13:9). So a pilgrim theology is also a modest theology.

But whatever is revealed by God, of that we can and must be certain. This is the meaning of the New Testament's strong and sometimes severe stress on *doctrine* (Matt. 16:12; Rom. 16:17; 1 Tim. 4:16; Tit. 1:9; 2 Jn. 9–10). St. Paul would have been baffled by the idea that Christian doctrine remains somehow nebulous and doubtful (Rom. 10:8). Christ told His church to proclaim the truth, not discover it (Matt. 28:19–20).

The New Testament words for "doctrine" always appear in the singular when they refer to Christian teaching. "Doctrines" in the plural are the erring and often conflicting inventions of men or demons (Matt. 15:9; 1 Tim. 4:1; Heb. 13:9). There is one, single, "sound" [healthy] (Tit. 2:1) Christian doctrine, and its proclamation must conform exactly to the apostolic pattern (2 Tim. 1:13). Christian doctrine constitutes an organic whole, not a loose assortment of unconnected items (Eph. 4:5; Jude 3). When speaking of parts or aspects of this one, seamless Christian truth, it is better therefore to speak of "articles of faith" rather than of "doctrines." The Latin word *articulus* means "joint," that is, an organic part of a larger whole.

According to ancient Christian usage, which reflects the New Testament (Matt. 13:11; 1 Cor. 4:1), the various articles of faith are *mysteries*. This word emphasizes the supernatural nature, content, and source of the faith. Its truths are not discoverable by human reason. They can be known only by the gracious self-revelation of the God Whose judgments are unsearchable and His ways past finding out (Rom. 11:33; Is. 55:8, 9).

The organic unity of Christian truth yields a further conclusion. If one looks atomistically at the differences among and within the various Christian churches—that is, if one counts so many versions of individual points of doctrine—the numbers can prove staggering. Such an approach, however, is wrong. Since Christian truth really forms an integrated whole, its various aspects must be seen as great interconnected "syndromes," not as independent atoms.

Here is help for Beginners' Doubt. Seen genetically and holistically, the basic alternatives total surprisingly few. Contrary to the pop-skepticism which counts hundreds of "denominations" and despairs at the odds against any one of them being right, there are for all practical purposes only three or four basic varieties, that is, "models" or "paradigms" of the Gospel and so of Christian doctrine: the Roman Catholic, the Lutheran, the Reformed, and perhaps the Anabaptist.[37] Everything else, exotic and eccentric sects aside, simply amounts to variations on the given themes. Therefore the basic choices are radically fewer and simpler than people often imagine. The first question is for or against the Reformation, then its

---

37. This classification will displease the Eastern Orthodox and the Anglicans, particularly, since they object to being lumped together with the Roman Catholic and Reformed churches, respectively. No offence is intended. Historically, however, the Church of England is a Reformed church, although its Calvinism is so mild that the English Church has been characterised as "Lutheranising." As regards Eastern Orthodoxy, its differences with Rome are of course important. Our classification is a rule of thumb only, and makes sense in light of the decisive issues raised by the Reformation. Also note however Oxford Prof. Michael Dummett's reference to "Catholics and Orthodox, who differ so profoundly in spiritual tradition, yet so insignificantly in doctrine" ("A Remarkable Consensus," *New Blackfriars* 809 [October 1987]:426).

two or three basic types. Differences between basic types can and should be faced frankly and fairly, then evaluated in the light of the Scriptures rather than by the heat of partisan passion.

These chapters seek to give a coherent overview of Christian doctrine.[38] But a generic Christian doctrine, apart from particular confessional "paradigms" or versions of it, is no more possible than are generalized fruit-trees without particular apple-trees, pear-trees, and the like. A choice among basic types is ultimately unavoidable. This book makes no secret of its Lutheran orientation. Yet the reader is urged to accept no assertion unexamined, but to follow the apostolic plea to "test them all; hold on to what is good" (1 Thes. 5:21). In the chapters that follow, the decisive appeal will always be to Holy Scripture. Whatever is not solidly grounded and founded in God's Word has no valid claim on the faith and loyalty of Christians.

---

38. Chapter Nine, "Why Christianity?" takes a Christian apologetic (defense) approach to Advanced Doubt.

Chapter Two

THE LIVING GOD

by Robert D. Preus

و❧

All of Scripture is "theology," language or talk about God. This chapter talks about the Trinity, and so rather obviously about God. Yet when the topic at hand turns to justification by grace or the Lord's Supper or eternal life or the lives of Abraham, Isaac, or Jacob, we are always and preeminently talking about God. Christian theology talks about God on the basis of Scripture. For God is a living and speaking God who has made Himself known to fallen mankind in various ways: through prophets and Old Testament Scriptures before the advent of His Son (Heb. 1:1) and through the apostolic Scripture of the New Testament after the death and resurrection of Christ.

Since there are many important and essential topics that we cannot discuss in the present chapter, this treatment of "The Living God" will seem—and will be—inadequate and incomplete. Here, we will attempt to answer three basic questions about God: (1) How do we know Him? (2) What is He like? and (3) Who is He?

HOW DO WE KNOW GOD?

To know God means not merely to know things about Him—that He is Father, Son, and Holy Spirit; that He is righteous, almighty, wise, good, and loving—important and fundamental as such knowledge is. According to Scripture, our knowledge of God is similar to our knowledge by acquaintance. It is a knowledge of the heart which results in love (Deut. 6:13; see Jdg. 2:10). Such knowledge is not merely factual but involves a relationship, a walking with God in communion (Mic. 6:8). It is personal and intimate like our knowledge of a dear friend, and it affects our lives. Where there is no knowledge of God there is neither truth nor mercy (Hos. 4:1), neither obedience nor sacrifice to Him (Matt. 9:13). "I know whom I have believed," St. Paul says, "and am persuaded that he is able to keep that which I have committed unto him against that day" (2 Tim. 1:12 KJV; cf. Rom. 8:38). Here we see that knowing God always involves personal trust and confidence. Christ knows His sheep, and His sheep know Him (John 10:14). When Peter denies Christ and says, "I know him not" (Luke 22:57 KJV), he cuts himself off from God and His grace and loses everything. When Jesus says, "This is life eternal, that they might know thee the only true God, and Jesus Christ, whom thou hast sent" (John 17:3 KJV), He declares that salvation and life eternal are the results of knowing God and what He in His grace has done for sinners. (See John 20:31; 1 Tim. 1:15.) The Old Testament teaches that one knows God only when one recognizes His redemptive activity. Philip Melanchthon echoes this truth when he says, "To know Christ is to know His benefits."[1]

Much modern theology has emphasized the personal, experiential, and relational aspect of our knowledge of God to the virtual exclusion of revealed facts and information about God and what He has done to save us. It tended to ignore, pooh-pooh, and deny the historicity of the mighty acts of God and the redemptive acts of Jesus as well as the pure doctrine of the biblical Gospel which recounts these acts and interprets them for us. This is not only contrary to every page of the Bible, which gives us facts and information about God, but also ends up as nonsensical. How can one know God without knowing anything about God?

In the Scriptures the existence of God is never questioned. The prophets and apostles and the saints of the Old and New Testaments take the existence and power of God for granted. They may deny God, defy Him, and rebel against Him, but they do not question His existence. When the house of Israel and of Judah dealt treacherously against the Lord, and the prophet says, "They have belied the Lord, and said, It is not he [literally, he is not]; neither shall evil come upon us'" (Jer. 5:12 KJV), they have not denied God's existence. However, they have become practical atheists, i.e., living as though there were no God, not bothering about Him or His commands (cf. Ps. 14:1).

According to Scripture, the knowledge of God is everywhere. "The heavens declare the glory of God; and the firmament sheweth his handywork" (Ps. 19:1 KJV). The glory and power of God are in nature and in history to be seen by all (Ps. 8; Is. 40; Jer. 10). But only God's people know Him and worship Him rightly. In a sense, even sin proclaims God. For sin is, above all, rebellion against God. The polemics in the Old and New

---

1. *Editor's note*: The most famous instance in which Melanchthon used this motto was in the first edition of his *Loci Communes*. See Wilhelm Pauck, ed., *Melanchthon and Bucer*, The Library of Christian Classics, vol. 19 (Philadelphia, PA: Westminster Press, 1969), 21. Compare Ap IV 101.

Testament are directed in favor of monotheism, the superiority of Christianity over other religions, and the pure doctrine of the Gospel.

There is no speculation in the Bible about the origin or development of God, although that sort of thing was quite common in ancient heathen religions. God does not evolve or emerge from something. The Bible does not give us a "history" of YAHWEH [that is, "the LORD," as today's English translations frequently say—Editor]. He does not change or develop. Neither is God a god among many, as in modern Buddhism and Mormonism. He is always portrayed in Scripture as the eternal and unchangeable God and Lord of all.

How, then, do we know God? The ready answer of Scripture is that we do not know Him by our reasonable efforts and investigations of His essence and attributes. Rather, He reveals Himself to us. How does He do this? In two ways. First, through the natural course of His created order (nature) and of human events (history); and second, through special acts of revelation.

God's creation bespeaks His goodness and wisdom (Job 38:41; Ps. 19:1). The mountains, sea, and waves are witness to the power and majesty of God; the seasons testify to His goodness (Ps. 65). His revelation in nature as a personal and providential creator God stands in contrast to the idols of the heathens and the false gods of deists and the philosophers (Is. 40; Jer. 10:11–15). This "natural knowledge" of God is very clearly addressed by Paul in Romans 1:19–20 (ASV): "Because that which is known [knowable] of God is manifest in [to] them; for God manifested it unto them. For the invisible things of him since the creation of the world are clearly seen, being perceived through the things that are made, even his everlasting power and divinity; that they may be without excuse." Paul tells us here that "the things that are made" gives evidence to all that there is a God who is highly exalted above the world and time, an eternal God who has created the ends of the earth (cf. Is. 40). The evidence is so clear that anyone may "see" (that is, know) that there is an invisible God who is all powerful and has created this visible order. But from this created order anyone can also know of God's divinity; His Godhead; His incomprehensible, incomparable, and glorious nature—what Luke calls the "majesty" or mighty power of God when he describes Jesus' divine healing miracles (Luke 9:43). Whoever does not recognize all this is "without excuse," for it is there to be known.

Yet all the knowledge that the unconverted sinner can gain from God's creation and His providence in nature and human events can never save a person. In nature is revealed God's power and majesty and wisdom, even His benevolence, but not His love that saves lost and condemned sinners and grants them eternal life. Our old theologians used to say that God's revelation in nature can bring us to a knowledge that there is a God with magnificent attributes but not a knowledge of who this God is—namely, Father, Son, and Holy Spirit, triune in His very essence, who is a gracious Savior, God, and Lord. That is revealed only in the Gospel of Jesus Christ, Paul says (Rom. 1:17). And even the Godhead, majesty, and wrath revealed from heaven are persistently and always distorted by people (Rom. 1:18, 21 ff.). All heathen and unbelievers, according to Scripture, may well know God in the sense that they have an awareness of His existence and presence and power. In another sense, though, they do not know Him (Gal. 4:8; 1 Thes. 4:5). This does not mean that they have an absolute ignorance of Him. It means that they are without Him. Paul calls them *atheoi*, atheists in the practical sense of having no God (Eph. 2:12).

But if man cannot know God from the created order and from his own futile searchings after the Deity (1 Cor. 1:21), how can he know Him, who He is and what He is really like? We know Him only when we are known by Him, Paul says (Gal. 4:9), when He chooses to disclose Himself to us not generally (as in nature) but specifically and specially in His Son and through His Gospel Word which comes to us today in the sacred Scriptures. Knowledge of salvation is only through Christ and the Gospel.[2]

It is important for us to emphasize this basic fact because it goes against the pride of our fallen sinful nature and the whole spirit of our times. In the modern Western world, our primary concern, seeking to follow ancient Greek thought, has been to understand, explain, and comprehend reality around us (including God), and this presumably for practical purposes, if there are any. Coupled with this concern is the desire to control environment and to escape the frustration of not understanding nature and everything about us. Such an attitude and approach to life is based on the assumption that the principles of the universe and of all reality can be grasped by the human intellect. In the area of modern science such a procedure has proved to be very fruitful. Yet where God and religion are concerned, such an attitude turns man in the wrong direction. For God cannot be found, analyzed, and understood by the speculative mind of finite and sinful man. He is simply not the object of speculation. Moreover, no speculation can tell us what God's Word says, that God is a lov-

---

2. John 1:18; Acts 4:12; Rom. 10:17; cf. also John 3:18, 36.

ing, personal creator God, Maker and Sustainer of "all things visible and invisible"; a Redeemer God, "begotten of His Father before all worlds . . . who for us men, and for our salvation came down from heaven, and was incarnate by the Holy Spirit of the Virgin Mary, and was made man, and was crucified also for us under Pontius Pilate"; and that He is a Comforter and Sanctifier who is the Lord and Giver of life and thus creates and sustains Christ's church on earth.[3] Only the revelation in Scripture shows us the true God, God as He really is and as He has really declared Himself in Christ, a Savior God.

In the Scriptures the knowledge of God and the knowledge of salvation are inextricably linked. And who brings us salvation? Jesus. The priest Zacharias sings by inspiration that Jesus brings the "knowledge of salvation" to God's people by procuring the remission of sins (Luke 1:77 KJV). Peter says that we grow in grace when we grow in the knowledge of our *Savior* Jesus Christ (2 Pet. 3:18). According to the apostle Paul, to be saved and to come to the knowledge of the truth (of God) are inseparable, and this is all because our Mediator, the God-man Jesus Christ, gave Himself as a ransom for us (1 Tim. 2:4–6).

To know our Savior Christ, therefore, is to have salvation and to know God[4]; and there is no other way to know God. "No man hath seen God at any time, the only begotten Son [better texts say "God"], which is in the bosom of the Father, he hath declared him" (John 1:18 KJV). Just prior to this text John had spoken of the Incarnation (1:14) and said that divine grace and truth are gained only through Christ. No man can see God and live. Yet the Son declares that God makes Him[self] known to all who know and believe in the Son. So Jesus can say that one who has seen Him, the incarnate Son, has seen the Father (John 14:9). In fact, He can assure believers in Him of eternal life because He and the Father are one in essence (John 10:30) and because He and the Father work in intimate union as He carries out the works of salvation (John 10:38). In Hebrews we are told that Jesus is the "very image of [God's] substance" (Heb. 1:3 ASV), and St. Paul says that the "light of the knowledge of the glory of God" is revealed "in the face of Jesus Christ" (2 Cor. 4:6 KJV). Thus, when the evangelist says that the Son, Jesus, "is" (ever existing) in the bosom of the Father (John 1:18), he is speaking of a direct seeing, or knowledge, of God which we have through Jesus. To know Jesus is to know God *Himself*. Jesus is not a mere reflection of God. Christ witnesses of the Deity, He

---

3. *Editor's note*: Quotations in this sentence are from the Nicene Creed.
4. Eph. 4:13; Phil. 3:8, 10; 1 Jn. 4:9; 5:20.

declares God to us because He *is* God. We have a knowledge of God and eternal life only when we know Christ (1 Jn. 5:20).[5]

But how do we know Christ? Not by a heroic act of faith, leaping blindly into the dark. Not by historic research. Certainly we cannot turn back the clock and walk with Him and talk with Him as the disciples did. We know Him and receive His grace through His Word, the informative and powerful Gospel word of Scripture. And this written word of the Old Testament which Christ fulfilled (Matt. 5:17 ff.; John 5:39) and of the New Testament which He guaranteed by the gift of the Holy Spirit to His apostles (John 14:26, 15:26–27, 16:13), this revelatory word, affords *knowledge*, knowledge of God, divinely revealed information about God.

Promoters of neo-orthodoxy deny that Scripture provides such cognitive knowledge about God, and devotees of modern logical positivism posit that all theology (language about God) is nonsense. We do not have time to refute these ideologies in this chapter.[6] Suffice it to say that such viewpoints spring from the matrix of secular materialism. And whether these ideologists believe in a transcendent God or in no God, they operate from the assumption that the finite is not capable of conveying or containing the infinite—whether we are speaking of the human Jesus or the human Scriptures.

WHAT IS GOD LIKE?

The Bible speaks less about the essence and attributes of God than about His works in history and in the lives of believers. One simply cannot get at the essence of God by speculation or by depicting Him in stone or wood, which was strictly forbidden in the Old Testament. God is holy

---

5. Luther says: "Scripture begins tenderly and leads us to Christ as a man, then to the Lord over all creatures and to a God. In this way I advance gently and learn to know God. But philosophy and worldly-wise people desired to begin at the top—and thereby they became fools" (WA 21:22). Cf. WA 1:362 [corresponding text in AE 31, 52–53]:

    It suffices and avails no one to know God in His glory and majesty, unless he knows Him in the humility and ignominy of the cross. . . . Thus when Philip, in the spirit of a "theology of glory" said, "Show us the Father" (John 14:8), Christ immediately restrained his wandering thought which sought God elsewhere and directed it to Himself, saying: "Philip, he that seeth me seeth my Father also." Therefore the true theology and knowledge of God is to be found in the crucified Christ.

6. I have attempted to analyze and evaluate these opinions in *Crisis in Lutheran Theology*, ed. John Warwick Montgomery (Grand Rapids, MI: Baker, 1967), 2:18–30.

and transcendent. He is the living God who cannot be caught by static images or conceptions. The emphasis throughout Scripture upon the actions of God, upon His intervention in history and His dealings with people, shows us that He is a living God. He fights for them and guides them (1 Sam. 17:26, 36); He loves His people and comforts them, and when they thirst after Him, He fills them (Ps. 42) and they find rest in Him (Ps. 84:3; Matt. 11:28–29). The living God is utterly dependable.

The living God is Author and Sustainer of all life: "In him we live, and move, and have our being" (Acts 17:28 KJV). It is significant that in the New Testament, Christ is called life and is the source of all life and all that is (John 1:1–2; Col. 1:17), thus showing that He is God. A central motif of Scripture is that God is the origin of life and all life springs from Him (Ps. 36:9). All life is a gift from Him (Ps. 104), and this is because God Himself is living. Life, activity, *presence for us* are fundamental to God's nature; He is not some pantheistic "ground of being." As the living God He is personally concerned about the world and His people (Ps. 18:47–48; Jer. 10:9–10; Hos. 1:10).

The living God is a *personal* God. The personal nature of God is brought out in many ways. Second Corinthians 4:6 [KJV] speaks of the "face" of Jesus Christ, that is, His personality. We pray to God and He answers. We trust Him as we trust a person. We say "thou" to Him and He to us. Throughout Scripture our relationship with Him is always personal. God has a will; He makes decisions. All His actions—*all* His actions—toward us are personal (see 1 Cor. 1). His grace and love and goodness, as well as His wrath and judgment, are personal actions (Rom. 2:4, 11:22; Tit. 3:4). When Scripture describes God as wise and true and good (John 3:33; Rom. 2:4, 16:27), it ascribes eminently personal attributes to God. Although love cannot be called the essence of Deity, still it can be said that the personal God is love. This is true in all His will and in all His work, expressly in Christ's work (John 3:16).

Biblical anthropomorphisms (expressions that ascribe human parts to God) and anthropopathisms (expressions that ascribe human affections or feelings or reactions to God) emphasize His personal nature in a striking way. In fact, the very transcendence of God is expressed by some anthropomorphisms, thus showing that even though God is one who is personally related to man, nevertheless, there is no common measure between God and man.[7] The anthropomorphisms bring out the uniqueness of God and at the same time tell us about Him cognitively. They are not

---

7.   Num. 23:19; Is. 43:13, 45:12, 23; Hos. 11:9.

mere naïve thoughts of primitive people concerning God but are God's own revealed descriptions of Himself and His actions in human terms which finite and sinful men can understand. These and other figures of speech must be taken therefore in all seriousness, for they tell of God as He really is and as He really acts.

The personal nature of God is brought out in Scripture also by the intimate relationship and dealings of God with man. This personal fellowship is expressed often by the verb "walk" in Scripture (Mic. 6:8 [KJV]). Adam walked with God in the Garden (Gen. 3:8). Enoch walked with God (Gen. 5:24). This means that Adam and Enoch had intimate communion with Him; no estrangement or disrupting factors broke the fellowship. A different but related word is used by Jesus and the New Testament: the word "love" which expresses the intimate relationship of husband and wife. Jesus says, "If a man love me, he will keep [cling to] my words: and my Father will love him, and we will come unto him, and make our abode [dwelling place] with him" (John 14:23 KJV).[8] Love is a personal act. The God who loves our fallen race is a personal God.

God's intimate personal association with men is seen also in the term "know" in Scripture. "I am the good shepherd, and know my sheep, and am known of mine" (John 10:14 KJV; cf. 10:27; 2 Tim. 2:19). Jesus knows us with the same intimacy that He knows the Father and the Father knows Him (John 10:14–15a). Such personal knowledge and love (communion) between God and man is unique to the Christian religion.[9]

Still another attribute and activity ascribed to God tells of His personal relationship with mankind: His presence among us. We are speaking here not so much of His immensity, His repletive ("filling") presence whereby He fills and sustains and upholds all things, as we are speaking of His gracious personal presence. For God's repletive omnipresence[10] also declares clearly that He is a personal God. Yet this comes primarily in terms of His sovereignty, His utter transcendence, and His awesome majesty and wrath. In the main, it is a preachment of Law.

As just noted, however, we are thinking more of God's gracious and loving presence with believers (Is. 57:15), His evangelical presence. This presence is marked by His promises to come to us who call upon Him for help and to save us, by the promises of Jesus that He will be with us, and by His promises of the presence of the Holy Spirit to guide and com-

---

8. Cf. John 3:16; Eph. 5:25; I John 4:7–21.
9. Isa. 52:6; Jer. 31:1 ff., 31 ff.; Hos. 2:23; John 17:3.
10. 2 Chron. 2:6; Ps. 113:4–7; Prov. 15:3; Jer. 23:24.

fort us.[11] This personal presence of God in and with believers is not some vague ubiquity, "there-ness," but a dynamic, gracious, real presence of our God Himself in His very essence, analogous to an eternal marriage (Hos. 2:19) or to a vine giving life to branches (John 15:1) or to a head and a body (Eph. 5:23). God Himself, not only His gifts, lives and is in the believer in a union whereby we become partakers of the divine nature (2 Pet. 1:4). The Holy Spirit dwells in all believers in Christ, not merely figuratively through His gifts, but personally (1 Cor. 3:16–17). And this means that the very Godhead dwells in believers in what our church fathers have called a mystical union with all the fullness of His wisdom, holiness, power, and other divine gifts (Eph. 3:17–19).

The personal God who is present for us through the atoning work of Christ and present in us through the sanctifying work of the Holy Spirit is an omniscient God. He has a perfect knowledge of His creatures and of His people. He knows perfectly our weaknesses, our needs, and the secrets of our hearts (Ps. 44:21). No desire for peace or forgiveness, no groaning is hidden from Him (Ps. 38:9). This knowledge is both personal and intimate, and this is of great comfort to us as we trust in Him.[12]

Every attribute and action ascribed to God in Scripture testifies that our God is personal. This is what God is truly like. God is as He has acted and revealed Himself. We know Him by His works. Werner Elert says, "The question to what degree God is personality or how His personality as such is to be described can be answered in no other way than through the consideration of His works."[13]

A fundamental fact of God's revelation of Himself in Scripture is that He, the Lord, is one and undivided in essence. A correlate of this fundamental truth is the biblical teaching of the uniqueness of God, that He alone is God and there are no other gods besides Him. The one truth involves the other. This "unity" and "unicity" of God (monotheism) is the foundation stone of the Christian religion. From the time of our first parents in the Garden, God has always revealed Himself as one God who is utterly unique. The unity of God is expressed by the great *Shema* of the Israelites' morning and evening prayer, "Hear, O Israel: The LORD our God, is one LORD" (Deut. 6:4, KJV). This oneness of God demands that we worship Him in our whole heart and being. For the passage goes on

---

11. Ps. 23:4; 91:14–16; 145:18–19; Is. 43:1–7; Matt. 18:10, 20; 28:20; John 14:23, 25–26; 15:26; 16:13–14.
12. Ps. 103:14; Matt. 6:32; 10:30; I John 3:20.
13. Werner Elert, *Der Christliche Glaube* (Hamburg: Furche-Verlag, 1956), 230.

to say: "And thou shalt love the LORD thy God with all thine heart, and with all thy soul, and with all thy might" (Deut. 6:5 KJV). The unity of God implies and demands unity of worship and doctrine. He cannot be worshiped in one way at one place and in another way at another place. God cannot be divided (John 4:24).

That God is one and cannot be divided means that He is absolute unity, free from all composition, not consisting of parts. When Jesus says He comes from God and is God, He does not deny the unity of God. "The early Christian monotheism is not threatened by the Christ-ology of the New Testament, but made secure."[14] Christ Himself speaks about only one God. He repeats the *Shema* (Mark 12:29, 32) and remarks that "there is none good but one, that is, God" (Mark 10:18 KJV)[15], and this even though He claimed to be one with God the Father (John 10:30; 17:21).

What about the fact that the Scriptures call the Son and the Holy Spirit God as well as the Father?[16] We can only reply that there can be no contradiction here but rather a mystery which transcends our understanding. We must simply hold to all the revealed data made known to us in Scripture.

Neither does the unity of God conflict with the many, sometimes seemingly contradictory attributes and actions Scripture ascribes to God, such as His wrath and His love, His judgment and His grace, His word of Law and His word of Gospel. Our infinite and transcendent God cannot be caught within the categories of our finite and fallen reason. Our minds cannot set limits to His being and works (Is. 40:18 ff.; Rom. 11:33 ff.). God cannot be defined.

Like the unity of God, monotheism is a fundamental premise of all biblical theology. There is no suggestion anywhere in Scripture of gods besides the one true God; throughout the history of God's people recorded in the Pentateuch, Yahweh reveals Himself as the only God. The first commandment of the Decalogue forbids worshiping or recognizing other gods (Ex. 20:2–3); and the punishment is imposed: "He that

---

14. Gerhard Kittel, ed., *Theologisches Woerterbuch zum Neuen Testament* (Stuttgart: Verlag von W. Kohlhammer, 1933–79), 3:103. *Editor's note:* The translation above is that of Dr. Preus, but a corresponding English translation may be found in Gerhard Kittel, ed., *Theological Dictionary of the New Testament*, trans. Geoffrey W. Bromiley (Grand Rapids, MI: William B. Eerdmans Publishing Company, 1965), 3:102.

15. Cf. 1 Cor. 8:4; Eph. 4:5–6; 1 Tim. 1:17; 2:5; 6:15–16.

16. See Is. 9:6; 11:2 ff.; 61:1; Jer. 23:6; Matt. 12:28; John 1:1; 1 Tim. 3:15; Tit. 3:5.

sacrificeth unto any god, save unto the Lord only, he shall be utterly destroyed" (Ex. 22:20 KJV).

Some scholars think that Moses or the Old Testament more generally recognized the existence of other gods besides the Lord but simply forbade Israel to worship them. This, however, is untenable. The first commandment indicates not the existence but the nonexistence of other gods. Only the Lord is the *living* God. His very name *Yahweh* is taken from the word "to be, to exist." When graven images are forbidden in Exodus 20:4, no one would assume that Scripture thereby attributes divine existence to graven images. No, only the Lord is God, and "there is none else beside Him" (Deut. 4:35 KJV; see Deut. 4:39; 32:39); all idols are no gods at all, "vanities," "nothing," "wind" (1 Kgs. 16:13; Is. 41:29; Jer. 8:19 KJV). God is transcendent, and His transcendence is His uniqueness (Is. 40:18; 45:5–6).

All the attributes ascribed to God in the biblical revelation tell us what God is like. He is holy, separated from all that is not God.[17] Holiness denotes God's radiance and purity, His absolute moral perfection in every direction (Job 15:15; Is. 1:4; Luke 5:8). It denotes His absolute transcendence and otherness (Hos. 11:9). Therefore His actions are a wonder to behold (Is. 29:14). Holiness denotes God's absolute power; what He does, only He can do (Is. 40:25–27; 41:1 ff). But God's holiness also marks His goodness, mercy, grace (Ex. 15:11; 1 Sam. 2:2), and glory.

God's glory is the manifestation of His holiness, of His absolute majesty (Ex. 33:18). And this glory fills men's hearts with wonder, fear, and confusion, but also with joy, peace, and anticipation (Is. 6:5; Luke 5:8).[18] The Holy One of Israel is the Redeemer, the Savior (Hebrew *goel*) of Israel,[19] and His holiness or His "holy name" finds its basis in His work to save. When Jesus is called "Savior" or "Redeemer" in Scripture, when He is called "the holy one of God"[20], when He is said to manifest His glory (John 1:14), then He Himself is declared to be God. (See Is. 42:8.) It is significant that the glory of God in the New Testament is always associated with Christ, the man (John 1:14), either in His birth (Luke 2:9), His activities (John 2:11), His transfiguration, His ascension, or even His death (John 16–17).

Like His holiness, omnipresence, and knowledge, previously mentioned, God's omnipotence embraces the whole spectrum of God's attri-

---

17. Is. 1; 6; 10; 40; 41; 43; 45; 48 ff.
18. Cf. also Ex. 3; Luke 2:8–14; John 1:14; Eph. 1:17–18; 1 Pet. 1:14–16.
19. Is. 41:14; 43:3, 14; 49:7; 54:5.
20. Luke 1:35; John 6:69; Acts 4:27, 30.

butes and actions. It reveals to us what kind of God He is: a living and personal God, a free God who does what He pleases and who can do anything.[21] God's power embraces His justice, His wrath against sin, His control of all things, His benevolence, and His saving grace (Eph. 1:19), even His eternity. His omnipotence may well frighten us because of our sins, but it also assures us that He is our God and that He is able to care for us in every way and to save us.[22]

God's power is eternal, and His eternity is omnipotent. There is an inextricable connection between all the attributes of God. All these attributes, however we might classify them, ascribed in Scripture to God and His works are really one with the divine essence. For, as we have seen, God is absolutely one and undivided. There can be no confusion or contradiction between the different attributes and works of God. As Scripture tells us that He is just, transcendent, good, righteous, immutable, truthful, omniscient in Himself and in all His works and ways, it tells us the truth about God and what He is really like.

WHO IS GOD?

As we have searched the Scriptures to learn what God is like, we have also learned His identity, who He is: Father, Son, and Holy Spirit. That is to say, He who has revealed Himself to be Creator of all things and who is the Father of our Lord Jesus Christ from eternity is called and is God; He who existed with God from eternity and has revealed Himself to be the only begotten Son of God and Savior of the world is called and is God; He who revealed Himself to be the Spirit of God proceeding of eternity from the essence of God, who came upon the Virgin Mary so that she became pregnant with the Son of the Highest, who anointed the Son of God to His ministry of redemption, and who calls, gathers, and enlightens Christ's church on earth through the Word of God is called and is God.

Here we stand on holy ground. We are confronted with the divine mystery of the Holy Trinity. The absolute unity of the divine essence is affirmed everywhere in Scripture. Yet God is three distinct persons, Father, Son, and Holy Spirit. These identifying names are never used in Scripture metaphorically. They never denote a mere attribute or activity or emanation of God, never a mere relation or force or mode of divine being. They denote always specific, concrete, real, distinct, identifiable, individual, conscious persons.

---

21. Gen. 18:14; Ps. 115:3; Jer. 32:17; Matt. 3:9.
22. Is. 50:2–3; Rom. 8:32 ff.; Eph. 1:18 ff.; 3:20 ff.; cf. also Gen. 17:1 ff.

The term *person* (Greek *hypostasis*, Latin *persona*) as it was used in the early church and to this very day by Christians is not explicitly found in the Old or New Testaments. But the idea which Christians have attempted to convey by this term, which was used and defined to combat misunderstanding and heresy, is certainly biblical. According to the Augsburg Confession, the Magna Carta of the Reformation, the three persons of the Godhead are "of the same essence and power, who also are coeternal, the Father, the Son, and the Holy Ghost. And the term 'person' they [the Reformers] use as the Fathers have used it, to signify, not a part or quality in another, but that which subsists of itself."[23]

This is precisely the unsophisticated and clear teaching of Scripture. Everywhere in the Old and New Testaments where the Father or Christ, the Son, or the Holy Spirit is spoken of individually, a conscious, real, individual, and distinct person is referred to, a person who creates, who wills, who loves, who judges, who has compassion, who comforts, who inspires prophets, etc. This is true also when one person of the Godhead is spoken of in Scripture in relation to another; a relationship of persons is always evidenced.

The personal relationship and thus the personal characteristics of the Father, Son, and Holy Spirit have been revealed most concretely in the ministry of Jesus, God's only Son. The Father and the Holy Spirit are intimately and personally involved in His incarnation, conception, and birth (Matt. 1:18–24; Luke 1:26–35), in His baptism and anointment into His redemptive ministry,[24] in His transfiguration (Matt. 17:5–8) and crucifixion. Jesus obeys (a personal act) the will of the Father; He promises and sends (personal acts) the Spirit. Throughout Scripture only masculine personal pronouns are used to denote Father, Son, and Holy Spirit.

The personal nature of Father, Son, and Spirit are most emphatically evidenced in Jesus' discourses in John 14–16. He urges His disciples to believe in the Father and in Him. If we know Him, we know the Father. If we have seen Him, we have seen the Father. He is in the Father and the Father is in Him—in Him in the most unique and divine communion and interpenetration[25] but without any confusion of the identity of the persons. The Father sends another Comforter, the Spirit of truth, who abides with the disciples and with His church. The world does not see Him or know Him, but we know Him. He is loved by all who love

---

23. AC I 3–4. *Editor's note:* The translation is that of *Triglot*, 43.
24. Matt. 3:13–17. Cf. Is. 61:1–3; 4:1 ff.; Matt. 12:18 ff.
25. What the Greek fathers called *perichoresis*.

the Father. The Father sends the Holy Spirit in Jesus' name. Jesus, too, sends the Comforter from the Father, and the Comforter testifies of Him. The Comforter comes and testifies and leads us into all truth. Now, it is persons—individual, intelligent centers of consciousness, "I[s]," "you[s]," "he[s]"—who are spoken of in this discourse of our Lord, not principles, relationships, events, attributes, or modes of being.

Just as Scripture witnesses to the fact that the names, activities, and attributes ascribed to the Father, Son, and Holy Spirit indicate that each is a true and individual person, so the testimony of Scripture teaches that each of the persons is true God. The Son and the Holy Spirit possess the fullness of the Deity with the Father. Divine names are ascribed to Christ, the Son, throughout the Old Testament (*Yahweh*,[26] *Adonai*,[27] *El*[28]). In the New Testament He is called both Lord and God in the absolute sense without any limitations.[29] To Him is ascribed the creation of all things (Col. 1:14–16). His work of redemption and everything pertaining to it is a work that only Almighty God can carry out. He is eternal with God (John 1:1), and is called "the only begotten Son" (v. 18 KJV) or the only begotten *God*. He possesses all the attributes of God, "for in him dwelleth all the fulness of the Godhead bodily" (Col. 2:9 KJV). He is the effulgence of God's glory and the image of His substance (Heb. 1:3). Therefore He is to be worshiped and believed just as the Father is to be worshiped and believed.[30]

The Deity of the Holy Spirit is also clear from the witness of Scripture. All personal characteristics ascribed to Him in Scripture—that He proceeds from God, that He witnesses, that He gives life, that He comforts, regenerates, forgives, and saves—are characteristics and works of God alone. His very name "Spirit" as ascribed to Him in Scripture suggests deity, and the common adjective *holy* is an essential attribute only of God. The gifts of the Spirit to the church such as confession of Christ, prophecy, inspiration, tongues and the interpretation of tongues, faith, love, unity, hope, baptism, etc.,[31] are all divine gifts, even as they are personal gifts. Everything pertaining to the Christian's spiritual existence has its origin in the Holy Spirit. There would be no church, no

---

26. Ps. 68:18; Jer. 23:6; Hos. 1:7; Zech. 2:8 ff.

27. Ps. 110:1; Mal. 3:1. See Is. 6:1 with John 12:40–41.

28. Ps. 95:7; Is. 7:14; 9:6; 35:4–6.

29. John 1:1; 20:28; Acts 20:28; Rom. 10:13; 1 Cor. 1:30–31; 2:8; 8:6; Col. 2:2; 1 Tim. 3:15; 6:14–16; Tit. 2:13; Heb. 1:8; 1 Jn. 5:20.

30. John 5:23; 6:29; 14:1; Rev. 5:13.

31. Rom. 12:6 ff; 1 Cor. 12; Gal. 5:22–25; Eph. 4:3 ff.

faith, no baptism, no forgiveness, no conferral of divine grace, and no enjoyment of salvation apart from the Holy Spirit and His work. That is why it is so important for us to believe that, as the Holy Spirit works, God is graciously and mightily at work with us and in us and for us, just as it is utterly crucial for us to know and believe that Christ's work of redemption is nothing else but the work of God Himself. Luther wrote in the Large Catechism:

> For neither you nor I could ever know anything of Christ or believe on Him and have Him for our Lord, except as it is offered to us and granted to our hearts by the Holy Ghost through the preaching of the gospel. The work is finished and accomplished; for Christ, by His suffering, death, resurrection, etc. has acquired and gained the treasure for us. But if the work remained concealed, so that no one knew of it, then it were in vain and lost. That this treasure therefore might not lie buried, but be appropriated and enjoyed, God has caused the Word to go forth and be proclaimed, in which He gives the Holy Ghost to bring this treasure home and apply it to us. Therefore sanctification is nothing else but bringing us to Christ to receive this good, to which, of ourselves, we could not attain.[32]

What Luther has just said is eminently biblical and of decisive importance. If Christ our Savior is not God, if the Holy Spirit our Sanctifier is not God, then there is no atonement, no salvation, no life after death, and no faith or hope for the Christian.

But is God really three divine persons, or does He only reveal Himself to be so? Christian theologians have distinguished on one hand between the eternal works of the Father, Son, and Holy Spirit, the inner relations within the Trinity, and on the other hand those works which Father, Son, and Holy Spirit do in relation to creation and mankind. When we refer to the former—i.e., the Father begets His own Son from eternity, the Son is eternally begotten of the Father and is identical with Him and is Light of Light, the Spirit proceeds from the Father and the Son[33]—we speak of the *immanent* Trinity. When we refer to the actions of the persons of the Godhead in relation to us, we commonly speak of the *economic* Trinity. The eternal inter-trinitarian works of the Godhead are no less real than His external and sometimes historical works toward

---

32. LC II 38–39. *Editor's note*: The translation seems to be Dr. Preus's somewhat altered version of that in *Triglot*, 689.
33. Ps. 2:7; 96:6; 110:4; John 1:1, 18; 3:16; 5:18; 8:29; 10:30; 15:26; Acts 16:7; Rom. 8:32; Gal. 4:6; Phil. 2:6; Col. 1:15; Heb. 1:3.

His fallen creation. Our one God is triune, three divine persons sharing the one divine essence, immanently as well as economically. "For," as Werner Elert says, "God cannot be anything else than what He has revealed Himself to be. If He has revealed Himself as three in one, then He is three in one."[34]

It is significant to note that throughout the history of doctrine when theologians have denied that the Father, Son, and Holy Spirit are persons, they have also lost the doctrine of the immanent Trinity just as surely as when they deny the Deity of the three persons. But they have lost more than what they think is just a relic of antiquated medieval metaphysics: they have lost the economic Trinity as well; they have lost God's mighty acts or muddled them beyond recognition. No longer do these theologians believe in a creation of all things, a redemption of the human race, and a sanctification of God's own people, all carried out by the living God Himself. And so they have lost God.

I am not simply talking here about Socinians, Jehovah's Witnesses, and modern Unitarians of recent generations who called themselves Modernists. I am also talking about contemporary theologians who reject the doctrine of the Trinity as unevangelical or unintelligible or for some other reason, who distort or try to "rehabilitate" the biblical doctrine, or who ignore the doctrine altogether. They have given up the Gospel which can only be proclaimed in a trinitarian matrix and setting. For the Gospel is nothing else than the proclamation of the external works of the economic Trinity, the Father, Son, and Holy Spirit.

The doctrine of God—that is, the Trinity—so firmly based on Scripture, is *the* fundamental article of the Scriptures and of the Christian faith in the sense that all biblical theology ought to be grounded upon and subsumed under this one article. It tells us everything we should know and believe about who God is and what He is like and what He has done. Really, it is all summed up beautifully by Luther in his commentary on the Apostles' Creed in his Large Catechism:

> In these three articles God himself has revealed and opened to us the most profound depths of his fatherly heart, his sheer, unutterable love. He created us for this very purpose, to redeem and sanctify us. Moreover, having bestowed upon us everything in heaven and on earth, he has given us his Son and his Holy Spirit, through whom he brings us to himself. As we explained before, we could never come to recognize the Father's favor

---

34. Elert, *Der Christliche Glaube*, 225.

and grace were it not for the Lord Christ, who is a mirror of the Father's heart. Apart from him we see nothing but an angry and terrible Judge. But neither could we know anything of Christ, had it not been revealed by the Holy Spirit.

These articles of the Creed, therefore, divide and distinguish us Christians from all other people on earth. All who are outside the Christian church, whether heathen, Turks, Jews, or false Christians and hypocrites, even though they believe in and worship only the one, true God, nevertheless do not know what his attitude is toward them. They cannot be confident of his love and blessing. Therefore they remain in eternal wrath and damnation, for they do not have the Lord Christ, and, besides, they are not illuminated and blessed by the gifts of the Holy Spirit.[35]

---

35. LC II 64–66 (quoted from Tappert, 419). *Editor's note*: On the translation of this section, see Edward Engelbrecht, *One True God: Understanding the Large Catechism II.66* (St. Louis, MO: Concordia Publishing House, 2007.

Chapter Three

THE INCARNATION OF GOD

Editor's Note: Unless otherwise indicated, all Scripture quotations in this chapter are from the King James Version of the Bible. All notes in this chapter have been added by the Editor.

"The Word was made flesh," writes St. John (1:14), "and dwelt among us, (and we beheld his glory, the glory as of the only begotten of the Father,) full of grace and truth."

God became Man. These simple words spell out the deepest mystery in heaven and on earth, the twin of that other sublime and incomprehensible truth: that the one true God is in fact three Persons. "Eye hath not seen, nor ear heard" such holy mysteries (1 Cor. 2:9; see Is. 64:4). They are beyond the ken of the greatest thinkers on earth, and they lie completely inaccessible to even the most sophisticated scientific equipment. Yet God has freely revealed them so that even simple children may confess them with their Hosannas. To those who saw our Lord in the flesh, He said: "Blessed are the eyes which see the things that ye see" (Luke 10:23). And of us, who came to faith through the testimony of eye-witnesses, He says: "Blessed are they that have not seen, and yet have believed" (John 20:29). Blessed indeed! For on this holy mystery of the Word made flesh depends our whole salvation.

FULLY GOD AND FULLY MAN

Pagan mythologies are full of demigods, legendary half-divine and half-human beings. The true God-Man, Jesus, is nothing like that. Not half God and half man, He is "true God, begotten of the Father from eternity, and also true man, born of the Virgin Mary."[1] In Him dwells not some supposed spark of divinity, but rather "all the fulness of the Godhead bodily" (Col. 2:9).

To us modern people it seems self-evident that Jesus was a human being. What does not stand out as so obvious to us is that He was and is the Almighty God, Who created the cosmos. The earliest Christians saw it the

---

1. SC Creed, Second Article explanation, *Triglot*, 545.

other way 'round, though. For those who lived in the immediate afterglow of His appearance on earth, "the glory of God in the face of Jesus Christ" (2 Cor. 4:6) remained a memory too vivid to let them lose sight of His divinity. It was His true humanity that seemed less obvious. Therefore St. John had to rebuke in the sternest terms the temptation to reduce Christ's human nature to a mere sham or illusion: "Every spirit that confesseth not that Jesus Christ is come in the flesh is not of God"; such a spirit is that of "antichrist" (1 Jn. 4:3). St. Paul, too, insists that our Lord was "made of a woman, made under the law" (Gal. 4:4), so much so that we Christians are "members of his body, of his flesh, and of his bones" (Eph. 5:30).

JESUS AS JEHOVAH

During the fourth century, Arius and his followers denied that Christ was really God. He was more than a man, yes—but, they said, not quite God. When pressed, these so-called "Arians" were even willing to call Jesus "God" in some sense, yet they denied that He was really the one true God Who created heaven and earth. Against their denials, muddles, and outright deceptions, the Councils of Nicaea (325) and Constantinople (381) put the biblical truth in the clearest language possible: "God of God, Light of Light, very God of very God, begotten, not made, being of one substance with the Father, by Whom all things were made." These great truths of the Nicene Creed we have solemnly confessed before God's altar ever since.

In our day the "Jehovah's Witnesses" have taken up the old Arian errors once more. They deny the Holy Trinity and the true Godhead of Jesus Christ. A mockery is made of St. John's profound confession that "the Word was God" (John 1:1) via the pretense that this means "the Word was a god"! The whole of St. John actually constitutes a sublime and glorious witness to our Lord's true divinity. It culminates, now in full view of the Lord's accomplished life, death, and resurrexion, in the same confession with which it opened: "My Lord and my God" (John 20:28).

St. John 8:58 takes us deeper still: "Before Abraham was, *I am*" [italics added]. The unbelieving Jews understood very well that Jesus with these words was making a claim to God's own name, Jehovah, which is based on the "I Am That I Am" of Exodus 3:14. They wanted to stone Him, saying: "thou, being a man, makest thyself God" (John 10:33).

For fear of misusing God's sacred name Jehovah (Yhwh is as close as we can get in English to the Hebrew original), the Jews had the custom of substituting another word which meant "Lord." That custom was followed when the Bible was first put into Greek. "Jehovah" became "Kyrios," Lord. When the New Testament calls Jesus "Lord," that is the meaning. He is

God, Jehovah. Old Testament "Jehovah" texts become "Kyrios" (Lord) texts in the New Testament, and are regularly applied to Jesus. So, for instance, Romans 10:13 ("For whosoever shall call upon the name of the Lord [Jehovah] shall be saved") directly applies to Jesus the words of Joel 2:32. The truth that Jesus is God is not found only occasionally here and there; it belongs rather to the very core confession of the New Testament that Jesus Is Kyrios (that is, "Lord"; see Rom. 10:9; 1 Cor. 12:3; Phil. 2:11).

Here, in embryo, are our trinitarian creeds. There is only one Lord (Jehovah, Deut. 6:4). Jesus is that one Lord Jehovah, yet so is the Father and so is the Holy Spirit (Matt. 28:19). Therefore God, Jehovah, is not one but three Persons.

GOD AND MAN, YET ONE PERSON

In the most Holy Trinity we must *distinguish* yet may not *separate* the Persons. So it is with the two natures of our Lord. On one hand, we must not imagine these natures confused or mixed up as though they were not *distinct*. Yet on the other hand, we must not *divide* or *separate* them, as though the Lord were two persons. He remains one indivisible divine-human Person. "He Whom the heavens cannot enclose does in Mary's lap repose," sings Luther in his famous Christmas hymn.[2] Accordingly, the ancient heretic Nestorius was wrong to deny that the blessed Virgin Mary is the Mother of God. Jesus is God, and Mary is His mother. Therefore, and in that sense, Mary is the mother of God (see Luke 1:43)—not the mother of a mere man who has some loose connexion to God.

This logic becomes even more important in the following sequence: Jesus died, Jesus is God, therefore God died. A mere man's death could not have saved us. "The blood of Jesus Christ his [God's] Son cleanseth us from all sin" (1 Jn. 1:7). No mere human blood can cleanse from sin. Does God then have blood? Yes, in Jesus, Who is God and Man in one Person. The holy blood of the Lamb of God (see also Rev. 5:12; 22:3) has infinite detergent power. That is why, despite some evasive modern translations, Scripture speaks of "the church of God, which he hath purchased with his own blood" (Acts 20:28).

LET HIM WHO BOASTS BOAST IN THE LORD

If Jesus is God and Man then it is wrong to divide Him from Himself as the (Calvinist) Heidelberg Catechism does in its Question 47: "With

---

2. This may have been Marquart's own translation. Compare "We Praise You, Jesus, at Your Birth," *LSB* 382, stanza 3.

respect to his human nature, he is no more on earth; but with respect to His divinity, majesty, grace, and Spirit, He is never absent from us."[3] To say that as Man Christ is present only in one place, and that everywhere else He is present only as God, is to try to undo the incarnation. By His ascension, the Lord—precisely in His human nature—became not more absent but if anything more present to us, since He "ascended up far above all heavens, that he might fill all things" (Eph. 4:10). "All things" is a Greek expression for the universe.

Of course the full divine majesty was in the Man Jesus all along. That did not begin with His resurrexion or ascension. So the Son of Man has the divine authority to forgive sin (Matt. 9:6), and is Lord of the Sabbath (12:8). And it was no one less than the Prince or Author of Life Who was killed, the Lord of glory Who was crucified (Acts 3:15; 1 Cor. 2:8). Yet during His earthly humiliation our Lord did not make full use of the divine glory He had in His human nature. He took upon Himself the form of a slave, humbly obedient even to the point of death (Phil. 2:7–8). Yet faith is not deceived by His lowly appearance: "Blessed is he [that is], whosoever shall not be offended in me" (Matt. 11:6). We are to imitate His self-denying lowliness (1 Pet. 2:21).

Our path, too, leads, by Baptism, through the cross to the crown (Rom. 6:5; 8:17). The grace of becoming, in Christ, "partakers of the divine nature" (2 Pet. 1:4) includes the gift of suffering (Phil. 1:29). We who seek the joy of the new without the death of the old must take to heart Luther's reminder that Christ must be grasped first as Man and then as God. The cross of His humanity must be sought before the glory of His divinity. Once we've got Christ the Man, He brings along Christ the God of His own accord.[4] Our own frightful times should teach us to glory in the Son of God Who for us and for our salvation did not evade suffering. As Edward Shillito put it after the horrors of World War I:

> "The other gods were strong; but Thou wast weak;
> They rode, but Thou didst stumble to a throne;
> But to our wounds only God's wounds can speak,
> And not a god has wounds, but Thou alone."[5]

---

3. The Heidelberg Catechism, *Book of Praise: Anglo-Genevan Psalter*, revised ed. (Winnipeg, Manitoba: Premier Printing, Ltd., 1984, 1987), 492.
4. WA 5, 128–129.
5. Edward Shillito, quoted in J. N. D. Anderson, *The Mystery of the Incarnation* (Downers Grove, IL: InterVarsity Press, 1978), 157.

Chapter Four

JUSTIFICATION AND SANCTIFICATION

FAITH AND LOVE

᷾

"How can I get a gracious God?" This haunting question did not mean for Luther what we moderns are so apt to think it meant: "How can I hit upon just the right mix in religion to make me feel good and 'upbeat' rather than depressed?" Luther despised play-religion of this sort. Nor was he asking as philosophers ask, comfortably, over coffee or cocktails: "Where do we come from? Where are we going?" and so on. Not puzzles and brain-teasers were on Luther's mind, but the most pressing emergency of our existence: How can a sinful human being find mercy and acceptance before the great and holy God Who hates and crushes all evil?

This cry "out of the depths" (Ps. 130:1) signals not a private neurosis, but the utter realism of one who has glimpsed something of his true standing before God. It echoes the plaint of the great apostle Paul himself: "Who will rescue me from this body that is subject to death?" (Rom. 7:24, author's translation). The Augustinian monk Martin Luther found his way to Paul's answer by way of the great St. Augustine (354–430 AD), who had written that human hearts are restless until they find rest in the Lord.[1]

Justification is Gospel-bedrock. It should not surprise us therefore to find here the very "epicenter" of that great upheaval known as the Reformation. Justification is the core of Christianity. Whatever one thinks and says here must affect one's understanding of everything else all along the line of Christian truth.

JUSTIFICATION AS IMPUTATION

Imagine a fever chart. Unlike the charts used in hospitals, this will be a spiritual fever chart (next page). It measures, let us say, spiritual goodness or righteousness.

The bottom line represents our starting level at birth: "dead in trespasses and sins ... by nature the children of wrath" (Eph. 2:1, 3 KJV). Now, what we need is not some half-way goodness—even if we could get that.

---

1. *Confessions*, I, 1.

To stand before God it is necessary to be totally good, one hundred percent. The only way in which we can have that is by way of a gift from God Himself. And this is precisely what happens in justification (represented in our diagram by the J-line). This justification is simply the forgiveness of our sins. Or, viewed another way, it is the exchange of guilt and innocence between Christ and ourselves. His perfect righteousness is credited to us and covers our sinfulness. God regards us no longer as we are in ourselves, that is, sinners, but as if we were His own dear holy Son, Jesus. All this happens in the first moment of faith. As soon as we believe in our Saviour Jesus, His whole great saving work for us becomes ours, as a free gift.

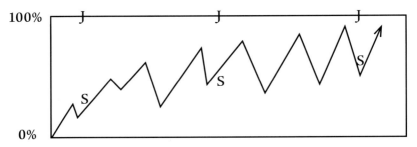

But justification, or the complete forgiveness of our sins, is not the only thing that happens. God does not simply forgive and accept us, and then leave us just as dead inside as we were before. Coming to faith is a new spiritual birth. Out of this new life, which is faith, there flow love and all good works, in the service of God and man. This effect of faith is called "sanctification" (the S-line in our diagram). Since the intensity of faith and love vary, sanctification (but not justification!) has ups and downs. The S-line is a zigzag, but its trend is upward, toward maturity.

This sharp distinction between justification, by which alone salvation is obtained, and sanctification, which follows as a result, was at the heart of the sixteenth-century dispute. On the basis of Scripture, the Reformation kept these two things quite distinct, while the opponents confused and collapsed them, so that sanctification (the S-line) was mistaken for justification. But this confusion works havoc with the biblical Gospel and misdirects people to seek justification and salvation in the wrong place.

In tabular form the main distinctions could be put like this:

JUSTIFICATION	SANCTIFICATION
1. Imputation	1. Transformation
2. Outside ourselves	2. Inside ourselves
3. Instantaneous, perfect	3. Gradual, imperfect

The word *imputation* is really the key to the whole thing. It means crediting or debiting something to someone, depending on whether it is a benefit or a debt. Other words for this, also used in various Bible translations, are "considering," "counting," "accounting," "reckoning," or "reputing." The point is that to be justified means to be *declared* righteous ("just"), not to be *made* righteous by an inner change. One can hardly think of a better explanation than that given by St. Paul in Romans 4:2–8 (RSV):

> For if Abraham was justified by works, he has something to boast about, but not before God. What does the scripture say? "Abraham believed God, and it was reckoned to him as righteousness." Now to one who works, his wages are not reckoned as a gift but as his due. And to one who does not work but trusts him who justifies the ungodly, his faith is reckoned as righteousness. So also David pronounces a blessing upon the man to whom God reckons righteousness apart from works:
>
> > "Blessed are those whose iniquities are forgiven, and whose sins are covered; blessed is the man against whom the Lord will not reckon his sin."

To be justified here means quite the same thing as to be forgiven. Since God is judge, justification is not a casual sentiment, but it is His favorable judgment or verdict. It is a judicial forgiveness, and therefore an "acquittal," as the Revised Standard Version calls it in Romans 5:18. Judicial verdicts of course happen in courtrooms. This is why justification is called a "forensic" (court-related) act. This is to distinguish it from processes which happen in us, such as sanctification, which could be compared to a medicinal or healing activity. But according to the Scriptures we stand before God not because of internal improvements or healings, but simply because of His gracious verdict of forgiveness spoken over us. That is justification.

Given that justification is by imputation, everything else follows. In contrast to sanctification, which is God's gracious renewal *in* us, the pardoning verdict of justification happens not in us but "about us," at the judgment seat of God. This verdict of course is an all-or-nothing affair. One is either forgiven and accepted by God or not, but never anything in between. Justification cannot increase or decrease because it consists of the perfect and unchangeable righteousness of Christ, credited to us. Faith does not add anything to this treasure, but merely receives it. Therefore justification does not fluctuate with the strength or weakness of faith. The weakest, tiniest spark of faith justifies as fully as does the mightiest mountain-moving kind. But sanctification does reflect the ups and downs of faith, and is therefore variable.

This should not be taken to mean, however, that justification is God's work, and sanctification our own. No, also sanctification is entirely the gracious work of God in us, as the Saviour Himself says: "I am the vine; you are the branches . . . . apart from me you can do nothing" (John 15:5).

BY GRACE

That justification and salvation are given us by grace is quite clear even from a surface reading of St. Paul's letters, particularly those to the Roman and Galatian congregations. In Reformation times even Luther's bitterest opponents had to admit that justification was by grace, although they gave a completely different explanation of what grace is. By "grace" they understood a supernatural power, a sort of spiritual electricity poured into people by God at their conversion, enabling them to produce the love and good works by which they were then justified! The question therefore became: Is saving grace this energy poured into men ("infused grace")? Or is it something in God, namely His unearned favor in Christ, as Luther taught?

Now, it is quite true that the Greek word *charis*, which through the Latin *gratia* becomes our English *grace*, is sometimes used in the sense of "gift of grace," that is, a gift bestowed on us by God's favor (for example, Rom. 15:15; 1 Pet. 2:19; 4:10).[2] But the question is not about special meanings. It is about the primary sense of the word, when it means the grace by which we are justified and saved. For this context St. Paul defines exactly what he means: "Now to the one who works, wages are not credited as a gift [literally: "according to grace"] but as an obligation" (Rom. 4:4). In other words, grace is the opposite of earning or deserving. Again: "And if by grace, then it cannot be based on works; if it were, grace would no longer be grace" (Rom. 11:6). "By grace," then, is the same as *gratis*, free of charge, without cost or payment on our part (although it did cost God a great deal).

These differences have far-reaching consequences. If with St. Paul and Luther we understand God's saving grace as His unearned favor in Christ, then grace and works as ways of salvation are opposites. They

---

2. *Editor's note:* The Greek word *charis* appears in 1 Pet. 2:19 and 20, yet it is not typically rendered as "grace" in most English translations of the Bible. (The English Standard Version comes close with "gracious thing.") In this reference and others, Marquart kept his eye on the original Greek text. He was determined to reflect it faithfully and fully.

exclude each other. Salvation must be either by grace or by works—not both. Since it is by grace, it cannot be by works. This is Paul's argument throughout. But if one is allowed to redefine grace as an inner energy which produces the works which in turn make us pleasing and acceptable to God, then one can turn the either/or of Paul and Luther into a both/and: Salvation is by grace, and therefore by works, because "grace" is now simply a code-word for a works-producing energy. St. Paul's logic, "if by grace, then not by works," is completely derailed into: "the more it is by grace, the more it is really by works." That is why it is so important to maintain the correct biblical understanding of saving grace as God's free favor, not as an infused something in us.

The right, biblical understanding of grace as favor corresponds exactly to the biblical sense of justification as imputation, rather than implantation, of righteousness. Before Luther understood this, the very idea of "the righteousness of God" (Rom. 1:17) had seemed tormenting and hateful to him. He had taken this, in good medieval fashion, to mean the righteousness by which God demands righteousness of us. Only when he saw that Paul was speaking here of the righteousness which God gives us as a gift did it dawn on Luther what the Gospel really is:

> At last, by the mercy of God, after I had pored over this night and day, I came upon the context of the words, "In it the righteousness is revealed, as it is written, 'He who through faith is righteous shall live.'" There I began to understand the righteousness of God as that by which the righteous one lives by means of a gift of God, which is truly by faith. And this is the meaning: through the Gospel is revealed the righteousness of God, namely the passive righteousness, by which merciful God justifies us through faith, as it is written: "He who through faith is righteous shall live." At that moment I felt that I had been born again, and that I had entered paradise itself through opened gates.[3]

THROUGH FAITH

If justification comes as a free gift, that is, by grace, then it must be through faith: "Therefore, the promise comes by faith, so that it may be by grace" (Rom. 4:16). A gift cannot be earned or paid for. It can only be received. And that is the entire function of faith in justification. It is simply the beggar's hand which takes hold of the precious present.

---

3. Luther's 1545 *Preface* to his works, as cited from WA 54:186 in Lowell C. Green, *How Melanchthon Helped Luther Discover the Gospel* (Fallbrook, CA: Verdict Publications, 1980), 62–63. See AE 34, 337.

The point is worth stressing, because a lot of loose "faith alone" talk makes faith into a piece of religious bravado, which "saves" on that account. So understood, or rather misunderstood, "faith" becomes the religious version of the secular boast "I did it *my* way!" This sort of faith is simply self-projection, inner stamina, optimism in the face of adversity, and the like. What matters then is the personal "quality of faith," its sincerity, intensity, or perhaps even its humanitarian concern. Never mind the thorny question of its objective truth! But this is a secular caricature. It makes faith into another work, only an easier and more self-indulgent one than the old monastic discipline.

All such notions that give to faith a weight of its own are foreign to faith's true nature. The whole saving gift and power is not in faith but in its object, Christ. Faith is but the humble setting which, having no value of its own, is precious only because it holds the priceless Jewel. It is this Christ-holding faith, not some dream about "self-fulfillment," which is imputed or credited as righteousness (Rom. 4:5).

GRACE ALONE AND FAITH ALONE

Granted that justification is by grace and through faith, must one add the "alone" in each case? Is that really biblical, or are we dealing here, as our modern "ecumenical" climate suggests, with one-sidedness and exaggeration on the part of the Reformation?

The fact is that the "alones" faithfully reflect the Bible's exclusion of everything else from justification. Typical texts are Romans 3:21: "apart from the law"; 3:28: "apart from the works of the law"; 4:6: "apart from works"; Ephesians 2:8, 9: "not from yourselves . . . not by works"; Titus 3:5: "not because of righteous things we had done." If works and law are excluded from justification, then *only* grace and faith remain. As St. Augustine put it, grace is not grace if it is not free [*gratis*]. Grace is not grace in any way unless it is grace in every way.[4]

One way of evading the clear force of the texts is to argue that St. Paul was excluding only the works of the ceremonial Old Testament law, not those of the Moral Law, or the Ten Commandments. Paul, however, makes it quite clear that the law which cannot save is precisely the Moral Law. He writes: "I would not have known what sin was had it not been for the law. For I would not have known what coveting really was if the

---

4. Quoted (in Latin) in Francis Pieper, *Christian Dogmatics*, trans. John Theodore Mueller and Theodore Engelder (St. Louis, MO: Concordia Publishing House, 1951) 2:519.

law had not said, 'You shall not covet'" (Rom. 7:7). The reference clearly is to the Ninth and Tenth Commandments, and so to the Moral Law. It is simply not the purpose of the law to give salvation, for "no one will be declared righteous [justified] in God's sight by the works of the law; rather, through the law we become conscious of our sin" (Rom. 3:20).

Another way to evade the exclusion of works from justification is to say: "Very well, Paul throws out works of the law. But he obviously means only works done before conversion, before a person has entered the state of grace. But works done once one is under the Gospel and in grace are different, and Paul does not exclude them." It is plain, however, that Abraham had been in the state of grace for many years, and that he was not justified by his good works of all those years (Rom. 4:2, 3; compare Gen. 15:6). Also, a literal translation of Titus 3:5 reads: "not out of the works which we did in righteousness"; in other words, even the works of "righteous" or justified persons do not save.

To conclude: If salvation is by grace at all, then it is by grace alone, and if through faith at all, then through faith alone.

FAITH AND WORKS

Although faith alone justifies, justifying faith is never alone! For faith is not a lazy opinion or a piece of dead mental furniture. A faith that does not produce love and good works is dead (Jms. 2:26). It is simply no faith at all.

Real faith *is* spiritual life. It is that Spirit-created wellspring from which flow "rivers of living water" (John 7:38). Like St. Paul (Rom. 3:8), Luther's Reformation has often been accused of encouraging sin and discouraging good works. Here, however, is what the Reformation itself officially confesses about faith and works:

> Oh, faith is a living, busy, active, mighty thing, so that it is impossible for it not to be constantly doing what is good. Likewise, faith does not ask if good works are to be done, but before one can ask, faith has already done them and is constantly active. Whoever does not perform such good works is a faithless man, blindly tapping around in search of faith and good works without knowing what either faith or good works are, and in the meantime he chatters and jabbers a great deal about faith and good works. . . . It is therefore as impossible to separate works from faith as it is to separate heat and light from fire.[5]

---

5. FC SD IV 10–12 (Tappert, 552–553).

If this is so, however, does not the whole Reformation dispute begin to look like a mere fuss about words? After all, Rome never said that faith did not have an important part to play, together with good works. And if the Reformation also insists that good works necessarily flow from faith, then do not both positions amount to the same thing: "faith plus works"? If there are differences left, are they not simply matters of emphasis?

This way of reasoning seems plausible on the surface, but breaks down upon further examination. If the debate turns on a "putting-the-cart-before-the-horse" kind of issue, it does not help to offer the solution "Well, in any case, it comes down to cart plus horse!" That misses the whole point. Similarly, the Reformation debate is not settled by showing that both parties held to "faith plus works" in some sense.

The real argument was about something else. Of course Christians must do good works. There was never any question about that. The question was about why the works had to be done and how they were related to Christ's saving work on the one hand, and to our faith and salvation on the other. The heart of the matter was this: Is salvation earned for us by Christ's work alone, or also by our works? Or one may put it like this: Granted that good works are to be done, are they a cause, or "input," which helps to bring about justification? Or are they a symptom, result, or "output" from a justification and salvation already received and possessed through faith?

This is the problem of the tree and the fruit. "Every good tree bears good fruit," says our Lord (Matt. 7:17). How then is the fruit related to the tree? Does the fruit make the tree alive, or must the tree not rather be alive in the first place in order to produce the fruit? And if a tree is dead, it cannot be revived by having fresh fruit tied to its branches. Yet a living tree will produce fruit from within. This is why Luther maintained that good works do not make a man good, but a good man does good works. Persons make works good, not the other way 'round.

Consider a Christmas tree and a living tree. The former is at first glance much more impressive. Decked out with all sorts of gaudy ornaments, it makes a living fruit tree look very ordinary and dull by comparison. Yet the Christmas tree is dead, despite the shiny trinkets. The humble fruit-tree is gloriously alive. Just so, Pharisaic religiosity may deck itself out in all sorts of impressive "good works." But like the Christmas tree, the Pharisee remains dead inside (Matt. 23:25–28). By contrast, genuine Christian faith is modest and self-effacing, not given to display. Yet faith, "expressing itself through love" (Gal. 5:6), busily serves God and man, even though its real life remains "hidden with Christ in God" (Col. 3:3).

Faith, then, wears two quite distinct "hats." Under its justification "hat" it simply takes hold of Christ's saving work. Under the sanctification "hat" faith actively produces love and good works. These two "hats" must not be confused. Faith justifies not because of the love and good works which indeed follow (under faith's "sanctification hat"), but only because faith alone can and does receive that Other One's righteousness which saves us. When Luther's opponents had to admit that according to the New Testament it is faith that justifies and saves, they took refuge in a special notion of faith, the so-called "formed faith" (*fides formata*). The idea was that faith had no saving power in and of itself but received this power from the love and good works it produced. Faith, then, saves because it is "formed," or given saving content and power, by love! This is quite topsy-turvy, though. It is not our works but Christ's saving work alone that gives faith its saving power. Faith saves because it grasps His work, not ours.

Faith's relation to justification on the one hand and sanctification on the other is not "even-handed." It may be illustrated by a well-known fable. A dog took a piece of meat to a creek. Seeing the reflection of the meat in the water, the dog wanted to grab the reflection as well. But as soon as he opened his jaws to snatch the reflected meat, he lost both the meat and the reflection. So it is with faith and works. If by true faith we hold on to Christ's forgiveness, we have both justification and its reflection, sanctification. If we want to have sanctification by itself, or for its own sake, then we lose both it and its source, justification.

When we say that sanctification "follows" upon justification, however, we are talking not about time but about logical order. It is not as if we were justified first for a time and then after a certain probationary period received the "second blessing" of sanctification. There is never a split-second when true justifying faith does not also produce love. That is why the thief on the cross begins to express love and good works as soon as he has come to faith (Luke 23:40–42).

MORE ABOUT SANCTIFICATION

A possible objection to the above discussion might run like this: "Love and good works are rather central in the preaching of our Lord Himself, and in the New Testament generally. To speak of salvation 'by faith and works' reflects the importance of good works better than to use 'faith alone' language." Yet the opposite is in fact the case. Paradoxically, good works can be done only if salvation is not by works but through faith alone. If salvation were due to good works, then good works would be impossible.

An example will show why this is so. Suppose a stranger comes to one's door, needing food and shelter. Now, if one believes that good works help to earn salvation, it will be impossible to avoid some such calculation as this: "How fortunate for me that this needy person came along, because in helping him I am adding to my deposits in heaven, which will ultimately get me there." Such selfishness would poison any help we might render and keep it from being a good work. It is hardly a good work to take advantage of other people's troubles by making them stepping-stones in the pursuit of our own interests. Indeed, it is just this misconception which enables modern Marxists to boast that they are more selfless than Christians since they, the Marxists, gladly serve the interests of mankind without any hope of eternal reward, whereas Christians have to be bribed with "pie in the sky" to do so!

It is only if we already have the free gift of justification through faith in Christ that we are truly free to help and serve others for their own sake, and from the love of God. Salvation by grace alone takes us off our own hands, so to speak, and liberates us for unselfconscious service (Matt. 25:37–39). A work is a good work only if it proceeds from that love and gratitude to God which flow from genuine repentance and faith (Ps. 51:16, 17; 1 Cor. 13:1–3). Without this source in a right relationship with God through justifying faith, our works are not God-pleasing offerings, but self-made religious junk (Luke 18:9–14; John 15:1–8).

This discussion of the right kind or quality of the Christian's motivation must not be confused, however, with a demand for perfection in degree or quantity. This latter easily becomes an excuse to do nothing at all. So for instance there is abroad today the idea that if one does not "feel" like doing something, then one should not do it, or it would be hypocrisy. Therefore if one is tired or generally out of sorts on Sunday morning, one reasons like this: "I'd better not go to church today, because if I don't really feel like it, but just go through the motions, I'd be a hypocrite." Such thinking makes us slaves to our moods.

Behind it lies a deeper confusion. It is that of the miser who never gives more than fifty cents to church because, he says, "the Lord loves a cheerful giver, and I can't be cheerful if I give any more than that." The trouble is that the flesh, or the "old Adam" in us, never wants to do good. The new creation in us, on the other hand, is always anxious to please God and be of use to our fellow humans. This is why there is a bitter civil war taking place within the soul of every Christian (Rom. 7; Gal. 5:17).

The inner conflict within believers must not be confused with the kind of struggles that philosophers and psychologists talk about. All people, not only Christians, must face conflicts between higher and lower faculties, or between crass self-seeking and a more altruistic posture. Such concerns are the stuff of good upbringing. But mere upbringing or pedagogy cannot do anything more with the "flesh" than rearranging, perfuming, and covering it up a bit. For the "flesh" in the biblical sense does not mean simply "body." Nor does its opposite, "spirit," mean "soul" in this connection. Rather, before conversion, both body and soul are flesh, that is, sinful, dead, and spiritually corrupt. After the new birth into Christian faith, the new life or "spirit" embraces both body and soul. That is why St. Paul urges Christians to present their *bodies* as living sacrifices (Rom. 12:1). It is after all too easy to think that one is offering the soul, while the body snores away lazily! Also among modern Christians there spooks about the false idea, derived from Greek paganism, that the soul is good because it is non-material, and the body evil because it is material. Salvation then consists in getting away from the physical as far as possible. But in the radical perspective of God's Word the body is relatively innocent. The flesh is at its worst not when illicitly indulging the bodily drives, but when it is most refined, respectable, and "religious" (Matt. 21:31; 2 Cor. 11:14). And for salvation Christianity points men not to the giddying heights of pure thought, but to the flesh and blood of Him in Whom the whole fullness of God dwells bodily (John 6:32 ff.; Col. 2:9).

The battle-line between good and evil then runs through every Christian, not around him. And it is a fight to the death, which therefore dare not be fought half-heartedly. The object is not an easy accommodation, but the constant and daily "crucifixion" or putting to death of the old evil nature (Luke 9:23; Rom. 8:13; Gal. 5:24). There can be no peaceful co-existence here. The conflict cannot end except in total defeat or in total victory. There may be and there are temporary setbacks for the Christian in this battle. But because Christ has already won the decisive victory over all the powers of hell (Col. 2:15), Christians can remain confident that they are fighting against a spent force. They can bravely bear the burden of this battle, whatever the cost, in view of the permanent triumph which awaits them (Rom. 8:18; 1 Cor. 15:54–57). Therefore the church sings in the words of St. Bernard of Morlas:

> Brief life is here our portion;
> Brief sorrow, short-lived care.
> The life that knows no ending,
> The tearless life, is there.
> O happy retribution:

> Short toil, eternal rest;
> For mortals and for sinners
> A mansion with the blest![6]

It is plain that there can be no such thing as "perfect" or "entire" sanctification during this earthly life. Even the most mature Christians must still carry the corrupt flesh with them to the grave. This is why even the best of good works are tainted with sin. The flesh always contributes corrupt and self-serving motivations, so that no matter how pure and holy the intention of the new nature in us, the "output" of actual, concrete behavior is always a mixture of good and evil. Even good works therefore need to be offered to God in deep humility and with a plea for forgiveness. They are pleasing to him on account of His fatherly love and mercy towards us in His Son.

If even St. Paul had to confess to his intense struggle against his sinful flesh (Rom. 7), how can any of us lesser Christians imagine ourselves to have surpassed the great apostle in holiness? Clearing the surface of a few outward vices is one thing; getting rid of their poisoned root and source (Jer. 17:9; Matt. 15:19) is quite another. The inspired apostolic words therefore apply without exception to all Christians: "If we claim to be without sin, we deceive ourselves and the truth is not in us" (1 Jn. 1:8). Indeed, those who in the judgment of their fellow-Christians have reached the highest levels of sanctification, have invariably had the deepest awareness of their sinfulness and helplessness before God. The closer they seemed to God, the farther they knew themselves to be, and the more fervently they grasped the life-line of His absolution. Thus St. Augustine died with a penitential Psalm on his lips, and Luther scribbled on a piece of paper found after his death: "We are beggars. That is true."[7]

In other words, we never outgrow in this life the need for justification. Forgiveness is not an early, immature stage of spiritual life, from which we later graduate into pure sanctification. No! Justification remains the life-giving sunshine, the bright sky of God's mercy and grace, beneath which alone our whole existence can and must be lived out. It is only in this sunshine that the blessed fruit of divine love can take shape and grow in us. "We love because he first loved us," writes the apostle of love (1 Jn. 4:19). Of course we are to be grateful (Col. 3:15–17). But love is something still more basic. Gratitude is a conscious indebtedness, but without love

---

6. "Brief Life Is Here Our Portion," *TLH* 448:1.
7. AE 54, 476.

indebtedness can easily turn into resentment and worse. Unlike gratitude, love does not arise from any sort of calculation. Children do not learn to love their mothers by counting the number of meals prepared, clothes mended, and the like, and then measuring out their affection accordingly. They love without any conscious reason, simply because they were loved long before they could know it. Just so the heavenly Father in our new birth or conversion embraces us in His love, from which He kindles our little responding loves with supernatural naturalness and spontaneity.

Of course, as we have already seen, the spontaneous outpouring of love and good works from faith does not mean the absence of effort and struggle. Sometimes one hears it said that good works follow "automatically" upon justifying faith. Such a choice of words is unfortunate, for it suggests machines, not organisms. But sanctification, as a life-process, is organic (John 15:1–8) rather than mechanical. And here the plant-analogy breaks down as well. For Christians dare not imagine that if only they will believe, then no great efforts at doing good works need to follow, since all the necessary consequences of faith will come about "automatically." Rather, "it is God who works in you to will and to act according to his good purpose" (Phil. 2:13, author's translation), and this new will seeks ever to serve and please Him more and more. It is prepared to "go through many hardships to enter the kingdom of God" (Acts 14:22).

Our otherwise self-indulgent, materialistic age has some appreciation for physical fitness and discipline. Should it not be obvious that spiritual discipline is infinitely more valuable (Rom. 12:1, 2; 1 Cor. 9:24–27; 1 Tim. 4:8)? No one has surpassed St. Paul in his passionate exclusion of all good works from justification. Yet no one has insisted more pointedly that good works must follow. The two themes are joined together like this by the great apostle of grace:

> For it is by grace you have been saved, through faith—and this is not from yourselves, it is the gift of God—not by works, so that no one can boast. For we are God's handiwork, created in Christ Jesus to do good works, which God prepared in advance for us to do (Eph. 2:8–10).

Chapter Five

LAW, GOSPEL, AND MEANS OF GRACE

ಎ

We have seen how the whole structure of Christian truth comes to a head in the work of salvation which God has accomplished for the whole world in His Son. We have also seen that only faith is able to receive all this. The most important practical question then is this: How does faith come about, and how does it stay alive?

The problem is that man after the Fall is spiritually dead (Eph. 2:1–3). Faith, on the other hand, is the very essence of spiritual life. As death cannot turn itself into life, therefore, so no sinful human being can stir up faith in himself or by his own powers. Faith is entirely a supernatural gift of God, and must come to poor sinners from outside themselves. The truth of the matter is that God gives faith through His Word (Rom. 10:17).

This preliminary answer, however, must be explained further. The fact is that there are two quite different Words of God. Only one of them, the Gospel, offers life and salvation, and therefore creates faith. The other is the Law, which cannot give salvation. To this most fundamental distinction we must now turn.

LAW AND GOSPEL DISTINGUISHED

"For the law was given through Moses; grace and truth came through Jesus Christ" (John 1:17). St. Paul insists everywhere that salvation comes not by way of law, but by way of promise (Gal. 3:15–21). The contrast is that between demand and gift. What an enormous difference it makes whether the saving "righteousness of God" (Rom. 1:17) is the righteousness which He requires of us, or the righteousness which He freely gives us in His Son! It is the difference between life and death (2 Cor. 3:6!), heaven and hell, salvation and damnation.

Knowing how to distinguish and apply these two very different things, what God demands (Law) and what He gives (Gospel), is the very vital art of all spiritual life. The afflicted must be comforted (with the Gospel) and the comfortable must be afflicted (with the Law). Between these two poles the Christian's whole existence oscillates. The "current" is produced precisely by the tension between the two poles. Trying to "even out" the contrasts by turning Gospel into Law or vice versa, or both into something neutral in between, destroys everything.

Although both Law and Gospel are both the Word of God, there is no equality or symmetry between them. God speaks His Law-Word for the sake of His Gospel-Word, and not the other way 'round. It is

> God's alien [strange, foreign] work to terrify because God's own proper work is to quicken and console. But he terrifies . . . to make room for consolation and quickening because hearts that do not feel God's wrath in their smugness spurn consolation. . . .
>
> These are the two chief works of God in men, to terrify and to justify and quicken the terrified. One or the other of these works is spoken of throughout Scripture. One part is the law, which reveals, denounces, and condemns sin. The other part is the Gospel, that is, the promise of grace granted in Christ.[1]

If this is so, then Law and Gospel are not simply major features among others in Holy Scripture, but its sole content: "All Scripture should be divided into these two chief doctrines, the law and the promises."[2] But this distribution into Law and Gospel must not be thought of in mechanical terms: so many verses Law, the rest Gospel. Some texts of course are clearly and expressly Law, while others are just as clearly Gospel. Yet the one always requires the other. The Law, since it cannot give life, calls for the Gospel. The Gospel assumes that there is dire need for mercy; in other words, sin and Law are understood.

It is futile therefore to snatch up some obscure verse in Leviticus or Numbers and ask: Is this Law or Gospel? It is probably both. Two things must be kept in mind here. One is that sentences in the Bible are not isolated logical atoms. They are part of an intricate tapestry of which Christ is the theme (John 5:39) and human salvation the purpose (2 Tim. 3:15 ff.). To tear biblical sentences out of the web of the grand design in which they are embedded is to destroy their meaning. Second, sentences and longer passages of the Bible are trivialised if they are taken simply as bits of information, however interesting. God's purpose in giving His Word is not to tickle curious minds, much less to satisfy academic pedantry, but to rescue sinners by calling them to contrition and faith. A genuine encounter with God's truth therefore dare never result in the shallow gasp "How fascinating!" It must rather wring from us St. Paul's twofold

1. Ap XII 51, 53 (Tappert, 189).
2. Ap IV 5 (Tappert, 108).

response: "O wretched man that I am! who shall deliver me from the body of this death? I thank God through Jesus Christ our Lord" (Rom. 7:24–25a [KJV]). Luther therefore urges "a garland of four strands"[3] as a fruitful approach to biblical study. This means finding in the text first some instruction, second, a reason for thanksgiving, third, an occasion for confession, and fourth, a cause of prayer. In this way God's personal address in Law and Gospel is heard, and the text does not become the plaything of cerebral games.

If Christ really is the all-pervasive theme of Scripture, and if God's written Word is not an impersonal philosophy but speaks to us judgment and salvation, then something very crucial follows. What follows is that not some "Lutheran insight" but Scripture itself demands the Law/Gospel distinction as "an especially brilliant light"[4] to reveal the true and intended sense of the biblical text. Texts that seem at first to lack any express Law or Gospel must therefore be seen as both rather than neither. Law and Gospel in such cases are related to each other not like adjacent patches of ground, but as different dimensions or aspects of the same ground. The Law is the Christian truth under the aspect of God's justice, severity, and wrath, while the Gospel is this same truth, but under the aspect of His undeserved grace and mercy in Christ. For the historical narratives in Scripture this means a great deal of "overlap" between Law and Gospel. The account of the Lord's suffering, crucifixion, and death, for example, is first of all the most terrible preaching of the Law, for it shows the full extent of God's just anger over sin. All this is still "Moses." It is Christ's "alien work," not the real point and purpose of His mission. His own real work is the grace and forgiveness which He has won by His cross, and which He now distributes through His Word and Sacraments. "And this is the preaching of the Gospel, strictly speaking."[5]

Like many other terms, *Law* and *Gospel* both have narrow and broad senses. In the broad sense *Gospel* means the whole doctrine of Christ, including the Law (as in St. Mark. 1:1). But when repentance—in other words, Law—is distinguished from believing the Gospel (as in St. Mark 1:15), then *Gospel* is used in its strict or narrow sense of forgiveness and life in Christ. In the broad sense, therefore, "Law" and "Gospel" mean the same thing, that is, Christian doctrine as a whole. In their proper or strict senses, however, "Law" and "Gospel" are the most irreconcilable

---

3. AE 43, 200.
4. FC SD V 1 (Tappert, 558).
5. FC Ep V 10 (Tappert, 479).

opposites—"more than contradictories" (Luther).[6] If the subscripts s and b stand for strict and broad senses respectively, a precise formula can be given: $L_s + G_s = L_b = G_b$.

This implies, it should be noted, that justification is the chief article but not the only article of the Gospel in the strict sense. A good rule of thumb is Luther's treatment of the first two Chief Parts in his Large Catechism. The Ten Commandments are the Law in the strict sense, and the trinitarian Creed confesses the Gospel in the strict sense.[7]

THE MORAL LAW

Within the Old Testament arrangements, we may distinguish three kinds of laws. The Ceremonial Law governed religious observance in great detail. The Civil Law regulated the Jewish nation as a political unit. The Moral Law finally set out man's permanent ethical obligations. Here we shall be concerned only with the Moral Law, since the other two have been fulfilled and abolished in Christ and His Kingdom (Col. 2:16–17).

That the Ten Commandments (also called the Decalogue) are the Moral Law is not as obvious as it may seem at first sight. These commandments, as given in Exodus 20 and repeated in Deuteronomy 5, were part and parcel of the covenant between God and the nation of Israel. This covenant contained detailed regulations for religious practice and for social and economic relations. The Ten Commandments form the direct basis for the Old Testament's Civil Law. Moreover, they themselves contain elements of the Ceremonial Law. So, for instance, the keeping of a special day, Saturday (Third Commandment), is not a part of the Moral Law. Under the New Testament this provision, together with the rest of the Ceremonial Law, is no longer in force (Col. 2:16–17). Another example is the rule against making any picture ("image") of anything in heaven or on earth (Ex. 20:4). The New Testament contains no such prohibition, since now the Son of God Himself, the very "image of the invisible God" (Col. 1:15), has taken on Himself our "nature," "likeness," and "appearance" (Phil. 2:7, 8).

How then can we tell what is permanent Moral Law in the Ten Commandments and what is not? For the answer we need to turn to the New Testament interpretation of the Decalogue.

Jewish tradition had divided the Law into 613 distinct commands and prohibitions, and moralists argued about which was the most important among these. When the Pharisees tried to entangle the Saviour in these

---

6. *"plus quam contradictoria"*; see the translation in AE 26, 337.
7. See LC II 1 (Tappert, 411).

slippery disputations, He, interestingly enough, by-passed the Decalogue completely. Cutting through to the heart of the matter, He quoted from the great creedal summary of Deuteronomy 6 and said, "Love the Lord your God with all your heart and with all your soul and with all your mind." This, He said, is "the first and greatest commandment." Next, He quoted from Leviticus 19: "Love your neighbor as yourself," and concluded: "All the Law and the Prophets hang on these two commandments" (Matt. 22:37–40). St. Paul boiled it down to one word: "Therefore love is the fulfillment of the law" (Rom. 13:10).

The fact that love interprets the Commandments, however, must not be taken to mean that it abolishes them. Otherwise we should end up with some sort of "situation ethics" in which there are no absolutes, but anything can be justified in the name of "love." In fact the demand for love is the very thing which makes God's Commandments so unattainably hard to keep. This is clear from the way in which our Saviour explains the real, spiritual core of the Decalogue in St. Matthew 5. Not only the overt acts of murder and adultery break the Fifth and Sixth Commandments, but even anger and lustful looks (vv. 21–28). For sin arises not at the surface levels of hands or eyes, but from the deepest layers of our being. "For out of the heart come evil thoughts—murder, adultery, sexual immorality, theft, false testimony, slander" (Matt. 15:19).

No doubt because the Saviour spoke of two "great" commandments, it became customary to divide the Ten Commandments into two "tables." The First Table, comprising commandments one to three, governs man's duties towards God. The Second Table, containing the remaining commandments, lays down our duties to our fellow human beings. It would be misleading, however, to describe the first set of duties as "religious," and the second set as "social." Actually, all these duties and obligations are "religious," since they are required by God Himself and are owed to Him. He has in fact made it very plain that a "religion" without "social" regard for our fellow humans is a sham (Jms. 1:27; 1 Jn. 4:20–21).

The First Commandment is really the fountainhead of all the others. Luther captures this truth in his classic catechism explanation: "We should fear, love, and trust in God above all things."[8] Certainly this embraces also that awe towards His name and His Word which the Second and Third Commandments require of us. But that is not all. To fear, love, and trust in God means also to honour authorities (Fourth Command-

---

8. Small Catechism, Ten Commandments, explanation of the First Commandment.

ment), human life (Fifth Commandment), the sacred bond of marriage (Sixth Commandment), property (Seventh Commandment), and reputation (Eighth Commandment), all of which have God's blessing and the protection of His Law. The Ninth and Tenth Commandments, which forbid even coveting, show that purity of heart and not mere external, civil compliance is what the Law of God is all about (Rom. 7:7–8).

When the Moral Law is correctly understood, no grounds at all remain for the illusion that sinful mortals can, perhaps with a bit of help, measure up to the just requirements of God. But what is the use of unattainable ideals and impossible standards? "Reality therapy" is precisely the central service which the Law must render to our opinionated egos, "so that every mouth may be silenced, and the whole world stand convicted before God" (Rom. 3:19 [author's translation]).

THREE USES OR FUNCTIONS OF THE LAW

Although the customary word is "uses," it may be better to speak of "functions" of the Law. The term "uses" may be mistaken to mean that we manipulate or control the Law, to bring about the sort of responses which we think fitting. In truth, however, it is God Himself who uses His Law to achieve His own purposes. According to God's revealed will, His Law is meant to function in several distinct ways. At times Luther distinguished two fundamentally different functions of the Law, the civil and the theological.[9] Further refinement identified a third function.

In its first function the Law serves as an incentive and a deterrent to promote, safeguard, and enforce the public attitudes and behaviour on which the existence and well-being of human society depend. This is the Law originally written into human nature at creation ("natural law"), and still discernible in its broad features even after the Fall, through conscience, reason, and philosophy (Rom. 2:14–15). Through this civil use or function of the Law, God preserves His created order despite and against the corrosive and destructive powers of evil. Here God rules not with His grace, but with His power, and His instrument is not the church, but the civil order, which includes elements like the marriage bond, parental authority, various social and economic forces, teachers, policemen, judges, statesmen, armed forces, and even executioners as a last resort (Rom. 13:1–6).

Because of its deterrent force, this first function of the Law is often called a "curb," that is, a leash or restraint. It is aimed not at God's own

9. For example, AE 26, 308 ff.

dear children, but against those who without such constraints would turn society into a rabble of living by the law of the jungle. The "law is made not for the righteous but for lawbreakers and rebels, the ungodly and sinful, the unholy and irreligious" (1 Tim. 1:9). On the other hand, it must not be forgotten that also Christians still have their old evil nature with them, with which they must struggle daily (Rom. 7). This old nature is a donkey which has no sense for the Gospel, but responds only to the stick and the carrot of the Law. Honor, health, and wealth impress this mulish nature more than heaven, God, or His love—and hell makes rather less of an impression than prison, cancer, or AIDS. The Law in its first function therefore is a valuable ally which Christians also need to keep their own sinful natures in check (1 Cor. 9:27).

The first function of the Law concerns the church only indirectly, insofar as Christians are also citizens. It is very different with the second or spiritual function of the Law, which is in fact the Law's real aim and purpose. Here the Law functions as a mirror, faithfully reflecting to the sinner his own inner bankruptcy. "By the law," writes St. Paul, "is the knowledge of sin" (Rom. 3:20 KJV). He explains: "I would not have known what sin was had it not been for the law. For I would not have known what coveting really was if the law had not said, 'You shall not covet'" (Rom. 7:7).

It is a great delusion to think that the Law can give salvation to sinners. On the contrary, the Law makes matters still worse (Rom. 4:15; 5:20; 7:5, 8–11, 13; 2 Cor. 3:6). Far from being a help or remedy, the Law is in fact "the power of sin" (1 Cor. 15:56), as the Funeral Service solemnly reminds us. The Saviour Himself warns: "Your accuser is Moses, on whom your hopes are set" (John 5:45).

This negative, accusatory force of the Law strips from us all self-reliance and false hopes. When even our prized moral and religious achievements are seen to be rubbish (Phil. 3:8), and we are destitute, then the Law has done its proper work. More it cannot do. It must lead us to Christ (see Gal. 3:24), yet not directly—for it knows Him only as Judge and Example—but indirectly, by impressing on us our urgent need or rescue. To quote St. Paul once more:

> Is the law, therefore, opposed to the promises of God? Absolutely not! For if a law had been given that could impart life, then righteousness would certainly have come by the law. But Scripture has locked up everything under the control of sin, so that what was promised, being given through faith in Jesus Christ, might be given to those who believe (Gal. 3:21–22).

God's "alien work" (see Law and Gospel Distinguished, p. 76) in the Law may be compared to a physician's diagnosis. No doctor simply pops medicines into a patient's mouth without first determining the nature of the complaint. Nor is anyone ever cured by the diagnosis itself. Much less does a doctor gleefully torment a patient with a gloomy diagnosis just for the sake of torture. The goal is healing. Yet a physician may need to speak very pointedly to a patient who disregards his condition and becomes frivolous about taking his medication. By analogy, even Christians need the faithful service of the Law's spiritual, diagnostic function, lest they give themselves to rosy illusions and neglect the means of salvation. If people are bored with the Gospel and want to turn church services into entertaining circuses, they have forgotten the deadly malady of their sin. The remedy, then, is not to whimper softly about "love," but to wield the Law very pointedly, like a dentist's drill, until it strikes the nerve that is festering beneath the decay. To "spare" the patient is to be cruelly kind.

Finally, the Law functions also as a rule or guide for the behaviour of Christians. This is the Law's so-called "Third Use." If it were not for this guidance from the Ten Commandments, as explained throughout the New Testament, we might invent all sorts of exotic performances and imagine them to be God-pleasing. In one culture it is considered an admirable discipline, for instance, to clench one's fists until the fingernails grow through the hand! The Ten Commandments curb our zeal by showing us how God really wants to be served. Left to our own devices, also Christians as sinners are prone to confuse our own fancies with the will of God. As Luther often pointed out, it seems so much more exciting to perform some high-minded work of public virtue or solemn ritual than to do ordinary things like farming, building, cleaning, taking care of babies, and so on. Religion is often used as a pretext for escaping the humdrum obligations of daily life into something more glamorous and "fulfilling." This is unhealthy, though. If we pay attention to God's will, "we shall have our hands full to keep these commandments, practicing gentleness, patience, love toward enemies, chastity, kindness, etc."[10] Such things are less impressive than an ostentatious religiosity, but they are what God commands and blesses. "The trivial round, the common task, will furnish all we ought to ask." Woe to us if we think that we can advance beyond the plain duties of God's Commandments to nobler, worthier causes! God's guiding Law punctures the balloons of our self-important and self-chosen religiousness, and brings us back to God's earth, where, for the time be-

---

10. LC I 313 (Tappert, 407).

ing, we belong. What matters is not spectacular feats but "faith express-ing itself through love" (Gal. 5:6).

Christians need all three functions of the Law, but only because they still have the sinful old nature with them. The new nature in us, "created in Christ Jesus to do good works" (Eph. 2:10) and "to be like God in true righteousness and holiness" (Eph. 4:24), does not need to have the Law presented in any of its uses. Animated by the life of Christ, this new nature spontaneously bears a precious harvest of the "fruit of the Spirit," which is "love, joy, peace, forbearance, kindness, goodness, faithfulness, gentleness and self-control. Against such things there is no law" (Gal. 5:22–23). This new nature, however, does not exist by itself, in a pure state, so to speak, during our earthly life. The concrete Christian person, saint and sinner at the same time (*simul iustus et peccator*), is therefore always in need of the Law. Christians' growing new nature presently remains locked in combat with their declining old nature in a contest unto death.

The Pharisees imagined that religion turned on the Law. To them, ask-ing the question about the greatest commandment raised the ultimate issue. The Saviour surprised them, though, by posing a question of His own just when they thought that everything had been settled: "What do you think about the Messiah? Whose son is he?" (Matt. 22:42). This truly central question cuts to the heart of the Gospel, and on this matter man's fate before God really hinges.

THE GOSPEL AS POWER

Words can carry powerful emotional charges. They can make us laugh or weep or buy one product rather than another, which is why fortunes are spent on putting words together in precisely the right way. Of course, words can communicate information on which life or death depends. The pen is indeed mightier than the sword. When Christians talk about "the power of the Word," though, they mean something much greater.

Much pop-religion indeed gives the impression of being some sort of mood-making voodoo. Faith is then psychologized into a harmless or even socially useful form of emotional escapism: even as "touching" sentiments in a greeting card with blurry pictures can evoke a smile or a tear, so the ap-propriate Scripture-verses can provide just the right uplift in times of stress. All this, however, is simply the power of words. It differs from the power of the Word as much as a stuffed museum exhibit differs from a real tiger.

The Word of God has power not because it is a word, but because it is God's word. Actors, witch-doctors, advertisers, and politicians may hold their audiences spell-bound, but their words cannot give life. God's

Word, whether announced by brilliant scholars or mumbled by illiterate peasants, has the power to make alive.

When God speaks, things happen. In the beginning, when there was nothing, God spoke, and everything came into existence (Gen. 1; John 1:1–3). At His Word a stormy sea turns calm (Mark 4:35–41), a few fish and loaves multiply to feed thousands (John 6:1–13), a dead man walks out of his tomb alive (John 11), and the very demons flee in terror (Mark 5:1–13). And at the end of time all the dead will appear before His Judgment Seat at His summons (John 5:28–29). This is God's living Word, not empty human talk.

Spectacular effects, however, are one thing, and real spiritual power is still another (1 Kgs. 19:11–13). "Which is easier," asked our Lord, "to say, 'Your sins are forgiven,' or to say, 'Get up and walk'?" Of course it is easier to *say*, "Your sins are forgiven." Who, after all, can test such a statement? It seems far more difficult to say to a paralytic, "Get up and walk," for everyone can see at once whether it worked. While medical technology can cure some forms of paralysis, what physician can heal the soul wasted by the deadly cancer of sin? That is in fact infinitely more difficult. As a sign and proof that He had this greater power, the Saviour exercised His lesser power and said: "Get up, take your mat and go home" (Matt. 9:5–6).

This power to impart God's own forgiveness, life, and salvation Christ has placed into His Gospel: "The words I have spoken to you—they are full of the Spirit and life" (John 6:63). Through His word the disciples were made "clean" (John 15:3), and by their repeating of this same word others will come to faith till the end of time (John 17:8, 20). In nature even the most promising soil remains dead and unproductive unless it receives a seed bearing within it the gift of life. Just so, the Word of God is that seed which alone contains and transmits the secret of spiritual life (Luke 8:11; 1 Cor. 3:5–7; 1 Pet. 1:23). Therefore St. Paul calls the Gospel, quite literally, the *dynamic* of God for salvation (Rom. 1:16). He also says that "faith comes from hearing . . . through the word about Christ" (Rom. 10:17). Through this Gospel, St. Paul had become father to the Corinthians, that is, had given them life in Christ (1 Cor. 4:15).

God is not content, however, to communicate His love to His holy Bride, the church, only in words. The Lord, whose mercies are new every morning (Lam. 3:23), surrounds His people with tangible tokens and proofs of His kindness. He has put his saving Gospel also into the form of *sacraments* (Baptism and the Holy Supper) in which the divine gifts and promises are attached to the earthly elements of water, bread, and wine. The one Gospel comes to us in the divinely given forms or modes of Word and Sacraments.

These various modes of the one Gospel we call the "means of grace." They are the channels through which the river of God's salvation flows to us.

WHAT IS THE FULL GOSPEL?

The Pentecostal movement has popularized the term "Full Gospel." This suggests that the "ordinary" Word and Sacrament are only half the Gospel, and that the other half is supplied by extraordinary "gifts," especially "tongues" and miraculous healings. One writer claims: "Healing was clearly one of the things Jesus had commanded them, and therefore as much a part of the [Great] Commission as preaching and teaching."[11] But the Great Commission (Matt. 28:19–20) must be distinguished from various local and temporary missions, such as the mission to the villages of Judaea (Matt. 10:1 ff.) or the command to fetch a donkey and her foal (Matt. 21:2). Physical healing is no more a part of the Great Commission of the universal Church than is fetching donkeys. If those who follow Jesus today—and who are not apostles (2 Cor. 12:12; Eph. 2:20)—must imitate His miraculous healings, then why not His walking on water?

Or why not His raising of the dead? When the Lord raised the young man of Nain from the dead, for instance, did He really intend that His ministers now should stop funeral processions with the command, "I say to you, get up" (as in St. Luke 7:14)? The Saviour's purpose instead was, as in the raising of Lazarus, to show that He is Himself the Resurrection and the Life (John 11:25), so as to invite and incite our total trust in Him. Having such trusting faith in Him clearly does not mean expecting His miraculous interventions every time physical death threatens. (Even the great apostles Peter and Paul, who had experienced many miraculous rescues, had to face death by execution.) It means, rather, trusting implicitly in the Saviour's promise: "He who believes in Me will live, even though he dies; and whoever lives and believes in Me will never die" (John 11:25–26 [author's translation]). Christians are assured here not that they are safe *from* cancer or plane crashes, but that they are safe even *in* cancer and plane crashes, because they are in Him over Whom "death no longer has mastery" (Rom. 6:9).

Nor does the Gospel offer political or economic "liberation," as is often claimed today. The Lord refused to be that kind of king (John 6:15; 18:36). Indeed, the Gospels used the title "Christ" (Messiah, Anointed One) very sparingly, no doubt because of the strong national and political overtones the term had acquired. But the Epistles are full of refer-

---

11. Larry Christenson, *The Charismatic Renewal Among Lutherans* (Minneapolis, MN: Bethany Fellowship, 1976), 98.

ences to "Christ." After the cross, the resurrection, and Pentecost, the strictly spiritual nature of His Kingdom was perfectly clear.

Nor does the Lord guarantee prosperity or even bare necessities at all times when He promises that "all these [temporal] things will be given to you as well" (Matt. 6:33). Else how could Christians ever die? Rather, the meaning is that He who owns and controls the whole universe, and is therefore perfectly able to give us anything He chooses, will in fact give us everything we need—but in His estimate, not in ours. He guarantees that He makes "all things," without exception, work "for the good" of His chosen people—including "trouble or hardship or persecution or famine or nakedness or danger or sword" (Rom. 8:28, 35)! That in Christ we have life "more abundantly" (John 10:10 KJV) has nothing whatever to do with material prosperity. It has everything to do with being "rich toward God" (Luke 12:21) and storing up "treasures in heaven" (Matt. 6:20). Poor Lazarus, with all his sores, had this abundant life, while his affluent neighbour did not (Luke 16:19–31).

That the Gospel is "spiritual," however, should not be taken to mean that it is spiritualistic. Worshiping "in spirit and in truth" (John 4:24 KJV) does not mean trying to evaporate into some state of "dematerialisation." It means, rather, seeking God where He wishes to be found, that is, in the Gospel. That Gospel is surprisingly "material" in several respects. It proclaims a God who has become flesh (John 1:14). It does so in outward, audible words, and with visible, tangible elements: water, bread, and wine. In the Holy Supper it actually communicates Christ's life-giving flesh and blood to our needy bodies. Since the body, being destined for resurrection and eternal life, also receives the holy means of grace, it clearly also participates, together with the soul, in the blessings there provided. However, bodily blessings are whatever our Divine Physician chooses for our temporal and eternal well-being. That has no necessary connection with medical health (2 Cor. 4:16)! The boundless blessing of God communicated and transmitted by the Gospel is to be received and treasured for its own sake and on its own terms (Matt. 13:44–46). It is frivolous to think of this blessing merely as a "religious" segment within a larger, secularly defined "holistic health."

The Gospel in its preached and sacramental modes *is* the "full Gospel." What, after all, was the real power and blessing of Pentecost? Long ago Elijah had discovered that God was not in the wind, nor in the earthquake, nor in the fire, but in the still, small voice (1 Kgs. 19:11–12). The remarkably parallel phenomena of Pentecost, the powerful sound of wind and tongues as of fire (Acts 2:2–3), likewise were "special effects." The real power of Pentecost was and is the preaching and Baptism by which the Holy Spirit distributes forgiveness, life, and salvation (Acts 2:36, 38).

This lavish Pentecost fullness is most obvious in the case of the sacraments. "This is My blood of the [new] testament, being poured out for many for the forgiveness of sins" (Matt. 26:28 [author's translation]), says the Saviour as He gives the blessed cup. Here is the very blood of God (Acts 20:28), which takes away the sin of the world (John 1:29). The priceless inheritance of the divine testament is here not merely commemorated but actually bequeathed, assigned, and paid out. Similarly, to be baptised is to be *co-buried* with Jesus. This term is used only twice in the New Testament, and both times it describes what happens in Baptism (Rom. 6:4; Col. 2:12). Baptism actually "saves . . . by the resurrection of Jesus Christ" (1 Pet. 3:21). In the sacraments, then, we have not wistful reminders of salvation, but the thing itself.

It was a great Reformation discovery that God's grace and salvation are offered and distributed not only in the sacraments, but also and even primarily through the Word, that is, through the proclamation of the Gospel itself. Indeed, the Gospel is first and foremost preaching, proclamation (Mark 13:10; 1 Cor. 1:17, 21; Col. 1:23; Tit. 1:3). It is the living and life-giving speech of God, not dead and death-dealing stone engravings. This Gospel is a glorious "ministry" (service, administration) of the Spirit, of righteousness, and of reconciliation, not simply because it talks about these realities, but because it actually contains, offers, and distributes them (2 Cor. 3:3, 6–11; 5:18). The "ministry of the Spirit" [2 Cor. 3:8] here refers not to "special effects" on the side, but to the very core-gifts of the Gospel, that is, life and justification (or righteousness; see 2 Cor. 3:6, 9). This is how and why the Saviour's words are spirit and are life (John 6:63).

The Gospel is an utterly unique form of communication. In Greek the words for "Gospel" and for "promise" are closely related. Unlike the Law, which threatens, the Gospel is pure promise. Fulfilled in Christ (2 Cor. 1:20), God's saving promises actually carry in and with them the very things promised. The word for "promise" can mean also "the thing promised," and these two senses can run together into one (as in Gal. 3:22; Eph. 3:6; Heb. 6:12, 17). As live divine promise, the Gospel is much more than information. This "more" may be compared to the difference between a letter and a check: the letter might promise a birthday gift, but the check actually conveys it. Here it is a case of the message being the medium—for imparting the very things the message names and describes. The Gospel, always including the Sacraments, in fact does two things: it gives the otherwise quite unattainable riches of Christ (Eph. 3:8) to needy sinners, and also creates in them the hand of faith with which to take these treasures!

THE GOSPEL AND THE SPACE-TIME GAP

There is a problem in popular Christianity which is as fundamental as it is largely unrecognized and unacknowledged. One symptom of it is a certain sense of unreality which for modern, technology-minded people surrounds persons, events, and situations from older cultures. The cultural gap between us and, say, Reformation times—let alone the age of the New Testament—is so dramatic that these other worlds strike us as outlandish. It is our own world that seems "real" and normal. One attempt to bridge these gaps is to dress up the church's ancient worship in the snappy sights and sounds of modern pop-culture. Such quick-fix solutions, however, rest on shallow views of the basic problem.

We need to dig deeper. Salvation has happened to the human race in Christ. In Him is all of God, and all of His grace. Whoever does not find God in Christ will never find Him anywhere else—even if he were to go over heaven, under hell, or into space, as Luther was fond of repeating.[12] As "the Way, and the Truth, and the Life" (John 14:6 [author's translation]), the Saviour is that one and only Bridge over which all the saving traffic between God and mankind must pass. In Him, God has *come into focus* for us (J. B. Phillips[13]). The "funnel" in the illustration (next page), coming to a point in the cross and resurrection of Jesus, expresses this evangelical truth in diagram form. So far all serious Christians are agreed. The problem arises when we go on to ask: How does all this come to us now? It happened two thousand years ago and, for North Americans, several thousand miles away. How is this space-time gap to be bridged? How does the salvation in Jesus *there and then* get to us *here and now*?

It is difficult to imagine a more crucial or practical question. One's whole understanding and practice of Christianity depend on the answer. Yet very different answers are given at this point. The usual answer in popular Protestantism (of the conservative kind) is that we must pray, or wrestle, or make a decision or a commitment, or in some other way "come to Calvary." The gap is to be bridged by our faith. "Faith" here seems to mean an exercise of mental, emotional, imaginative, or ethical powers, the exact "mix" depending on the local theology. According to this think-

---

12. *Editor's note:* See AE 34, 207. Compare AE 23, 123: "I know not where to find God, either in heaven or on earth, except in the flesh of Christ."

13. *Editor's note:* See J. B. Phillips, *When God Was Man* (New York, Abingdon, 1955), 15: "... God, focused in human form...."

ing we must shut our eyes, as it were, concentrate as hard as we can on Christ, and so "experience" Him and His cross. This meeting takes place, however, in the realm of mind or religious imagination—a realm highly suspect for all who lost their innocence in Psychology 101. Hence, a nagging sense of unreality and malaise!

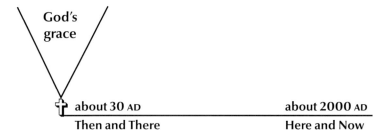

Completely different is Luther's recipe for encountering God. To modern religious nerves attuned to televised exhortations to "come to the cross," it is jarring to be told: "If now I seek forgiveness of sins, I do not run to the cross, for I will not find it given there."[14] Of course Luther knew, better indeed than most others, that the cross is everything. But where is this cross now? The event is beyond our reach, and if we could find the original cross somewhere in Jerusalem, it could in principle do no more for us than the Shroud of Turin. Luther explains that we must not muddle together two quite different aspects of forgiveness, namely, its source and its distribution. On the cross Christ achieved and won forgiveness for all, but He does not distribute it there. In His Gospel and Sacraments, Christ distributes forgiveness, although that is not where it was won. We are not left to our own devices here. The cross is not to be captured with mental exercises. Its treasures are distributed by God in His holy Word and Sacraments, and this not mentally but really and truly:

> Christ on the cross and all his suffering and his death do not avail, even if, as you teach, they are "acknowledged and meditated upon" with the utmost "passion, ardor, heartfeltness." Something else must always be there. What is it? The Word, the Word, the Word. Listen, lying spirit, the Word avails. Even if Christ were given for us and crucified a thousand times, it would all be in vain if the Word of God were absent and were not distributed and given to me with the bidding, this is for you, take what is yours.[15]

---

14. AE 40, 214.
15. AE 40, 212–213.

Luther's severe words to those he derisively called the "heavenly proph-ets" of his day are very timely in our confused age. God did not plant His cross on earth and then leave us to struggle toward it as best we could. He has provided the access Himself. The space-time barrier between the cross and us cannot be pierced from our side. God Himself penetrates it with His holy means of grace. This means that Christian faith and life or-bit around two poles, not one. The cross is the "input" pole, and the Gos-pel the "output" pole. Our diagram will therefore need a second "funnel," showing that just as all God's grace is given in Christ, and there alone, so all God's grace in Christ is given in the Gospel, and there alone (see illustration). There can be no more conflict or competition between these two poles than there is between an electric power station and the wires and outlets that convey the current to the consumer. The Gospel is simply Christ's own way of giving Himself.

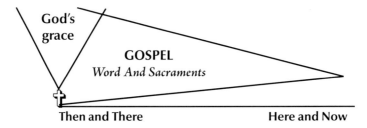

The two poles or "funnels" come together beautifully in 1 John 5:6–8: [1.] Christ "did not come by water only, but by water and blood. . . . [2.] For there are three that testify: the Spirit, the water and the blood; and the three are in agreement" (or: "intent on one and the same thing"). In the first statement St. John makes it clear that the Son of God un-derwent not only His Baptism, but also His actual death as signaled by the separation of blood and water (John 19:34). Some ancient heretics imagined that the Son of God spared Himself the supreme disgrace by withdrawing from the man Jesus before the crucifixion! But then, in a dramatic switch from past to present, St. John goes on to note that spirit, water, and blood are actively testifying here and now. The most obvious meaning is that "Spirit" here is the evangelical truth told by the Holy Spirit (1 Jn. 5:6b), or the words which are Spirit and life (John 6:63); the "water" is Baptism; and the "blood" is Jesus' blood of the New Testa-ment, given in the Sacrament. Truly, the Lord "then and there" does not need us to "make Him real" to our contemporary world. He Who is "the same yesterday and today and forever" (Heb. 13:8) really gives Himself and His benefits in real means of grace.

Those who teach the New Testament, therefore, have the obligation to show not only how all the promises and prophecies are fulfilled in Christ, but also how all this now reaches us by means of His Word and the sacraments. Unlike other histories, the Gospel stories which we hear every Sunday are not "dead histories of the dead," but as Luther said, "sacraments,"[16] that is, sacred signs which communicate the very blessings they describe.

Here are the "greater things" (John 14:12) that the Lord promised His followers would perform. Every baptized baby is a greater miracle than Lazarus raised from the dead (John 11). Lazarus received only physical life and had to die again. Baptism, however, bestows eternal, spiritual, heavenly life. Again, those who receive the Sacrament of the Altar take part in a wonder far greater than that of Cana, with its miraculous wine (John 2), or that of the miraculous feedings (e.g., John 6). The Lord's own body and blood are treasures infinitely more wondrous than even the most miraculously multiplied loaves and fish! And those who receive the divine Absolution (John 20:22–23) are there cleansed from defilements vastly worse than mere leprosy (Luke 17:12 ff.). The humble earthy words, water, bread, and wine are for us today the counterparts of those lowly servant-forms of Baby-in-the-manger and Man-on-the-cross, under which God gave His best and dearest.

To conclude: neither Law nor Gospel is simply correct information about God, although each is that too, of course. The Law is God acting, commanding and condemning. The Gospel is God acting, forgiving and saving. These are not theories about death and life, but the realities themselves. The Gospel is not, as in Reformed Protestantism, an anemic "plan of salvation," awaiting implementation or compliance with its conditions. Instead, the Gospel presses upon us the ready fact and gift of salvation. It is the invitation which is already part and parcel of the banquet itself (Matt. 22:1–14).

WHAT THEN IS FAITH?

It is now easy to see what sort of thing saving faith must be. It is not an exercise in spiritual ingenuity or religious heroics. Faith is from beginning to end a gracious gift of God. It has no existence apart from the Word of God which creates it and which it embraces (Rom. 10:17). It is not as though God had done His part in providing salvation in Christ and now it were up to us to do our part in response. Even the response—that is, the

---

16. WA 49, 21 and WA 9, 440.

reception of God's gift—is itself a gift (Phil. 1:29) from the Father Who through His Spirit (1 Cor. 12:3) draws people to His Son (John 6:44).

Faith's beginning in us (conversion) does not come from our own resources. Neither does its continuation. Bringing a person to faith is every bit as much a creative act of God as was the production of light out of darkness (2 Cor. 4:6; cf. Gen. 1:3). The unbelieving sinner, dead in trespasses and sins (Eph. 2:1–3), can no more "make a decision for Jesus" or decide to "co-operate with the Holy Spirit" in conversion than could the dead Lazarus wish himself alive after carefully considering the pros and cons (John 11). Faith is spiritual life, and can be given only by the creative voice of Him Who is the Resurrection and the Life. Psychologically, to be sure, we may experience something like a "decision." If so, it is only a sign that we were already alive through the Gospel.

Faith is a theological mystery. It does not lie open to psychological inspection. This means that on the one hand the newly baptised baby or the sleeping or comatose believer, and on the other hand the brilliant Christian scholar all have the same Spirit-given faith. It also means that people must not be put through torture-mills about some particular experience, as though it were the only right way of conversion. There is no standard conversion experience. Personal experience can be as varied as are human personalities. Whatever we may think we can trace experientially, God's workings within us are hidden and will elude us (John 3:8).

Faith is "born of the Gospel, or of absolution."[17] It saves in the same way that eating nourishes: the Gospel is the food, faith is the God-given act of eating (John 6:50–51). Against all forms of *synergism* (the idea that natural man can co-operate with God in his conversion, as though he had spiritual powers even before faith), we confess strict *monergism* (the doctrine that everything belonging to our salvation is entirely God's doing) in the catechism explanation of the Creed's third article:

> I believe that I cannot by my own reason or strength believe in Jesus Christ, my Lord, or come to Him; but the Holy Spirit has called me by the Gospel, enlightened me with His gifts, sanctified and kept me in the true faith. . . .[18]

---

17. AC XII, 5 (Tappert, 34).
18. Small Catechism, Apostles' Creed, explanation of the Third Article.

Chapter Six

THE SACRAMENT OF HOLY BAPTISM

WHAT DOES *SACRAMENT* MEAN?

As noted earlier, our word *sacrament* comes from the Latin translation of the word *mystery* in the Greek New Testament. Echoing 1 Corinthians 4:1 ("stewards of the mysteries of God," KJV), the ancient church fathers called the great life-giving truths or teachings revealed in God's Word the "mysteries" of the faith. Gradually the word *sacrament* came to be narrowed down to only one kind of Christian mystery, namely, God-given actions in which the promise of forgiveness and salvation is attached to outward elements like water, bread, or wine. The New Testament knows two special such "sacraments."

Consider the remarkable conversation in St. Mark 10:35 and following, Ambition ran high for the sons of Zebedee, not to mention their mother (as St. Matthew 20:20 and following does). Might the sons be awarded the privilege of sitting, one at the Lord's right hand and one to His left, in glory? As so often, the Lord replies with a question: "Can you drink the cup I drink or be baptised with the baptism I am baptized with?" [author's translation]. Misunderstanding the whole thing in a trivial, ceremonial sense, James and John reply in effect: "Yes, yes, we can drink anything, and of course we'd be glad to undergo any baptism." Yet here the Lord means by "cup" and "baptism" His own redemptive sufferings, culminating in His cross. (On "baptism" see St. Luke 12:50 and compare St. John 19:30; for the "cup," see St. Mark 14:36.) Clearly the Lord chose these words to describe His saving work because He was going to establish for His Church these two, a baptism and a cup, as wondrous ways in which His cross and the salvation gained there might come to us and be given to us.

St. Paul does something similar with the exodus theme, the crossing of the Red Sea. He describes this great founding event of the people of Israel in terms of a baptism and a spiritual banquet in which Christ is food and drink (1 Cor. 10:2–4). These repeated couplings of baptism with "the cup" or with spiritual food and drink cannot be accidental.

Baptism and the Lord's Supper stand in a class by themselves in the New Testament. We call them "sacraments," meaning divinely instituted actions in which God has attached the heavenly gifts of forgiveness and salvation to humble earthly elements.

It is not enough to define a sacrament as a "visible sign of an invisible grace" as the "Reformed" (non-Lutheran Protestants) do. For, as we shall see, in the sacraments God not only gives us signs, pictures, and reminders of His blessings. He gives *these blessings themselves!* The sacraments have this power in and through the concrete Gospel-Word that God has placed into them, as in St. Augustine's famous saying: "The Word comes to the element and makes it a sacrament."[1]

CHRIST'S BAPTISM AS THE SOURCE OF OURS

The Baptism of our Lord, which opens His public ministry, is reported by all four evangelists. It must be of major importance.

The first thing to be noted is that at the Baptism of Jesus the three Persons of the most holy Trinity appear together. The Father's voice is heard. The eternal Son stands, incarnate, in the Jordan. The Holy Spirit shows Himself in the shape of a dove. This explicit trinitarian *theophany* (appearance or manifestation of God) at Jesus' Baptism is unique. There is nothing quite like it anywhere else in the entire Bible. This same Triune God meets us in our own baptism. Interestingly, the precise formula "in the name of the Father and of the Son and of the Holy Spirit" occurs in Scripture only in St. Matthew 28:19, and there as part of the Lord's baptismal command. Baptism is thoroughly trinitarian!

Yet there seems to be, on the face of it, a problem here: If baptism is for the forgiveness of sins, and if Jesus is sinless (both of which Scripture clearly teaches!), then what can be the meaning of His baptism? Surely it is not enough to say that the Lord was simply setting a good example.

We may begin with the clue He gave in St. Luke 12:50: "I have a baptism to be baptised with, and how pressed I am till it be completed!" [author's translation]. The Saviour cannot be speaking here of His baptism in the Jordan, which had already happened (Luke 3:21). He must mean that great "baptism" which was to culminate on the cross, where it would be finished (John 19:30) or completed. For Jesus, baptism means the cross.

For us the cross means quite the opposite of what it meant for our Lord: death for Him but life for us. On the cross He is the Testator. We are the beneficiaries. His holy life and death provide the "input." The "output" of full and free salvation comes to us.

---

1. Quoted in LC IV 18 (Tappert, 438). Note what was said earlier on "The Means of Grace" in the previous chapter, especially in connection with 1 John 5:6–8.

Christ's baptism and our baptisms are related, then, through His cross. They are alike in that both His baptism and ours point to His cross. Yet they differ in the "direction" of this "current" of salvation. For they stand on opposite sides of His cross.

We may think of our Lord's baptism as a great tide that washes the world's sins onto Him and sweeps Him (and them) *to* the cross. It is precisely at His baptism, therefore, that Jesus stands revealed as "the Lamb of God, who takes away the sin of the world" (John 1:29). *From* the cross, however, flows to us the saving tide of our baptisms (1 Pt. 3:20–21!), full of God's mercy, forgiveness, and life.

An analogy from photography suggests itself. From one single negative, many "positive" pictures may be made. The "negative" differs from the positives only in that black and white are completely reversed. In the terms of this analogy, Christ's baptism is the unique "negative" from which God makes all the "positive" copies, our baptisms. Through the cross, His baptism is the *reverse* of ours.

This biblical understanding of the relation between Christ's baptism and ours is solidly entrenched in the mind and worship of the church. The ancient Christian poet Coelius Sedulius put it like this in his great Epiphany hymn:

> Within the Jordan's crystal flood
> In meekness stands the Lamb of God
> And, sinless, sanctifies the wave,
> Mankind from sin to cleanse and save.[2]

Luther expresses this same common understanding of the church when he takes over this language for baptismal prayer: ". . . through the baptism of thy dear Child, our Lord Jesus Christ, hast consecrated and set apart the Jordan and all water as a salutary flood and a rich and full washing away of sins . . . ."[3]

The old Eastern liturgies give beautiful visual expression to all this when a crucifix is dropped into a body of water at the annual Epiphany observance of the "blessing of the Jordan." The point is that it was the Jordan which received the blessing from Christ and His cross, not Christ from the Jordan!

---

2. This is John Mason Neale's superb translation (*TLH* 131:3).

3. Both Luther's orders of Baptism from 1523 and from 1526 contain these words (AE 53, 97 and 107). *Editor's note*: Similar wording is found in the order for Holy Baptism in *LSB*, p. 269.

As for us today, we need not travel to Palestine, nor would we be "closer" to Jesus if we did. The Jordan of His Baptism flows to us freely through the baptismal font of every parish church throughout the whole wide world (Matt. 28:18–20)!

WHAT IS BAPTISM?

"Baptism is not just plain water, but it is the water included in God's command and combined with God's word."[4] So the Small Catechism teaches. It makes explicit reference to St. Matthew 28:19: "Go and make disciples of all nations, baptising them into the Name of the Father and of the Son and of the Holy Spirit . . ." [author's translation].

A valid baptism requires the application of water in the name of the Holy Trinity. It is neither the amount of water that matters, nor the manner of its application. Curiously, those who take a "low" view of what happens in baptism will often fuss a great deal about how this supposedly unimportant thing is to be done.

It will not do to insist, for instance, that a person must be totally submerged to be truly baptised. Now, it is true that the word *baptise* comes from a Greek word meaning "to dip." The forms *baptise* and *Baptism* are used only of religious washings, though. In such cases the reference is to any sort of application of water, as the usage in St. Mark 7:4 makes clear. Even the meaning "dip" or "immerse" in and of itself need not imply complete submersion. The most ancient depictions we have of our Lord's Baptism in the Jordan show Him standing in the water up to His waist, with John the Baptiser pouring water on His head from a shell.

It may be noted in passing that the Israelites are said to have been "baptized . . . in the cloud and in the sea" (1 Cor. 10:2). However, the only people who were "immersed" or submerged there were Pharaoh's pursuing armies! (It should also be observed that the usual mode of baptism in the Lutheran Church is a threefold *pouring* of water on the head, not "sprinkling.")

Water by itself is not yet baptism. It needs to be applied in the thrice-holy name of the Father and of the Son and of the Holy Spirit. This baptismal "formula," however, must not be mistaken for a magical incantation or mantra, where everything depends on correct recitation of the right syllables. In the Word of God it is not the sounds or syllables that matter, but the right sense or meaning. Therefore the baptismal Word is not a bit less effective in English than it is in New Testament Greek.

---

4. Small Catechism: Baptism, First Section.

This stress on the sense rather than the sounds implies something else too. What if the trinitarian words, or sounds, are used, but the doctrine of the Trinity is denied? For instance, what if one says "in the name of the Father and of the Son and of the Holy Spirit," but adds that this really means "in the name of Liberty, Equality, and Fraternity," or some other non-trinitarian content? Then we have not a baptism but a mockery.

Baptisms performed with water in trinitarian churches must be accepted as valid even if the churches are confused or even wrong about the power and benefit of baptism. But purported "baptisms" done by churches that deny the blessed Trinity cannot be regarded as valid. In the former case, those previously baptised are not to be baptised again, for the one baptism (Eph. 4:5) of the New Testament (like circumcision, Col. 2:9–13) is once-and-for-all. In the latter case, it is not a question of re-baptising anyone but simply of baptising those who in truth had not been baptised before.

THE BENEFIT OR POWER OF BAPTISM

Various churches hold basically two views of baptism. According to what we might call the "low" or "empty" view, baptism is essentially an act of obedience on our part. It amounts to a sign, symbol, or picture which gives nothing. It reminds us of the new birth, God's grace, and the like, but these must actually be obtained in some other way. In this view, baptism is essentially Law, not Gospel. This view is taught by the "baptistic" churches, but not only by them.

The other view of baptism, which might be termed "high" or "full," is confessed in Luther's Small Catechism: Baptism "works forgiveness of sins, rescues from death and the devil, and gives eternal salvation to all who believe this, as the words and promises of God declare."[5] Here baptism actually offers and gives—it does not merely symbolize—God's saving gifts.

Which of these two opposing views is taught in the Bible? If we were to classify relevant baptismal texts of the New Testament in a two-columned table representing the two different understandings, we would find that all the texts belong in the "high" or "full" column, and not a single one in the "low" or "empty" column (see table on next page).

All the texts in this table teach not that baptism only means or signifies something or other, but that it actually offers and gives something. It gives forgiveness, the new birth, the Holy Spirit, and salvation. Baptism

---

5. Small Catechism: Baptism, Second Section.

THE HIGH or FULL VIEW	THE LOW or EMPTY VIEW
God's Action: Baptism as Real Gift	*Man's Action: Baptism as Picture or Reminder*
GOSPEL	**LAW**

St. John 3:5: Unless someone is *born again out of water and Spirit*, he cannot enter into the Kingdom of God.

Acts 2:38: Be *baptised . . . into the forgiveness of your sins and receive the gift of the Holy Spirit.*

Acts 22:16: Be *baptised* and *wash away your sins.*

Rom. 6:4: *We have been buried together with him through baptism into death,* so that as Christ was raised from the dead . . . we likewise might *walk in newness of life.*

1 Cor. 6:11: But you have been *washed, . . . sanctified, . . . justified . . . .*

1 Cor. 12:13: For in one Spirit we all have been *baptised into one body.*

Gal. 3:27: As many as have been *baptised into Christ have put on Christ.*

Eph. 5:26: . . . that He might *sanctify her by cleansing her by means of the bath of the water in the Word . . .*

Col. 2:12: . . . *having been buried together with Him in baptism, in which you have also been raised together with Him* through faith . . .

Tit. 3:5: . . . He *saved us through the bath of rebirth and of renewal of the Holy Spirit . . .*

1 Peter 3:21: *Baptism, being the antitype (fulfillment) of the flood-water, now saves you also . . . through the resurrection of Jesus Christ . . .*

Editor's note: All passages in the left column are the author's translation.

is *into forgiveness*, not into symbols of it. Paul actually *washes away his sins* in baptism. Baptism *buries and raises* us with Christ, *saves us*, and so on. It is wrong to change this *real* language into picture language, as for instance the so-called *"Living Bible"* does without any basis in the text at all.

The Small Catechism asks, "How can water do such great things?" and answers:

> Water certainly doesn't do it, but the Word of God, which is with and in the water, and faith, which trusts such Word of God in the water. For without God's Word the water is mere water and no baptism. But with the Word of God it is a baptism, that is, a Water of Life, rich in grace, and a "bath of the new birth in the Holy Spirit."[6]

This must not be taken to mean that while the water happens to be there, it might just as well not be there, imagining that the Word does everything by itself apart from baptismal water. Rather, God's baptismal Word works *through* the water, not apart from it. Baptism is the "water-in-Word" bath. (See Eph. 5:26.) Therefore faith "trusts such Word of God *in the water*," not simply some Word-of-God-in-general apart from the baptismal water. For this reason the *Formula of Concord* specifically *rejects* this proposition: "That the water of Baptism is not a means whereby the Lord God seals the adoption of sons and works regeneration."[7]

BAPTISM AND DAILY LIFE

Having been made participants in the death and resurrection of Christ by baptism (Rom. 6:4 and Col. 2:12), His forgiven and reborn people are now called to live a new life of service to God and man (Eph. 2:8–10), and this by the power of that same risen Jesus Christ Whom they have "put on" in baptism (Gal. 3:26–27). The Small Catechism puts it like this:

> What does such baptising with water signify?

> Answer: It signifies that the old Adam in us must by daily contrition and repentance be drowned and die with all sins and evil lusts, and again daily a new man come out and arise, who is to live before God forever in righteousness and purity.[8]

---

6. *Editor's Note*: This seems to be the author's rendering of the material found in SC Baptism, Third Section.
7. FC SD XII 31 (Tappert, 635).
8. *Editor's Note*: This seems to be the author's rendering of the material found in SC Baptism, Fourth Section.

In an age like ours (2 Tim. 3:1–4!), when all that is holy, good, and noble is trampled underfoot in a demon-ridden Gadarene stampede (St. Mk 5:1 ff.) into unbridled self-indulgence, the practical implications of Holy Baptism must ever be kept before our eyes. In all facets of life—whether money, clothes, work, education, politics, cars, entertainment, or anything else—and in every decision involving these, Christians need to strive *with* their baptism against their flesh, not with the flesh against baptism and the Spirit!

Christ has defeated the powers of hell and freely gives us this liberating victory in baptism (Gal. 3:27–28; Col. 1–3). Luther therefore would hurl a defiant "I am baptised!" in Satan's teeth whenever the latter would seek to torment him. By the power of Christ's gift in baptism, Christians must daily assert their precious liberty as children of God and courageously do battle against the devil, the world, and their own flesh. Against the impudent pretensions of occult and demonic powers in our day we sing with Luther:

> This world's prince may still
> Scowl fierce as he will:
> He can harm us none,
> He's judged, fore'er undone!
> One little word can fell him.

THE BAPTISM OF BABIES

Infant baptism ("pedobaptism," as it is technically known) does not stand apart as a separate, independent issue. Rather, its pros and cons must be settled further "upstream," in the very question of what baptism is and does. Everything here will depend on what one thinks of baptism itself. If baptism is taken in the "low" sense of a mere picture or symbol, then of course it will be difficult to see the point of baptising babies. But if one takes the "high," biblical view of baptism as a powerful Gospel-gift, then why should babies be denied its heavenly benefits?

While the question about the very nature of baptism is basic, neither should one overlook particular points like these:

a. *The scope of our Lord's baptismal command is universal.* He said, "all nations" (Matt. 28:19). St. Peter noted that "the promise is to you and your children" (Acts 2:39 [author's translation]). Moreover, the Lord Himself welcomed and blessed the little ones, whom St. Luke expressly calls "babies" (Luke 18:15–16). Since Christ established for His church not child-blessing ceremonies but baptism, it is by baptism that babies must be allowed and not forbidden to come to Him today.

b. *Children need the very thing offered by baptism.* To Nicodemus Christ says not that wickedness sets in with old age, but that "that which is born of the flesh is flesh" (John 3:6 KJV) and needs to be "born again," that is, "of water and the Spirit" (John 3:3, 5). St. Paul describes man's condition from birth as "dead in trespasses and sins" (Eph. 2:1 KJV) and "by nature . . . children of wrath" (Eph. 2:3 KJV). Baptism, as the "bath of rebirth and of the renewal of the Holy Spirit" (Tit. 3:5 [author's translation]) is just the right antidote.

c. *It is a great mistake to assume that babies can have no faith simply because their conscious understanding and language use are as yet undeveloped.* In no case is faith a human achievement for which adult abilities are required. Faith is a Spirit-worked miracle of divine grace in the adult no less than in the newly baptised baby. Grace alone! And even in adults, faith cannot be made completely dependent on conscious intellectual activity. For instance, faith evidently continues in sleeping adults, while their conscious minds are "closed for repairs," or else they would need to be re-converted every morning! Neither sleep, therefore, nor unconsciousness, coma, or mental derangement in and of themselves affect faith. As the very core of all spiritual life, faith is safely "hidden with Christ in God" (Col. 3:3). He who created the extraordinary spiritual life of John the Baptiser when he was yet unborn (Luke 1:15, 41, 44) is fully able to create ordinary spiritual life in born children through Holy Baptism.

Parents who glibly talk of waiting until "the child is old enough to make up his own mind" should consider this: What would be the disastrous results of not feeding a baby till he can read a menu and "choose for himself"?

d. *Baptism is the normal entry into the New Testament people of God, as circumcision was the initiation into the Old Testament Israel. Note how St. Paul connects the two in Colossians 2:9–13.* Circumcision was to be performed on male babies when they were eight days old (Lev. 12:3). Now, the New Testament is not narrower but broader and much greater than the Old Testament, which was but a shadow of the New (John 1:17; Col. 2:17; 2 Cor. 3:4–18). If it pleased

God even in the more restrictive and exclusive Old Testament to receive little eight-day-old babies into His Kingdom, how much more now in all-universal, all-embracing New Testament? And just as circumcision, intended for babies, was performed mainly on adults when God initially established it (Gen. 17:23–27), it is not surprising that baptism, at the time of its institution and in the first generation of the church, was given first of all to adults. Yet whole families or households were baptised (Acts 16:15, 33; 1 Cor. 1:16), which normally would have included children of various ages. We also know from history that the Jews at the time of Christ practised "proselyte baptism" (baptism of converts, a Jewish tradition but not a God-given sacrament) which was administered to whole families including the babies. Had our Lord intended a different practice for the baptism He gave, He would have had to make a special point of excluding babies. He did no such thing.

Christ established neither "adult baptism" nor "infant baptism": He simply established baptism. How this sacred gift is to be applied and administered must be determined from what His authorized spokesmen (the inspired apostles and evangelists) teach about what baptism is and does. Proper baptismal practice cannot be deduced by a shallow and logistic reading of unexplained "precedent" from the Book of Acts! It must flow from a believing appreciation of the New Testament's *theology* of baptism.

THE NECESSITY OF BAPTISM

The Lutheran Church confesses that "Baptism is necessary for salvation."[9] This assertion reflects biblical statements such as "Whoever believes and is baptized will be saved" (Mark 16:16) and "unless a man is born of water and the Spirit, he cannot enter the kingdom of God" (John 3:5 [author's translation]).

The necessity of baptism for salvation must not be taken to mean, however, that without the act of baptism no one can possibly be saved. For example, if someone were instructed with a baptism planned for Easter Sunday but that person died as a believer during Holy Week, no one should doubt his salvation. Our church's Smalcald Articles make the point that "those who have come to faith before they were baptized . . . came to their faith through the external Word which preceded."[10]

---

9. AC IX 1 (Tappert, 33).
10. SA III viii 7 (Tappert, 313).

Consider a modern electrical analogy. Anyone who has ever struggled with defective bulbs on strings of Christmas tree lights will avoid like the plague the kind of strings on which all the lights go out if one of them fails. The problem is that such lights are hooked up "in series," so that the current can be broken by any bulb for all the others. Good strings are connected "parallel." There even if one bulb fails, the electricity still reaches all the others. We may think of the holy Means of Grace as connected "parallel." The divine gift and blessing of forgiveness, life, and salvation remains the same in all the various forms in which the one Gospel comes to us. Whether we receive baptism, preaching, absolution, or the Holy Supper, we get the same Gospel content. Only the mode of application varies.

Nevertheless, baptism remains *the* anchor or reference point for our entry into Christ. Faith, after all, deals not with a Christ-in-general but with the Christ Who gives Himself in concrete words and acts of promise. Thus faith looks back to baptism as its source (Gal. 3:27, etc.), and not to various emotional experiences. Similarly, a faith that comes into existence before baptism looks forward to baptism and to all that is given there. Faith can never say, "I already have Christ through the Word; therefore I do not need baptism." Also, no one desiring to have Christ for his Saviour should ever be told, "In your case, baptism is not necessary." All are invited to be joined to the Lord by way of baptism. This is what is meant by the "necessity" of baptism for salvation.

However, if baptism, though desired, cannot be obtained (say, for lack of water, or lack of a person able and willing to baptize), no one will be lost on that account. Luther appeals to the Old Testament, in which circumcision was to be administered on the eighth day. Yet babies who died before that day, therefore without circumcision, were never considered lost on that account.

Nevertheless, we have the responsibility to see to it that from our side everything possible has been done to make baptism available. We may not trifle with it or make light of it. Christian parents must be taught to have their babies baptised as soon as possible, not to wait until it is convenient for some far-away relative to attend. In case of imminent danger of death, any Christian present ought to administer emergency baptism. If there is doubt whether the person to be baptized is dead or alive, he should be given the benefit of the doubt and thus be given baptism. (Medical death and "theological death" are not the same. Many people are revived hours after medical death has occurred, which would not have been possible had they died "theologically.")

Sometimes people say, whether in effect or in these actual words, "Either Christ or baptism" or "Either faith or baptism." These amount to false alternatives, though. They are attempts, and not very clever ones, to suggest that a "high" understanding of baptism violates either "Christ alone" or "faith alone." Of course it is Christ alone Who saves, but He has chosen to use baptism as a means. Nor is there any competition at all between baptism and faith. Baptism is God's *giving* means, while faith is our *taking* means.

"BAPTISM IN THE HOLY SPIRIT"?

"Pentecostal" (and, since 1961, "Charismatic") churches and teachers hold that in addition to the Sacrament of Baptism, which they call "water baptism," there is also a "Spirit baptism" or a "Baptism in the Holy Spirit," of which "speaking in tongues" is the usual sign. This second, or "Spirit baptism" often happens to people years after they have already become Christian believers and have received "water baptism."

The first thing to be observed here is that the whole scheme of two different baptisms, one with water and the other with the Spirit, is quite foreign to the New Testament. There we have, pointedly, only "one Lord, one faith, one baptism" (Eph. 4:5). This one baptism of the New Testament is neither a water-only nor a Spirit-only, but a water-and-Spirit baptism (see the texts in table, page 92). If the New Testament taught two different sorts of baptism, then it could never speak simply of "baptism" or being "baptised," but would have to specify which one was meant each time. Yet the New Testament speaks quite simply of "baptism" and "baptising," because there is only one baptism.[11] Nor does the New Testament know the fantasy of two different classes of Christians, a "first class" consisting of those who have "tongues" and the "Baptism of the Holy Spirit," and another, a sort of "economy class" with only "ordinary" faith and "water baptism"! There is only one holy, baptised, priestly, royal people of God, the Body of Christ (1 Cor. 12; Eph. 2 and 4, etc.).

A shallow reading of texts like St. Matthew 3:11 may indeed give the impression that there are two different baptisms. The confusion disappears, however, the moment it is realised that the contrast here is not be-

---

11. Hebrews 6:2 does not teach several baptisms. The word used here is not the usual New Testament word for Christian baptism, but a word meaning ceremonial washings generally. It is so translated in many modern Bible versions. The idea is that Christian baptism must be distinguished from all sorts of religious washings, Jewish and pagan, which abounded in the ancient world.

tween the Sacrament of Baptism and a Pentecostal experience, but rather between John's Baptism and Christ's own work, culminating in Pentecost. Today we no longer have John's baptism, nor do we live before Pentecost. We have the complete Christian Sacrament of Baptism, with all the power and blessing of Pentecost in it![12]

As usual, we get the "depth dimension" in St. John's Gospel. Here John the Baptiser is quoted as contrasting his own baptising with the work of Jesus, "the One Who is baptising in the Holy Spirit" (John 1:33 [author's translation]). This has nothing to do with tongues. It is not even a direct reference to Pentecost, which lay some three years in the future. The present tense ("He is baptising") means that this "baptising in the Holy Spirit" was something then already happening in the work of Jesus. As God the Son, Jesus had the Spirit "not by measure" (John 3:34 RSV). From one perspective, His entire work may be described as winning for death-bound human flesh the heavenly gift of the life-giving Spirit of God. This Spirit-fulness could not be released upon the human race until Christ's redemptive work had been completed and He had been glorified (John 7:39). Pentecost is the signal that all this has been fulfilled, and that the spiritual treasures of life and salvation are now ready for distribution "to the ends of the earth" (Acts 1:8). The real power of Pentecost is not the sound as of a mighty rushing wind, nor the tongues of fire, nor the strange languages. All these are "special effects." The real and permanent dynamic of Pentecost is the Gospel (Rom. 1:16) in the forms of preaching, baptism, and the Lord's Supper. This remains in the church to the end of time, even though the "special effects" of the apostolic age (and peculiar even then to the apostles, and not to every Tom, Dick, and Harry, Acts 8:14–18; 2 Cor. 12:12; cf. Eph. 2:20) have long ceased.

The usual Pentecostal "guided tour" of the Book of Acts is designed to show that "speaking in tongues" or the "baptism with the Holy Spirit" is a normal stage of spiritual development to which every Christian ought to aspire. A closer look at Acts does not bear this out, though. We notice that "tongues" or some visible manifestations of the Spirit occur not generally or indiscriminately, but that a few "extensions" of Pentecost occur in a handful of highly significant situations. We find that these special occurrences in fact mark the transition of the Gospel to a new stage of the missionary programme given by the risen Saviour Himself: Jerusa-

---

12. A very helpful discussion by a non-Lutheran is Frederick Dale Bruner, *A Theology of the Holy Spirit: The Pentecostal Experience and the New Testament Witness* (Grand Rapids, MI: Eerdmans, 1970).

lem and Judea, Samaria, and the uttermost parts of the earth (Acts 1:8).
And so we have a "mini-Pentecost" when the Gospel crosses into Samaria
(Acts 8:4–24), and again when it reaches the Gentiles in Caesarea (Acts
10:44–46). The only other occurrence is the special case of Acts 19:1–7,
where it is a question of the superiority of the full and permanent Christian baptism over the temporary, provisional baptism of John. The necessity of these special demonstrations of the oneness of the Christian
church, regardless of race and nationality, is evident from the great difficulty with which the great apostle Peter learns this lesson and lets go of
old prejudices and scruples (Acts 10:9–28; Gal. 2:11–14).

In the post-apostolic church we are to take Pentecost on faith, just as
we take the resurrection on faith (John 20:29) in the living Gospel and
sacraments of Christ. It is sacrilege to suggest that humble believers in
Christ, who are complete in Him in Whom dwells "all the fulness of the
Godhead bodily" (Col 2:9 KJV), either need or can have something supposedly "more" here on earth.

Chapter Seven

THE SACRAMENT OF THE ALTAR

On the most solemn night of the Lord's life on earth He placed into the midst of His church the true New Testament Holy of Holies, the Sacrament of His body and of His very blood of the new Testament. Since this Sacrament is the very embodiment of the Gospel, differences in the understanding of the Gospel must show up as divisions over the Sacrament.

Church history has borne this out. The main issues may be sorted out under four heads: (1) The Real Presence of Christ's Body and Blood; (2) Sacrament or Sacrifice?; (3) Preparation and Confirmation; and (4) Sacrament, Church, and Confession.

THE REAL PRESENCE OF CHRIST'S BODY AND BLOOD

The Saviour's founding words are clear: "This is My body. . . . This is My blood of the Testament [or: the New Testament in My blood]" (author's translation; see Matt. 26:26–28; Mark 14:22–24; Luke 22:19–20; 1 Cor. 11:23–25). With the church of all ages, Luther's Small Catechism therefore confesses that the Sacrament of the Altar is "the true body and blood of our Lord Jesus Christ under the bread and wine, instituted by Christ Himself for us Christians to eat and to drink."[1]

It is faith's way to say the deepest things in simple, straightforward language. Faith is satisfied to know *what* God is saying, giving, or promising; it is not interested in prying into the *how*. As in all the other great mysteries of our salvation, so also in that of the Holy Supper, faith gladly takes God at His Word. Christ gives exactly what He says He gives, His body and blood. How He does this must be left entirely to Him. It is far beyond our ken.

We may of course help ourselves with fitting analogies, up to a point. The ancient church was very fond of comparing the Sacrament with the Incarnation: as Christ is God and Man in one Person, so His body and blood are sacramentally united with bread and wine in His Supper. This does not "explain" the mystery, nor is it meant to. The comparison stays

---

1.   Small Catechism: Sacrament of the Altar.

modestly within the bounds of God's Word, and takes off on no clever flights of fancy.

Later a different attitude arose. When philosophising became a consuming interest during the high Middle Ages, the Christian mysteries were also put under the microscope of inquisitive human reasoning. There developed a detailed explanation of how the Real Presence comes about. The bread and wine, it was claimed, are changed or "transubstantiated" into Christ's body and blood, in such a way that they are no longer bread and wine at all. Only their "accidents" are left behind, that is, colour, taste, shape, and the like. This theory of "transubstantiation" lacks all basis in God's Word, and therefore the Reformation rejected it.

Unfortunately Zwingli and Calvin, and the "Reformed" churches which followed them, threw out the baby with the bath-water, as it were. They rejected the Real Presence along with transubstantiation. For Zwingli the bread and wine presented only pictures or reminders of the absent body and blood of Christ. Calvin tried to upgrade this bare symbolism. He could even talk about a "real" and "substantial" presence of Christ's body and blood, but only for "faith." Objectively—that is, for the hand of the celebrant and the mouth of the communicant—nothing was there except bread and wine. Calvin's difference with Zwingli, then, was more rhetorical than real. In the "Zurich Consensus" Calvin agreed with the Zwinglians that the body and blood of Christ were as far away from the bread and wine as heaven was from earth.[2] Since Christ's body was detained far away in heaven, it could not also be in the Holy Supper. In this view whatever may be offered to the communicant in the bread and wine, no matter how beautifully garlanded in flowery language, it is not the body and blood of Christ. For Calvin, to "place Christ in the bread" would be to "drag Him from heaven."[3]

From the preceding it may well seem that three basic positions exist concerning the Holy Supper. There is the Roman Catholic view of transubstantiation, which holds that no bread and wine remain at all. Then there is the opposite, "Reformed" extreme, according to which the Lord's

---

2. *Editor's note:* "The *Consensus Tigurinus*," trans. Ian D. Bunting, *Journal of Presbyterian History* 44 (1966):58. Reprinted as an appendix in Hermann Sasse, *The Lonely Way: Selected Essays and Letters*, trans. Matthew C. Harrison et al (St. Louis, MO: Concordia Publishing House, 2002), 2:437–449. For the present citation, see the last page.

3. John Calvin, *Institutes of the Christian Religion*, ed. John T. McNeill, The Library of Christian Classics, vol. 21 (Philadelphia, PA: Westminster Press, 1960), 1403.

body and blood are not really in the Supper, but only in heaven. Finally, there is the Lutheran "middle-ground," that the Sacrament includes bread and wine as well as the body and blood of Christ. All this is trivially true enough. Beneath the surface, however, the picture is simpler still.

Actually, it makes more sense to think of only two basic positions: either confession or denial of the Real Presence of Christ's body and blood. Here lies the big division. Some of those who confess the Real Presence also have a false theory about it, yet that is not the same order of importance as the basic difference over the Real Presence itself. Whether bread and wine are present obviously matters not nearly so much as whether Christ's body and blood are there. Transubstantiation is simply a silly attempt to explain the unexplainable. Luther always regarded the matter thus. He rejected transubstantiation, of course.[4] Yet this was not, as we shall see, his major objection to the Roman Mass. Forced to choose between the two errors, Luther would quip: "Sooner than have mere wine with fanatics, I would agree with the pope that there is only blood."[5]

There is still another interesting point about transubstantiation. It is sometimes claimed that if the Lord's Words of Institution are really taken literally, only transubstantiation will do. According to this claim, Luther departed from the literal sense. In reply, Luther gave counter-examples like these:[6] If I point to a glass containing a beverage and say, "This is water," or "This is beer," I am obviously not saying that the glass container itself has now been transubstantiated into water or beer. Or if I were to hand someone a leather-purse full of gold pieces and say, "Here's the gold," no one would take me to be asserting a transmutation of leather into gold. When we say "This is water" (or beer, or gold, or what have you) we are simply naming the important part, the content, without bothering to mention the container. To say instead "This is a glass plus beer" or "This is cowhide plus gold" is not being more literal. It is just being pedantic.

Not only do the Words of Institution *not* teach transubstantiation, but transubstantiation is not even the most straightforward reading of these words.[7] For if we ask what it is that changes in transubstantiation, we are told that it is the "substance" of the bread which turns into the "substance" of Christ's body. If we ask further what is meant by "substance," we learn

---

4. *Editor's note*: See SA III vi 5.
5. *Confession Concerning Christ's Supper* (1528), AE 37, 317.
6. AE 37, 302–303.
7. This matter is discussed in some detail in Tom G. A. Hardt, *On the Sacrament of the Altar* (Fort Wayne, IN: Concordia Theological Seminary Press, n.d.), especially pp. 18–20.

that it means something "intelligible"—something that only minds can grasp, but not the senses. Perhaps we have here the first few steps away from sacramental realism. Zwingli and Calvin later went much farther in reducing the Real Presence to something mental. Rome and Geneva often have more in common than may appear at first glance. It turns out that the most direct, most realistic understanding of Christ's words is found in Luther's stress on the presence of Christ's "true, natural body," the same body which was born of the Virgin Mary and was crucified for us, not a new body made up somehow from bread!

However mistaken the whole scheme of transubstantiation, outright denial of the Real Presence of Christ's body and blood stands out as much worse. It is the nature of Christian faith to receive God's revealed mysteries with simplicity or "singleness of heart" (Acts 2:46 KJV). The opposite of singleness is doubleness, from which we get our words *doubt* and *duplicity*.[8] To make the Lord's words "This is My body" mean in effect "This is not My body" is indeed to depart from the simplicity of faith.

Those who refuse to take "This is My body" at face value must find an opening somewhere in this sentence for a non-literal, or figurative, interpretation. Since the sentence has only three basic elements, "This," "is," and "My body," one of these three must be given some unusual, non-obvious sense. All three possibilities were actually tried already in Luther's lifetime. His refutations may still be read with profit today.[9]

First, there was a short-lived attempt to explain "This" as not referring to the sacrament at all. In this view, Christ handed His disciples the bread, then pointed to Himself and said, "This (which you see sitting before you) is My body." Unlike modern preachers, however, the Saviour never uttered platitudes or trite truisms. The idea is just as silly as when Adventists or Jehovah's Witnesses make Him say to the thief on the cross: "Verily, verily, it is today that I am telling you that (someday) you will be with Me in Paradise." (See Luke 23:43.) We hardly need the Son of God to teach us that today is today. His body is His body.

---

8. I follow here the argumentation of Werner Elert, *The Lord's Supper Today, Contemporary Theology Series*, trans. Martin Bertram (St. Louis, MO: Concordia Publishing House, 1973), 22.

9. See especially: *Against the Heavenly Prophets*, 1525 (AE 40, 79–223); *That These Words, "This is My Body" Still Stand Firm against the Fanatics*, 1527, (AE 37, 13–150); *Confession Concerning Christ's Supper*, 1528, (AE 37, 161–372); and *Brief Confession concerning the Holy Sacrament*, 1544 (AE 38, 287–319). See also Charles Porterfield Krauth, *The Conservative Reformation and its Theology* [*Editor's update:*] (St. Louis: Concordia Publishing House, 2007), 585–830.

More ingenious was the idea that "My body" really meant "symbol of My body," or even "fruits and benefits gained by means of My body." This is fanciful, however, and clearly does violence to the text. The Lord, after all, refers to the body "given for you" and to the blood of the [New] Testament, "shed for you." There is not the slightest excuse in the text for taking away the things themselves of which the Saviour speaks, and putting in their place pictures or effects of these things.

Doubtless the most influential of the three re-interpretations was Zwingli's theory that "is" means "represents." In this thinking Christ then meant to say: "This represents, or symbolises, My body." When challenged to give examples of "is" meaning "represents," Zwingli offered sentences like Christ saying "I am the Door" and "I am the Vine." A moment's thought shows, however, that the interpretations "I represent the Door" and "I represent the Vine" are impossible. When one thing represents another, such as a flag representing a country, then the thing being represented is always greater than the one representing it. So where is the huge door, or cosmic vine which Christ is supposed to represent? Clearly, as Luther pointed out, the figure of speech in such sentences lies not in the word "is," but in the words "Door" and "Vine." These have become "new words," Luther said, like "Fox" in the sentence "Herod is a Fox." The meaning is not that Herod is or represents a furry quadruped, but that he is clever as a fox. He is a Fox with a capital F. Just so, the Lord does not represent parts of buildings or plants. Rather, He really *is* the Entrance to heaven and the very Source of life for His branches. *Door* and *Vine* are metaphors. They are "new," capitalised words, if you will. "Is" still means *is*, though.

More plausible at first sight are examples taken from dreams, visions, or parables. Take the sentences "The seven good cows are seven years" (Gen. 41:26) and "The seed is the word of God" (Luke 8:11). This translates, supposedly, into "The seven good cows mean seven years," and "The seed means the Word of God," respectively. On such grounds even the Oxford English Dictionary gives "signify, amount to, mean" as a possible use of "to be."[10] Others would argue, however, that "to be" never has the sense of "to mean." We are dealing here, they would say, not with real cows or real seed, but with dream-cows and dream-seed. And unlike their ordinary cousins from daily life, which might "mean" something or other, dream-cows and dream-seed, in their settings, do not merely "mean" years and the Word, but actually *are* those things. The analogy of a picture may

---

10. *The Oxford English Dictionary*, second (1989) ed., s. v. "Be."

help. I may point to a drawing and say, "This represents Charles." By "this" I obviously mean the pattern of lines and dots appearing on a piece of paper. But if I say, "This is Charles," I clearly mean by "this" not the markings on the paper, but the person they represent. And that person does not merely "mean" Charles, but he is Charles. I may say "This represents Charles," and I may also say "This is Charles," but the two sentences do not mean the same thing.

Be that as it may, in the Lord's Supper we are not dealing with dreams or parables but with sober narrative. The Words of Institution have a legal, testamentary force and solemnity ("blood of the [New] Testament"). One may not play fast and loose even with a mere human being's last will and testament (Gal. 3:15). How much more are we bound to take the Son of God at His word and to accept that on this awesome occasion He said exactly what He meant and meant exactly what He said. Imagine the following scene in a secular court: John's last will and testament had left the farm to Mary, and the rest to all sorts of other people. Thereupon greedy relatives ask the court to rule that by "the farm" John had meant not the farm itself but an aerial photograph of it which had hung for years over the mantelpiece and had great sentimental value. Which human court would put up with such tricks? In the Words of the Sacrament, One greater than Solomon speaks (Matt. 12:42)!

The Words of Institution are clear in and of themselves. Their official interpretation, moreover, by Christ's authorised and inspired apostle, St. Paul, leaves no doubt about their literal, intended sense: (1) St. Paul in 1 Corinthians 10:16 calls the sacramental bread and wine the "participation" in the body and blood of Christ. One cannot participate or share in something that is not there. (2) To abuse the Holy Supper is to "be guilty of sinning against the body and blood of the Lord" (1 Cor. 11:27), clearly present, therefore. (3) To receive the Sacrament "without discerning [distinguishing, differentiating] the body" of the Lord is to receive it to judgment (1 Cor. 11:29). (4) A purely spiritual "eating and drinking" of Christ, which is simply believing in Him (John 6:50), can never harm anyone, and no one should be warned against it. If one can eat and drink the Lord's body and blood "to judgment," then this cannot be the purely spiritual eating and drinking of faith. (5) The parallels of Jewish and pagan sacrificial meals make it clear that the participation meant there is one that happens through physical eating and drinking, not by some mental or "spiritual" process (1 Cor. 10:14–22).

More generally, it is wrong to apply St. John 6:63, "The Spirit gives life; the flesh counts for nothing," to Jesus, and then to play off the Spirit against *His* flesh. Of course our own sinful flesh "counts for nothing"! What of His flesh, however, which He had just characterized as life-giving (John 6:51–58)? When "the Word became flesh . . . full of grace and truth" (John 1:14), so that in Him "all the fulness of the Godhead lives *bodily*" (Col. 2:9 [author's translation]), it is sheer sacrilege to suggest that *this* holy and saving flesh "counts for nothing." Nor does the Holy Spirit despise outward, tangible things as such, as imagined by a false spiritualising. When He acted in the miracle of the Incarnation, the blessed Virgin conceived not an occult "spirit-being," but the flesh-and-blood Saviour (Luke 1:35). The Spirit likewise distributes life and salvation through outward words and speech (John 6:63; 20:22–23; 2 Cor. 3:6 ff.; Gal. 3:2–5), and in holy and intimate union with "the water and the blood" (1 Jn. 5:8).

One must finally consider the whole relation between the Old and New Testaments. They stand to each other as a provisional shadow to the permanent reality (John 1:17; 2 Cor. 3:7–11; Col. 2:17). The words of the Supper are clearly intended as a great counter-thrust to the ancient words of Moses: "This is the blood of the covenant [testament]" (Ex. 24:8). The Passover meal formed the setting for the Last Supper, and it should be noted that at the Passover real bread and flesh were eaten. Now, if even the "shadowy" Old Testament types gave real flesh and blood, how could the New Testament fulfillment and reality possibly give less? How could it offer mere pictures, symbols, or reminders? No! In the New Testament Holy of Holies the Lamb of God Himself feeds us with His own flesh and blood, once and for all sacrificed on the cross for our salvation.

It remains only to tidy up some matters of language. To talk simply of the "Real Presence," for instance, clearly is not enough. No Christian ever denied that Christ as God is present everywhere. Moreover, when we pray, "Come, Lord Jesus, be our guest," we clearly have in mind our Lord's real, personal presence. Yet breakfast cereal is not the Sacrament!

In the Lord's Supper, not a generic "Real Presence" lies at issue, but the unique sacramental presence of Christ's body and blood in the consecrated bread and wine. A simple three-point test will tell a genuine confession of the sacramental presence from mere sound-alike rhetoric: (1) *Sacramental union:* Is it confessed that the Lord's body and blood are so united with the bread and wine that the latter are truly the "participation" [communion] in this body and blood (1 Cor. 10:16)? If not, if Christ's body and blood are thought of as given in some other way than by the external eating and drinking of the sacramental elements, then we have spiritualising rhetoric instead of the New Testament reality. (2) *Oral reception:*

Are the body and blood of Christ said to be received with the mouth, or only "spiritually," by faith? If the latter, then again we have only rhetoric. (3) *Reception by the unworthy:* Is it confessed that everyone who takes the sacrament thereby receives Christ's true body and blood, regardless of his faith, sincerity, or other personal qualities? If not, if it depends on "faith," then no objective presence is confessed, whatever the rhetoric.

This whole discussion is concerned not with the "mode or manner" of Christ's presence, as is sometimes claimed, but with whether His body and blood are really there at all. If one person were to insist that Charles himself had been in the room on a certain occasion, while another says that only Charles's picture had been there, then it would be dishonest to pretend that the quarrel is only about *how*, not *whether*, Charles had been there. The Charles-party might have to "smoke out" the picture-party with questions like these: Was Charles there three-dimensionally? Did he move? What did he say? The more fudging about the issue, the more seemingly far-fetched and hair-splitting the questions might need to become. The object of these questions would be not to quibble about technicalities but to keep fancy talk about a picture from passing as genuine discourse about Charles.

It is tragic that many modern Lutherans have so far forgotten their Confessions, that they can endorse weaselley-worded compromises like the *Leuenberg Concord* (1973)[11] and the "Lima Statement" (1982).[12] Some even allege that both "Reformed [Calvinist] and Lutheran traditions" have "strongly affirmed the real presence of Christ in the Sacrament" and that the real differences were about the mode of Christ's presence,[13] but these should not divide the churches. Such claims directly contradict the Book of Concord.[14] One cannot knowingly advance them and at the same time swear to uphold the Lutheran Confessions without thereby perjuring oneself.

---

11. "In the Lord's Supper the risen Christ imparts himself in his body and blood, given up for all, through his word of promise with bread and wine" ("Agreement Between Reformation Churches in Europe [*Leuenberg Agreement*]," *An Invitation to Action: A Study of Ministry, Sacraments, and Recognition,* The Lutheran-Reformed Dialogue Series III, 1981–1983, James E. Andrews and Joseph A. Burgess, eds. [Philadelphia, PA: Fortress Press, 1984]), 68.
12. "It is in virtue of the living word of Christ and by the power of the Holy Spirit that the bread and wine become the sacramental signs of Christ's body and blood" (*Baptism, Eucharist, and Ministry,* Faith and Order Paper No. 111 [Geneva: World Council of Churches, 1982], 13).
13. Andrews and Burgess, eds., 16; see 14.
14. See FC SD VII 2–11 (Tappert, 569–71).

The unhappy example of transubstantiation should serve as a warning to avoid all attempts to explain the sacramental presence. But does not the traditional Lutheran "in, with, and under" formula also fall into that trap? Actually, these words explain nothing, nor are they meant to. They serve simply to avoid transubstantiation on the one hand while stressing on the other hand the fact that the Saviour has attached the gifts of His body and blood to external bread and wine, not to intangible transactions between "faith" and who knows what. The Small Catechism and the German of the Augsburg Confession have the word "under," and the Large Catechism has "in and under." The word "with," used by Melanchthon in his Altered Augsburg Confession of 1540, is too weak to stand by itself, and lends itself to slippery evasions. "In, with, and under" language is misunderstood if it is taken as a retreat from the blunt statement of the Smalcald Articles that "the bread and the wine in the Supper are the true body and blood of Christ."[15] A famous rhyme, attributed to Queen Elizabeth I, puts it rather well:

> 'Twas God the Word that spake it,
> He took the Bread and brake it;
> And what the Word did make it,
> That I believe and take it.

The "what" of the sacrament, then, is all-important. The "how" holds no interest. Since we can know nothing about this mode of presence, we simply call it "sacramental" and let matters stand at that. The term "sacramental" signals that this presence of Christ's body and blood is unique to the Sacrament of the Altar and cannot be explained. It also distinguishes this mode of presence from the ordinary, visible sort, for of course the sacred elements are not present in pounds or inches. Unlike the bread and wine, the truly present Lord's body and blood are not present in a gross, material, quantifiable way but rather in a supernatural and incomprehensible manner. That becomes important because the enemies of Christ's Supper have always burlesqued this holy mystery in coarse, cannibalistic, butcher-shop terms. Such crass, sacrilegious fantasies are usually rejected as a "Capernaitic" eating and drinking, so named because of the scoffers at Capernaum (John 6:59).[16] Yet God will not be mocked (Gal. 6:7).

---

15. SA III vi 1 (Tappert, 311).
16. *Editor's Note*: See FC Ep VII 15.

SACRAMENT OR SACRIFICE?

What is to be done with the holy gifts in our Lord's Supper? His instructions to us are: "Take, eat . . . given for you . . . Drink . . . poured out for you." This Supper is pure gift. All we can do with it is to receive it. It is offered by God to us, not by us to God.

To be sure, the receiving is to be done "in remembrance" of Him. Yet the remembrance happens by the very reception and celebration of what is here given. To proclaim Christ's death (1 Cor. 11:26) is to announce, preach, and distribute the treasures of salvation which come to us through His blessed death. (Compare 1 Pet. 2:9.) "For you, for the forgiveness of sins," says the Lord. Of course, "where there is forgiveness of sins, there is also life and salvation."[17]

How did this downward direction of the Sacrament come to be reversed into the upward thrust of the "sacrifice of the mass"? In part, it occurred through misunderstanding. In the ancient church the love offerings were often given in kind. Actual food was brought for distribution to the poor. Naturally, not all of this could be placed on the altar. Some of the bread and wine, to be used for the sacrament, was brought forward to represent the rest. So St. Augustine, for instance, pointed to the cup of wine-offering and told his congregation: "You are in that cup." We do the same today when we present offering plates full of money and ask God to receive these gifts together with our bodies, souls, and all that we are and have. For the offering is nothing if it is not a token of a larger whole, that is, of our self-giving. (See Rom. 12:1, and compare 2 Cor. 8:2–5.) This offering of ourselves, whether with money or with bread and wine, is not the sacrament or any part of it. It constitutes rather our feeble response to God's great gifts. And the sacrament is not God's response to our offering. Rather, our offering responds to His sacrament!

During the Middle Ages the response came to be confused with the sacrament itself. The end result was the bizarre idea that Christ's body and blood are being sacrificed anew in the sacrament, for the sins of the living and the dead. Some even claimed that although Christ's one sacrifice on the cross paid for original sin, the oft-repeated "sacrifice of the mass" made up for daily, actual sins! Modern Roman Catholic scholars themselves are often unhappy with the language of the Council of Trent, which insisted on the mass being a "true" and "proper" and "propitiatory" sacrifice.[18]

---

17. Small Catechism: Sacrament of the Altar.
18. James F. McCue, "Luther and Roman Catholicism on the Mass as Sacrifice," *The Eucharist as Sacrifice*, Lutherans and Catholics in Dialogue III, (N.p.:

There are two possible kinds of sacrifice, the "propitiatory" and the "eucharistic." A sacrifice is propitiatory if it actually makes up to God for human sin, and so satisfies His justice. Eucharistic sacrifices do not atone or pay for sin, but offer praise, adoration, and thanksgiving to God for mercies received from Him. The word *eucharistic* comes from the Greek word for giving thanks. Since it is rude to receive even ordinary gifts without saying "thank you," how much more so in the case of God's gift in the Sacrament! The communion Preface rightly exhorts us: "Let us give thanks to the Lord our God." This is why the whole sacramental action came to be called the "Eucharist." Indeed, it is most appropriate to "concentrate" our thanksgivings here where Christ gives Himself to us bodily. One can, of course, offer thanks anywhere. Yet Christ praised not any general gratitude of the nine lepers, but instead the specific thanksgiving of the tenth who returned to honor the Savior in His bodily presence (Luke 17:18). Nevertheless, just as the tenth leper did not confuse his own thanksgiving with the prior mercy and gift of Jesus, so we must beware of regarding our eucharistic sacrifices as a part of the Sacrament itself.

When it comes to propitiatory sacrifices, there was only one such in the whole history of the world. Christ's one sacrifice of Himself was unique, perfect, complete, and unrepeatable. The Book of Hebrews therefore insists that "by one sacrifice he has made perfect forever those who are being made holy," and that once all sins have thus been forgiven, "sacrifice for sin is no longer necessary" ([Heb.] 10:14, 18).

One may ask at this point: Did not the Old Testament sacrifices take away sin? Well, yes and no. God had in fact attached His promise of forgiveness to those sacrifices (Ex. 30:10; Lev. 17:11). In themselves, though, they were "only a shadow of the good things that are coming—not the realities themselves." It is, after all, "impossible for the blood of bulls and goats to take away sins" (Heb. 10:1, 4). Such animal sacrifices, however, served as types or signs, pre-figuring the one sacrifice of the Lamb of God. Yet they were not empty signs, as we have seen; they actually gave forgiveness. In today's terms we might say that the Old Testament sacrifices "worked" somewhat like credit-cards: the plastic cards have no value in themselves, but are accepted as payment on the understanding that satisfactory arrangements have been made for a full cash settlement in the

Representatives of the U.S.A. National Committee of the Lutheran World Federation and the Bishops' Committee for Ecumenical and Interreligious Affairs, 1967), 69n. For careful analysis of the issues, see M. Chemnitz, *Examination* II, 439–498.

future. Those sacrifices, therefore, "which can never take away sins," had to be offered "day after day . . . again and again" (Heb. 10:11). Now the one great Settlement has been made, once and for all, on the cross. That is final. "It is finished" (John 19:30).

To talk now of having to sacrifice Christ's body and blood again somehow in the celebration of the Sacrament is to suggest that the one sacrifice on the cross was not quite enough after all. Such a belittling of the Lord's own self-offering once and for all is, frankly, intolerable. That explains the Reformation's rather strong and uncompromising language in rejecting the "sacrifice of the mass" as blasphemous.[19]

Is it not true, however, that Christ's one propitiatory sacrifice is present in the Sacrament of His body and blood? Yes, but all depends on the "direction" one has in mind here. The Lord's body and blood are not present in the Sacrament to be offered up anew somehow by way of a propitiatory sacrifice. Rather, they are being "offered down" by God as the finished, completed sacrifice, now being distributed with all its benefits to its beneficiaries! Consider again the Old Testament animal sacrifices. Certain of these sacrifices would be divided up into three parts: one part to be burned on God's altar, one part to be given to the priests for food, and one part to be returned to the family bringing the offering, for their sacrificial/sacramental meal. (See 1 Cor. 10:18.) But in the case of Christ, "Himself the Victim and Himself the Priest,"[20] the entire sacrifice is offered to God. He returns this entire completed sacrifice to us in the sacrament, and we are asked to give ourselves to Him entirely in return (Rom. 12:1). The New Testament goes by wholes, not by halves or by sevenths or by tithes (tenths). The gift is without reserve: "He who did not spare his own Son, but gave him up for us all—how will he not also, along with him, graciously give us all things?" (Rom. 8:32). Or, in the sublime words of St. John: "God has given us eternal life, and this life is in his Son" (1 Jn. 5:11).

False ideas of sacrifice can also take more subtle forms. Given our inborn illusions about self-salvation, it is not surprising that God's gracious visitations (Luke 19:44) come to be twisted into celebrations of our own religiosity! This happens in the Holy Supper when what we do or how we respond looms larger than what God gives in His banquet of grace. A case in point is the immensely popular "Four Actions" scheme, derived from Gregory Dix's *The Shape of the Liturgy.*[21] The four actions thought to

---

19. See, for example, SA II ii (Tappert, 293–297).
20. *TLH* 307:1. *Editor's note: LSB* 637:1.
21. Gregory Dix, *The Shape of the Liturgy* (London: Dacre Press, 1945).

be essential to the Supper in this view are the offertory procession ("He *took* the bread"), the Eucharistic prayer (which absorbs the Words of Institution), the breaking of the celebrant's host (a large wafer), and the distribution. Much too much is made here of ceremonial formalities. How important, really, can it be whether the elements arrive in procession, or whether a wafer is ceremonially broken? The emphasis here falls on what we do. The Supper is understood as the church's action toward God, not as God's unilateral, testamentary gift to His church. Indeed, the ritual action is made to weave a pattern so compelling in its own right, that in the end it no longer matters whether Christ's body and blood are there or not.

Compare with all this the sober stress on the essentials, as found in the Formula of Concord: The three actions which together make up the "divinely instituted use" of the Sacrament are the consecration, the distribution, and the reception.[22] The consecration, or blessing, happens through the repetition of the Words of Institution over the bread and wine, according to St. Augustine's famous formula: "The Word comes to the element, and it becomes a sacrament."[23] Not our action, faith, or eating is central here—certainly not a pretty collage of symbolic rituals—but the all-powerful Word and promise of the Supper's divine Founder and Host! Just as His creative words "Be fruitful and increase in number" (Gen. 1:22, 28) have lost none of their power, but still make sea and land teem with sub-human and human life, so His Words of Institution will until the end of time make bread and wine His body and blood in the Sacrament whenever we invoke these words at His command.[24] For in this sense, as Luther put it, Christ "has attached his own command and deed to our speaking."[25]

No longer, then, are Christ's Words of Institution to be whispered or muttered secretly at the altar, as in the Middle Ages. (Our term *hocus pocus* comes from the misunderstood Latin for "This is My body.") Rather, these words are to be publicly spoken or chanted, for they are the "sum and substance of the whole gospel," accomplishing the very mysteries they describe.[26]

PREPARATION AND CONFIRMATION

St. Paul warns against receiving the Sacrament "in an unworthy manner," which leads to "judgment" (1 Cor. 11:27–29). What is "worthy" or

---

22. FC SD VII 86, 87 (Tappert, 584–585).
23. *Editor's note:* Cited in LC V 10.
24. See FC SD VII 76 (Tappert, 583).
25. Quoted in FC SD VII 78 (Tappert, 584).
26. AE 36, 277; see FC SD VII 79–80 (Tappert, 584).

"unworthy" here is not the person of the communicant, but his manner of reception, that is, his treatment of the body and blood of Christ. No one is ever "worthy" of Christ's great gift of Himself. The *Small Catechism* therefore puts it well: "Fasting and bodily preparation are certainly fine outward training. But that person is truly worthy and well prepared who has faith in these words: 'Given and shed for you for the forgiveness of sins.'"[27] Bodily discipline and reverence for the Sacrament are not to be sneered at, least of all in an age obsessed with physical fitness and beauty. It is just that such external exercises by themselves are hollow (1 Tim. 4:8).

The whole point is to repent of one's sin and to turn for help and healing to the "medicine of immortality" (St. Ignatius[28]) in the body and blood which have taken away the sins of the world. That, and not a sickly concentration on internal inventories, is the purpose of the self-examination (1 Cor. 11:28) before Communion. Delaying until one feels worthy (or unworthy) enough is to leave faith for feelings. It is like a deathly ill patient gasping: "Thank you, doctor, for the antibiotics. I'll take them as soon as I feel a little better."

The two things which are to draw us often and regularly to the Sacrament are our own need and the great value and power of the divine remedy. And what if people feel no particular need? One can hardly improve on Luther's answer:

> I know no better advice than to suggest that they put their hands to their bosom and ask whether they are made of flesh and blood. If you find that you are, then for your own good turn to St. Paul's Epistle to the Galatians and hear what are the fruits of the flesh: [Luther then quotes Gal. 5:19–20]. . . .
>
> If you cannot feel the need, therefore, at least believe the Scriptures. They will not lie to you, and they know your flesh better than you yourself do. . . . But the fact that we are insensitive to our sin is all the worse, for it is a sign that ours is a leprous flesh which feels nothing though the disease rages and rankles. . . . In short, the less you feel your sins and infirmities, the more reason you have to go to the sacrament and seek a remedy.

---

27. *Small Catechism*: Sacrament of the Altar.
28. "The Letter of Ignatius, Bishop of Antioch to the Ephesians" (20.2) in Cyril C. Richardson, trans. and ed., *Early Christian Fathers*, The Library of Christian Classics, vol. 1 (Philadelphia, PA: Westminster, 1953), 93.

Again:

> If you could see how many daggers, spears, and arrows are at every moment aimed at you, you would be glad to come to the sacrament as often as possible.[29]

Elsewhere Luther reminds us of a vital truth so often neglected:

> If you find that the words and the sign of the Sacrament are softening your heart and moving you to be kind to your enemy, to receive your neighbour, and to help him bear his distress and sorrow, all is well. If this is not the result of your partaking of the Sacrament, you cannot be certain that you have profited from the Sacrament, even if you were to partake of it a hundred times a day with the greatest of devotion and were overwhelmed with tears of joy. Such wondrous devotion which carries on in this manner counts for nothing with God. It is also very dangerous, because it is so completely self-centered and misleading.[30]

Great as our own need is, the Lord's goodness is greater still (Rom. 5:20). The accent must fall on the latter more than the former. We can never prize and honour enough the treasures to which He so urgently invites us in this feast.

Why then the false anxiety, as if the Sacrament were like x-rays —to be taken rarely and in small doses? Rather:

> We must never regard the sacrament as a harmful thing from which we should flee, but as a pure, wholesome, soothing medicine which aids and quickens us in both soul and body. For where the soul is healed, the body has benefited also.[31]

Self-examination is not the only weighty matter that arises here. There is also the duty of pastors, as "stewards of the mysteries of God" (1 Cor. 4:1 KJV). As householders over these mysteries, and therefore also administrators of the sacraments, Christ's under-shepherds are accountable to the Good Shepherd Himself for how and to whom they dispense the sacred things entrusted to their care. They are to see to it that the sheep

---

29. LC V 75–78, 82 (Tappert, 455, 456).
30. P. D. Pahl, trans. and ed., *Luther for the Busy Man: Daily Devotions from Luther's Sermons on the Standard Gospels* (Adelaide, Australia: Lutheran Publishing House, 1974), 94.
31. LC V 68 (Tappert, 454).

and lambs of Christ's flock are rightly fed (John 21:15–17). Responsible self-examination and participation in the Holy Supper are possible only on the basis of proper instruction in the saving truths of God's Word. Pastors must satisfy themselves that those who ask for admission to the Lord's Table know what they are doing there. Neither pastors nor people may trifle with the holy body and blood of Christ by irresponsibility in either distribution or reception.

Illustrations from daily life abound. Suppose, on a dark and stormy night, one came upon barricades with signs: "Stop! Bridge out ahead!" Would one grumble resentfully: "Fascist country! Can't even drive where one pleases anymore"? Of course not. Or, if no barriers had been put up, would one's last thoughts be, while plunging towards the raging river: "What glorious liberty! Even this is allowed"?

If it is possible to incur judgment by desecrating the Lord's body and blood in the Sacrament, then carefully supervised access to His table becomes a necessary service of love. Of course, if the Lord's Supper consisted of nothing but bread and wine, it would not matter much who did what with them.

In light of all this, the custom of Confirmation makes very good sense. Confirmation is not a sacrament. It was not instituted by God. Confirmation is a church custom marking the end of a period of instruction that prepares a person for responsible participation in the Holy Supper of the Lord. It has no independent weight whatever beside Baptism and the Sacrament of the Altar. Everything was given already in Baptism. To that, Confirmation adds nothing. Thinking that it can add something is to steer into the "second blessing" theology of Methodism and Pentecostalism.[32] Such a misconception is why the Reformation at first rejected Confirmation, which the medieval church had listed among its seven sacraments. Later Confirmation came to be accepted without superstition, not as a sacrament but simply as an opportunity to provide the basic instruction in the one faith (Eph. 4:5) needed for responsible self-examination at Communion. This basic instruction and first communion took place at a relatively early age: between six and twelve years, according to one authority.[33]

---

32. It is particularly clear in Acts 19:1–7 that the laying on of St. Paul's hands was not a "second blessing," but a part of the baptismal action itself, signaling its nature and power by special apostolic sign (2 Cor. 12:12; compare Acts 8:17).

33. Arthur C. Repp, *Confirmation in the Lutheran Church* (St. Louis, MO: Concordia Publishing House, 1964), 56–57.

SACRAMENT, CHURCH, AND CONFESSION

In the Old Testament the details of public worship were carefully prescribed by law. The New Testament has no such levitical regulations.
Worshiping God "in spirit and in truth" (John 4:24), however, is not an
excuse for shapelessness and whim. Public worship in the New Testament is in fact shaped by the one external observance of which the Lord
said: "Do this in remembrance of me" (Luke 22:19). This forms the pivot
of the church's life and action, the focal point 'round which she gathers
(1 Cor. 11:20–33). Together with the preaching for which it is the context,
the Supper gives the basic frame of the church's public liturgy or service.
When we speak of *"the* Liturgy" we mean the Service of Holy Communion. This service, says the Augsburg Confession, "is preserved among us
in its proper use, the use which was formerly observed in the church and
which can be proved by St. Paul's statement in 1 Corinthians 11:20 and
following and by many statements of the Fathers."[34]

Unlike the Jewish Passover, or the Day of Atonement, which took
place only once a year, our New Testament banquet is to be celebrated
often. In apostolic days the Jerusalem church seems to have observed the
Holy Supper daily. The Gentile congregations celebrated it at least once a
week, a practice also taken for granted in the Augsburg Confession and its
Apology.[35] The Lord's Supper marked the Lord's Day, the day on which
He had risen from the dead (Acts 20:7). The Resurrection is the great
fact that supports the whole Christian faith and church. Easter was the
first Christian celebration, observed every Sunday from the beginning.
(In Russian, for instance, even the word for "Sunday" is "Resurrection").
Later a special annual observance of Easter and its associated events was
added, and so the foundation was laid for the Christian liturgical year.

Modern scholars like Oscar Cullmann have reminded us of two important facts in this connection.[36] First, in the New Testament and the
entire ancient church, the Sacrament was not an occasional extra, but a
regular and central feature of congregational worship. Second, given that
the Resurrection appearances of our Lord took place at meals or meal-
times (Luke 24:30; John 20–21; Acts 1:4), the ancient church understood
the Meal which her Lord had given her to observe as the occasion when
the resurrected Lord Himself again "came and stood among them," but

---

34. AC XXIV 35 (Tappert, 60).
35. Ap XXIV 1: "every Sunday and on other festivals" (Tappert, 249). Compare
    AC XXIV 34 (Tappert, 60).
36. See Oscar Cullmann, *Early Christian Worship* (London: SCM Press, 1966).

now invisibly. Indeed, the guests at His table until the end of time have the special blessing of "those who have not seen and yet have believed" (John 20:19, 29). The Lutheran Apology of the Augsburg Confession reflects this aspect as well: "We are talking about the presence of the living Christ, knowing that 'death no longer has dominion over him.'"[37] In this Supper the "glory and mystery of the incarnation combine . . . as they combine nowhere else."[38] As a medieval Communion hymn put it, the divinity of Christ was concealed at the cross, but here in the Sacrament even His humanity lies hidden.[39]

St. Luke includes (14:16–24) a parable quite similar to the parable of the wedding banquet for the King's Son in St. Matthew 22:1–14. In the former we read: "At the time of the banquet he sent his servant to tell those who had been invited, 'Come, for everything is now ready'" (Luke 14:17). When is this "now"? Clearly it is this present time, beginning with Christ's coming in the flesh. For centuries the advance invitation had gone out through the prophets. But now "the time of the banquet" has come, and "everything is now ready." We are meant to think, in other words, not of a far-off future, but of what is happening right now, as Christ gathers His church around Him from all parts of the world through His divine means of grace.

It is not an accident that Christ pictured His Kingdom as a banquet. For He knew that He would, in that final, solemn night with His disciples, go beyond pictures and parables, and establish an actual, literal banquet, the Sacrament, in which He, the Lamb of God, is both Host and Food. Here we have, "with angels and archangels and with all the company of heaven," a foretaste and participation in heaven itself, and in the Tree of Life (see Heb. 12:22–24; Rev. 19:7; 22:19). In this banquet we "proclaim the Lord's death until he comes" (1 Cor. 11:26). Past and future come together here in one great present stream of salvation.

A prominent feature of the sacramental feast is its social, corporate nature. To be sure, each penitent sinner receives here his own most personal portion of forgiveness, life, and salvation. Yet this never takes place in isolation. The bonds forged and renewed here between the heavenly Father and His children on earth at the same time bind them to each

---

37. Ap X 4, citing Romans 6:9 (Tappert, 180).
38. Krauth, 655.
39. *Editor's note*: The hymn is "Adoro Te Devote" by Thomas Aquinas ("Thee We Adore, O Hidden Savior," *LSB* 640). The particular stanza to which Marquart referred does not appear in *LSB*.

other as brothers and sisters in "the Son he loves" (Col. 1:13). The church as the mystical Body of Christ is united most closely and solemnly by His sacramental body: "Because there is one loaf, we, who are many, are one body, for we all share the one loaf" (1 Cor. 10:17). All this is given in the *communion* or *participation* in Christ's body and blood (1 Cor. 10:16).

It is clear therefore that receiving the Sacrament together is a public confession of unity in the Gospel. For the apostolic church it would have been unthinkable to observe "the breaking of bread" together with those who rejected or falsified "the apostles' teaching" (Acts 2:42). St. Paul warns against that very thing (Rom. 16:17; see the sacramental context suggested by the "holy kiss" of the previous verse). Far from being a private, individual act, the celebration of Christ's Supper is in fact the church's most public and most solemn confession (1 Cor. 11:26).

Quite different, secular ideas lie behind the common view that it is really everyone's own personal business where to "go to Communion," and that if one "has the right idea about it," one may go to the Sacrament wherever one likes, even in heterodox churches. As if nothing mattered but one's own thoughts, feelings, impressions, and intentions! The fact of the matter is that a person's Christian identity is established not simply by what he may at any given moment think or say he believes. It is shaped, rather, by the altar—and its pulpit!—at which he regularly confesses (1 Cor. 10:16–17; 11:26). The question here is not simply about worthy reception but also about the integrity of the genuine, apostolic Gospel. "Close" or "closed" Communion therefore was self-evident for the ancient church, and needs to become so again:

> By his partaking of the Sacrament in a church a Christian declares that the confession of that church is his confession. Since a man cannot at the same time hold two differing confessions, he cannot communicate in two churches of differing confessions. If anyone does this nevertheless, he denies his own confession or has none at all.[40]

---

40. Werner Elert, *Eucharist and Church Fellowship in the First Four Centuries,* trans. N. E. Nagel (St. Louis, MO: Concordia Publishing House, 1966), 182.

Chapter Eight

ONE HOLY CHURCH, ON EARTH AND IN HEAVEN

Editor's note: Marquart's entire typescript for this chapter was intact, with two exceptions: (1) the absence of a couple of diagrams, and (2) more important, that the page or pages are missing which contained the endnotes he wrote. Thus, while we know where Marquart planned to place note numbers in the text, we do not always know what the corresponding notes were supposed to say. In the chapter below, wherever a note immediately follows a quotation, we have provided the appropriate reference. However, no attempt has been made to speculate about what content Marquart had in mind for discursive notes.

FAMILY TIES

Christian faith is deeply personal, yet never a private affair "just between me and God." He Who "sets the lonely in families" (Ps. 68:6) makes His Christians into a chosen race, a royal priesthood, a holy nation, God's own people (1 Pet. 2:9), yes, into "members of his household" (Eph. 2:19). Christians are not footloose individuals, but a holy family (Matt. 12:48–50; 19:29), a brotherhood (1 Pet. 2:17), who pray: *"Our Father . . . ."* If English had kept the distinction between "thou" for the singular and "you" for the plural, it would be clear at a glance to every reader of the New Testament that the Lord and His apostles almost always address "us" as the body of believers, not simply "me" individually. The Bible does not treat people as so many separate atoms, each on a private quest for "identity" or "fulfillment." As there is a solidarity in sin, so there is a solidarity of salvation. From Adam the first man we have inherited sin and death, but in Christ the Second Adam we are a new human race, living with God forever (Rom. 5, 1 Cor. 15).

This new humanity is the church. Far from being an optional little extra to be faced perhaps after one has "come to know Jesus personally," the church is in fact quite central to the doctrine and practice of Christianity. The Jesus of the Bible founded not a loose federation of clubs for the cultivation of private religiosity, but a preaching, teaching, sacrament-dispensing church, against which the very gates of hell cannot prevail (Matt. 16:18). To despise the Lord's church is to despise Him (Luke 10:16). Therefore if a person under admonition refuses "to listen even to the church," says the Savior, treat him "as you would a pagan or a tax collector" (Matt. 18:17). So closely does the Lord identify Himself with His church that He asks a persecutor of the church, "Saul, Saul, why do you persecute *me?*" (Acts 9:4, emphasis added).

The connection between Christ and His church could not be closer. She is His Bride. On the analogy of marriage, these two are one in a way that is "a profound mystery" (Eph. 5:32). There is, further, a deep inner connection between the church being the temple of God (Eph. 2:21) and her being the Body of Christ, for His body is that temple which men destroyed but which He Himself raised up again in three days (John 2:19)! Unlike all other temples, the Temple of the church is built out of "living stones" (1 Pet. 2:5), and each stone is itself a holy shrine for the Triune Majesty. (See John 14:23 and 1 Cor. 6:19.)

Enough has been said to show that the church comes into being not from below, but from above. That is, the church is not a voluntary association of individuals who have banded themselves together for common purposes. It is rather a supernatural creation of God, a beach-head of heaven on earth. To it, people are "added" (Acts 2:41) by God's power and action as He works through His Gospel and sacraments. To become a Christian is to become a member of the church. To abandon Christ's church is to abandon Christianity.

The church is "the mother that begets and bears every Christian through the Word of God."[1] This remains her divinely given duty and function (Matt. 28:19–20; 1 Jn. 5:6–12). It is not as though Christians first "found salvation" privately, then decided to join together in the church for mutual support. This would make the church far too "horizontal," too dependent on persons. The church's main dimension is "vertical": as the Bride of Christ she has and she distributes, according to His command, all the rich treasures of salvation He has given her. The Word and Sacraments she administers by His command and institution form the river of life from which Christians draw continual renewal. Only from these spiritual resources can Christians live and exercise their priesthood (1 Pet. 2:9).

> Glorious things of thee are spoken,
> Zion, city of our God;
> He whose word cannot be broken
> Formed thee for His own abode.[2]

---

1. LC II 42 (Tappert, 416).
2. *TLH* hymn 469:1. *Editor's note:* See *LSB* 648:1.

One often hears it suggested today that "going to church" lacks importance. What matters, people think, is the practice of charity in one's personal life and of ethics in business. This general view was well put by a critic who said that Christians going to church reminded him rather of an army that constantly runs about parading and saluting but never carries out orders! No doubt, this bitingly entertaining image contains some truth. How self-evident it seems to modern people that church-going amounts to simply a bit of ceremonial icing on the cake, a matter of parading and saluting!

This might indeed be the case if there were no such things as means of grace. If God's Word and Sacraments really did not do anything but only served as symbols or reminders of spiritual blessings to be obtained in some other way, then of course church services would amount to little more than religious ceremonialism topped with bits of ethical advice. But if Christ's Gospel and sacraments constitute the very fountain of life and the river of salvation, and if Christians as poor sinners stand in need of these divine mercies, then it becomes quite impossible to maintain a "low" view of what happens in church. Belittling church attendance resembles scoffing at automobiles being serviced by saying, "Cars are made to travel, not to sit in service stations!" True, but unless they visit service stations regularly, they cannot fulfill their purpose at all. Similarly, church is the indispensable life-support system of Christians, not mere window-dressing.

All this can be so, however, only if what actually happens in church is what is supposed to happen according to the New Testament. Of the apostolic church we read that its life revolved about four basic elements: the apostles' doctrine or teaching, the fellowship, the breaking of bread, and the prayers (Acts 2:42). The life-giving apostolic doctrine or Gospel on which the church is built (Eph. 2:20) has priority over everything else in the church (Gal. 1:8–9). Hence the Reformation's great stress on the centrality of preaching. The second item, "fellowship," does not merely involve affability or camaraderie, as suggested by the "fellowship halls" of modern churches. The word means sharing or participating, and therefore often means concrete aid and support (Rom. 12:13; 15:26; Gal. 6:6; Phil. 1:5; 4:15). The likely meaning of "fellowship" in Acts 2:42 is gifts or offerings, out of which the needs of fellow-believers would be met. As for the breaking of bread, this refers ultimately no doubt to *the* breaking of *the* bread in the Sacrament, although it probably includes that fellowship meal (*"agape"*) that often preceded the Sacrament and caused the problems of which we read in 1 Corinthians 11:17 and following.

The last item is *the* prayers, rather than simply "prayer" without the definite article (as in some translations). It suggests set liturgical forms, not a shapeless "praying." First-century Jews recited set prayers at stated times of the day. These forms of prayer included also certain psalms, for instance, Psalm 63 at the time of the morning sacrifice, Psalm 141 ("Let my prayer be set forth before thee as incense; and the lifting up of my hands as the evening sacrifice," KJV) at the time of the evening sacrifice, and Psalm 4 at bedtime. There were also hymns and spiritual songs (Col. 3:16), not camp-fire ditties, but deeply theological, confessional compositions like the New Testament canticles (Luke 1:46–55, 68–79, etc.) and probably creedal hymns like Philippians 2:6–11 or 1 Tim. 3:16. The apostolic church kept the customary hours of prayer (Acts 2:15; 3:1; 10:9; 12:12). These developed into a cumbersome system in the medieval monasteries, simplified by Luther into daily Matins and Vespers (see also Morning and Evening Prayers in the Small Catechism) with the full Service of Word and Sacrament on Sundays and holy days. Personal prayer and devotion grew within this larger frame, shaped and supported by the daily, weekly, and annual rhythm of the church's abundant life in the Word of Christ.

We may say that the four elements of Acts 2:42 marked the worship of the apostolic church as doctrinal, sacrificial, Sacramental, and liturgical. Two of these, preaching and the Sacrament, move from God toward us. This "downward" mode of worship is more generally called "sacramental." The "upward" mode, in which we offer our gifts and prayers to God, is called "sacrificial." God and His grace take the initiative. Then, having received forgiveness, life, and salvation, we respond in love and service. (See Rom. 12:1.) Therefore God's holy means of grace, not fickle human moods, belong at the centre of the church's life. The order and reverence of the church's worship must not yield to pop-religious itches for sentimentality or entertainment.

THE ONE CHURCH AND THE MANY CHURCHES

At Pentecost Christ launched His holy church. Within three hundred years it had conquered the mighty Roman Empire. Today the church is split into many different factions, most of which seem more conquered than conquering in the face of modern cultural pressures. How can one square a divided and apparently retreating Christendom with the one, holy, catholic, and apostolic church confessed in the Creed?

Intuitively, the reunion of the separated Christian churches appears urgently necessary against all obstacles and at almost any cost. This urgent drive towards Christian reunion is embodied in the modern Ecumenical Movement, the chief institutional expression of which is the World Council of Churches. The impact of this movement on all churches today cannot be overestimated.

The important issues involved are best clarified by comparing the Ecumenical Movement's basic approach with that of the Reformation. We may begin with the famous sentence by one of the Ecumenical Movement's founding fathers, an Anglican: "I believe in the Holy Catholic Church, and sincerely regret that it does not at present exist" (Archbishop of Canterbury William Temple, 1881–1944). This suggests what may be called the apple-pie theory of the church: The pie has come apart into many slices and slivers, and by themselves none of these are the church. Only when all the pieces get put together again will there truly be one catholic church.

If putting everything under one organisational roof becomes the top priority, it looms as almost inevitable that the means to this end will take some form of ecclesiastical bartering: Can you say this if we say that? Will you give this up if we give up that? It can hardly be surprising that theological statements arrived at by this process prove stretchable enough to fit the broadest landscape.

Luther's approach stands out as totally different. For him, the church was not an organisation but an organism. As a part of the mystery of Christ, the church shares in the Lord's hiddenness. In the Creed we confess not, "I see one holy Christian church," but "I believe one holy Christian church." Faith believes what it does not see, on the basis of God's word (Heb. 11:1). Only believers are saints, that is, holy in Christ, and the church consists only of such saints or believers. (See St. Paul's salutations, like 1 Cor. 1:2 and Eph. 1:1, and what is said about the church in Eph. 2:21.) Only God can look into a human heart to see whether or not faith is there. (See Rom. 11:4 and 2 Tim. 2:19.) We humans cannot be sure who really is a believer, therefore a member of the church, and who is not. So for us the church remains in this life an article of faith, not of sight.

We believe one holy church, even though what we see is division, sin, and the full range of human behavior from the altruistic to the cantankerous. Concealed beneath the cross and human frailties and offences, the church is a high, deep and hidden thing. It may neither be perceived nor seen, but can be grasped only by faith. Like the other Christian mysteries the church lies inaccessible to human reason, however many spectacles reason may wear.

Luther's biblical, evangelical understanding of the church differs markedly from the modern ecumenical approach. Clearly no one visible organisation, least of all the entity called "the Lutheran church," can be equated with the one holy Christian church. But even if all the bits and pieces could be put together again, under the chairmanship, say, of the Bishop of Rome, the resulting "commonwealth of churches" would still not form the one church of Christ. Instead, this one church remains hidden within all the external bodies in which enough of the Gospel and sacraments "get through" to enable the Holy Spirit to work faith, and thus to give birth to Christians and to the church. This church is already one, just as Christ is one.

Two difficulties appear to arise at this point. First: if the church can nowhere be seen, how then can anyone find it? Second: if Christians are more or less in all churches, then what difference does it make to which church one belongs? Both of these difficulties must be referred to a crucial reality, the "marks of the church." On these marks everything depends here.

Although the church eludes human wisdom, "thank God, a seven-year-old child knows what the church is, namely, holy believers and sheep who hear the voice of their Shepherd."[3] These words of Luther from the Smalcald Articles refer to the Savior's speech in St. John 10:

> I am the good shepherd; I know my sheep and my sheep know me. . . . I
> have other sheep that are not of this sheep pen. . . . They too will listen
> to my voice, and there shall be one flock and one shepherd. . . . My sheep
> listen to my voice; I know them, and they follow me. I give them eternal
> life. . . . (John 10:14, 16, 27–28a).

To find the flock, we must look for the Shepherd. More precisely, we must listen for His voice. If we try to find the sheep directly, or look for the largest numbers or the best qualities of the sheep, quite likely we will be deceived by "sheep's clothing" (Matt. 7:15 [KJV]). Only the Shepherd's voice is reliable. It comes to us only in His holy Gospel, including the sacraments. Therefore these holy means of grace are called the *marks of the church*. Where they are found, the church is found, for these means or marks are her sure foundation (Eph. 2:20). Any falsification of Christ's Gospel counterfeits His voice, is destructive, and has no rights in the church (Gal. 1:8–9).

Two distinctions must be made. Distinction A is between the church in the strict or proper sense (the "association of faith and of the Holy Spirit in men's hearts"), and the church in the wide or larger sense, comprising

---

3. SA III xii 2 (Tappert, 315).

the outward gathering around particular pulpits, fonts, and altars (that is, the "association of outward ties and rites").[4] Sometimes the church in the strict sense is called "the invisible church," and the outward gathering about the marks is termed "the visible church." If this terminology is used, one must be careful not to suggest that there are two churches, one visible and one not. There is only one church of which we speak in different respects, either in a stricter or a looser sense.

Roman Catholicism, at least until Vatican II, declined to make Distinction A. It simply identified the church with the visible institution headed by the papacy. Reformed (Calvinist) theology, on the other hand, virtually separates an "invisible church" from the "visible church." The Calvinist "invisible church" consists only of those predestined to salvation, so it cannot be "discernable by [any] signs" or marks (Geneva Catechism)[5], while the "visible church" is understood as a law-enforcing institution. In contrast to both of these approaches to the church, the Lutheran church makes Distinction A. She *distinguishes* between the church in the strict and in the wide senses, yet she does not *separate* them into two churches.

Since the means of grace are the sole instruments through which God creates believers, the church in the strict sense can exist only within the matrix of the church as "association of outward ties and rites." With this point we can address the first difficulty noted above, namely, how to find the church. The church's marks show where the church is. Far from being empty or inert sign-posts, though, the marks of the church are faith-creating means of grace. They are the marks not simply of some secondary "visible" church, but of the one holy church herself.[6]

Not all churches, however, have the same relation to the marks of the church. Hence our second vital distinction, Distinction B: between orthodox ("right-teaching") and heterodox ("other-teaching") churches. The pure marks of the church, that is, the purely taught Gospel and the rightly administered sacraments, document for us the orthodox church. Impurity of the marks documents heterodoxy.

It is important to see not only what is meant here but also what is *not* meant. Belonging to an orthodox church does not mean that one is a better Christian than others. Again, calling a church heterodox does not

---

4. Ap VII/VIII 5 (Tappert, 169).
5. *Calvin: Theological Treatises*, trans. J. K. S. Reid, The Library of Christian Classics, vol. 22 (Philadelphia, PA: Westminster, 1954), 103.
6. See Apology VII/VIII, 20 (Tappert, 170–171).

mean that there are no real Christians in it, or that these Christians are less sincere or devout than orthodox Christians, whom they may often surpass in love, joy, peace, and the like.

So if orthodox and heterodox churches both include good and bad, sincere Christians and hypocrites, why fuss about the difference? If salvation may be found in most churches, does it not amount to a petty purism to insist on orthodoxy? We now find ourselves at the second difficulty mentioned earlier: what difference it makes to belong to one church or another.

Let us turn to a thought-experiment. Imagine an old-fashioned kerosene-lamp. Let the lamp be filled with kerosene, and it will of course burn brightly. Now suppose that as the kerosene level falls, we bring it back to its former level by pouring in sand, tea-leaves, coffee-grounds, and similar things. Will the lamp still burn? Of course, so long as enough kerosene is able to reach the wick. This appearance may mislead a superficial observer, for it may seem that sand and tea-leaves work just as well as kerosene. Of course, the lamp keeps burning not *because of* such additives but *in spite of* them. It burns only because of whatever kerosene remains. Substitute "Gospel" for kerosene, and the analogy explains itself. There is only "one Lord, one faith, one baptism" (Eph. 4:5). The Holy Spirit works the very same faith in all Christians, and He does so through the same Gospel truth. He never works through error. Where false teachings intrude themselves, there is set up a counter-force which stands in competition and conflict with true Spirit-worked faith and poses a threat to it.

To the extent that false doctrine is given official licence, standing, and approval under the sacred name "church," to that extent misshapen counter-churches, pseudo-churches, or sects result. Needless to say, God commands that His Word and truth alone be taught in His church. The church's members, and especially her public teachers, should flee misrepresentations of His Word and avoid all complicity with them (Matt. 7:15; 15:6–9; Rom. 16:17–18; Gal. 1:8–9, etc.). For only God's Word has the right to hold sway over the church. Where the skull and crossbones of spiritual piracy (that is, false doctrine) flies on equal terms with the flag of divine, evangelical truth, conflict results. The Zion of the church is everywhere in principle at war with the Babylonian captivity forced upon her by the false teaching.

Two points must be observed in this fight of the church militant. On one hand, she must always remember that her warfare is spiritual. After all, "our struggle is not against flesh and blood" (Eph. 6:12). Care must be taken not to injure captive Zion while opposing Babylon. On the other hand, the presence of naive, well-meaning people in objectively wrong causes and movements (like Absalom's two hundred, who "went quite innocently, knowing nothing about the matter," 2 Sam. 15:11) cannot be allowed to paralyse the church's energetic defence against the encroachments of these causes and movements. Thus, opposing false doctrine and the official institutions that represent it somewhat resembles resisting tyrannical regimes. Such resistance does not mean that one hates or opposes the people held captive by the system.

This emphasis on truth, rather than outward union, constitutes the hallmark of the Reformation's return to the biblical understanding of the church. In high school we learned that we could solve an equation with two variables if we knew the value of one of them. The two variables in the "ecumenical equation" are the Gospel and the church. If one is known, the other can be calculated. For Luther, as for Scripture, the Gospel is the known element. It is "given." The Savior did not say, *go into all the world to find the truth*, but rather *go and proclaim* it! Wherever this saving Gospel (together with the sacraments, of course) is purely proclaimed, there the true church is to be found.

The Ecumenical Movement, on the other hand, turns this topsy-turvy. There the Gospel is treated as the unknown, the *x*. The starting point rather is the church, understood as so many visible, historical institutions. Whatever they can ultimately agree on must be the Gospel. (A famous claim by twentieth-century German New Testament scholar Ernst Kaesemann holds that there are contradictory doctrines and theologies even in the New Testament itself.[7] If so, then there exists no reliable standard by which to measure doctrinal truth or error.)

Here lies the great watershed dividing the Reformation from the modern Ecumenical Movement. The Lutheran Reformation contents itself to *believe* the holy church, walking strictly by faith in the light of God's Word. The Ecumenical Movement thinks it can *see* the church. It exchanges faith for sight. A false tension then arises between truth and unity. In the New Testament unity is created by the truth of the Gospel. Unity on any other basis is a human illusion. However sincerely intended, such unity must be resolutely resisted. (See Matt. 16:22.)

What has been presented above in broad outline is the simple, yet profound ecumenical program of Article VII of the Augsburg Confession, which rests squarely on St. Paul's great exposition of the mystery of the

---

7. *Editor's Note*: See, for example, Ernst Kaesemann, "The Canon of the New Testament and the Unity of the Church," *Essays on New Testament Themes*, trans. W. J. Montague (London: SCM Press, 1964), 95–107.

church in the letter to the Ephesians. Here is the crucial sentence, following the German text:

> For this is enough for the true unity of the Christian church, that the Gospel be unanimously preached there according to its pure understanding, and the sacraments administered in accordance with the divine Word.[8]

Centuries of repetition have made these words seem like a self-evident truism among Lutherans. Actually they are far from self-evident, for packed into them is a surprising weight of evangelical content. Article VII, in which our sentence occurs, is in fact the first dogmatic definition of the church and of its unity.

The church had to grapple with the problem of dissension and disunity from the very beginning. (See texts like Rom. 16:17; Gal. 1:6; 1 Jn. 2:19.) After the apostles died, it was thought that the bishops could serve as guarantors of the church's unity. "Stick to the bishop," advised the early fathers, "and do nothing without him." But then bishops fell into false doctrine and led opposition churches. One answer to that might be the church council, in which the bishops of many churches acted together collegially. Yet what if councils of bishops disagree with each other? The Western church tried to solve such problems with the idea of the papacy: The Bishop of Rome is the successor of St. Peter, goes the claim, who is in turn the personal representative of Jesus Christ among the apostles and in the church generally. The pope, then, becomes the divinely appointed arbiter of truth. The orthodox church is thought to be the one which is in communion with him and which recognizes his authority.

This scheme seemed to work for centuries, at least in the West. By Luther's time it had in principle broken down, though. During the century before Luther, the "Great Schism" had featured, at one stage, three different popes, each claiming to be the true one. Clearly it was time to start over again and to approach the whole problem of Christian unity in a fundamentally different way.

Struggling with a half-political power claiming to be *the* church forced Luther back to basics. He saw that no organisational solution to the problem of unity was possible. Human crutches, no matter how steeped in tradition, are simply incapable of supporting superhuman weight. Only the church's divinely given foundation itself (Eph. 2:20), only God's own saving truth can bring about the unity of the church, therefore also preserve

---

8.   AC VII 2 [author's translation].

and guarantee it. The church and her authentic public manifestations as well as her unity are all determined by the divinely revealed Gospel and sacraments, not the other way 'round!

How does the church of Christ, which is "the pillar and foundation of the truth" (1 Tim. 3:15), keep itself from becoming a debating society? The answer lies neither in human autocracy or aristocracy on one hand. Nor, on the other, does it lie in mass democracy with its fickle majority opinions. The answer lies rather in the church's own inner dynamic as Christ's constitutional monarchy. The church is His Kingdom, which He Himself has constituted upon His saving Word, the one thing needed (Luke 10:42).

The Augsburg Confession's "it is enough" simply reclaims Christ's own evangelical Magna Carta or "Bill of Rights." No one has any right to demand more for Christian unity than what Christ Himself established as His church's bedrock: the pure Gospel and sacraments. "It is not necessary that human traditions or rites and ceremonies, instituted by men, should be alike everywhere."[9] This is not to say that Christian tradition simply does not matter. It is in fact very important that every church do its utmost to order its life as well as possible, and in the greatest possible harmony with other orthodox churches, taking full account of the church's past experience (1 Cor. 14:36). Still, differences in details neither commanded nor forbidden by God may not be allowed to divide the church:

> churches will not condemn each other because of a difference in ceremonies . . . as long as they are otherwise agreed in doctrine and in all its articles and are also agreed concerning the right use of the holy sacraments. . . .[10]

As the above quotation from the Formula of Concord shows, one may also not demand *less* for the true unity of the church than consensus in the pure Gospel and sacraments. The contrast in Augsburg Confession VII is not between the Gospel and other, less important doctrines, but between the Gospel—all of it—and human traditions. The doctrine of justification is the "chief article" that holds all the others together, but it is not the only article. A moment's reflection will show that a "justification" without the Trinity, the incarnation, the redemption, and the Sacraments, for example, would simply be meaningless nonsense. The full dogmatic content of the biblical Gospel is what is meant in Augsburg Confession VII. No cut-rate or mini-gospels will do.

---

9. AC VII 3 [author's translation].
10. FC SD X 31 (Tappert, 616).

On the other hand, it is also clear that Article VII speaks pointedly of the Gospel, not of the Law. For the Law is not distinctively Christian. The church shares the Law, in however distorted a form, with the Jewish synagogue, the Muslim mosque, and the humanitarian Red Cross. Although the Law is always a necessary presupposition of the Gospel, the Law creates and governs neither the church nor its unity. Only the Gospel does this. The Gospel, not the Law, is the church's only source of life and unity. That Gospel is strictly unique to the church. Even the holy angels have to learn of it, with great surprise, from the apostolic proclamation of the church (Eph. 3:10)!

This is all well and good in theory, some may say, but does it not get bogged down in the sheer number of churches from which to choose? Given the hundreds of different churches in existence—with new ones arising regularly in California alone—statistically, is it really likely in all this confusion that the average person could be in a position to find and identify a "true church," assuming there is one?

Yet the picture is not as confused as it may appear at first sight. Exotic cults and eccentric sects aside, there are actually only three basic versions of Christianity: the Roman Catholic (with which, for convenience, we may here lump Eastern Orthodoxy), the Lutheran, and the Reformed. These comprise the three great theological types, or paradigms, representing three alternative "models" of the Gospel. Everything else amounts to variations, sometimes considerable, on these three basic themes. The choices are therefore fundamentally few and relatively simple. There is no fuzzy "generic" Gospel in the New Testament which everyone might then flavor to his own liking. The Gospel is from the beginning controversial, because its doctrinal contours are sharp.

Contrary to popular impression, the real differences among the churches do not turn on obscure texts, or trivial ceremonies, or the exact wordings of prayers. The differences between Rome and the Reformation, for instance, are both weighty and clear-cut: (1) Is salvation strictly a free gift for Christ's sake, or must we also earn it somehow? (2) Does final authority in the church reside only in God and His inspired Word, or does it reside also in church officials? The choices between the Lutheran and the Reformed understandings of the Gospel are also at bottom simple. For instance, does Holy Baptism really offer forgiveness and regeneration, or not? Is the Gospel only correct information, or does it actually carry and convey all the blessings it describes? Is the Lord's Supper really His body and blood, or are the Lord's own words to that effect (and those of St. Paul) to be taken in some other way, as some sort of picture language?

No serious interpretation of the Gospel can avoid such questions or leave them unanswered. The idea of a doctrinally neutral Gospel therefore is a self-contradiction.

Finally, something should be said about the name "Lutheran." It may well give the wrong impression at first, as though the church of the Reformation were built on Luther and his personal authority. Interestingly, Lutherans were given that name not by themselves but by others. Luther himself did not want people calling themselves by his name, for he had been crucified for no one. [11] Nor was anybody baptised into him. What is more, the official Lutheran confessional writings, collected in the Book of Concord, never speak of a "Lutheran Church," but use words like "evangelical," "reformed," "catholic," and "orthodox." By and by, the word "catholic" came in popular usage to identify the Church of Rome. "Reformed" was claimed by the Calvinists, and the identifier for the Lutherans evolved from "evangelical" to "Evangelical Lutheran," or even to plain "Lutheran." (It would be a pity today to surrender that beautiful word "evangelical" to those who rob the "evangel" [Gospel] of its crowning glory in Holy Baptism and the Lord's Supper!)

Lutheran theology by its nature stresses content rather than form and substance over names (or "images," as we say today). While with St. Paul boasting only "in the Lord" (1 Cor. 1:31), the Lutheran church modestly accepts the sectarian-sounding nickname, knowing that this sort of thing has happened before in Christian history. When, for example, the great St. Athanasius had led the church to reject the Arian heresy that Jesus is not really God, the Arians pretended that the trinitarian Creed of the Councils of Nicaea (AD 325) and Constantinople (AD 381) taught new-fangled, "Athanasian" ideas. Again, when St. Augustine (354–430) stood up for salvation by grace alone against Pelagius, those who confessed the truth were called "Augustinians." In the sense in which the one holy, catholic, and apostolic faith was once nicknamed "Athanasian" and "Augustinian," the heirs of the Reformation willingly bear the reproach of being "Lutheran."

Not Luther's personal opinions, however, but the public confessions composing the Book of Concord define what the Lutheran church believes and teaches on the basis of Holy Scripture alone. In keeping with the blunt and honest nature of Luther's Reformation theology, these confessional writings are not satisfied with mere lip-service on ceremonial occasions. What matters is not which documents are officially mentioned

---

11. *Editor's note:* See, for example, AE 45, 70.

in church constitutions, but whether the Gospel is actually preached and taught in its truth and purity and the holy sacraments are administered according to their divine institution.

Nor should anyone be impressed simply by the Lutheran name, as such. The last and most detailed of the Lutheran Confessions, the Formula of Concord, is directed almost entirely against nominally "Lutheran" positions, that is, views given out as being in harmony with the Augsburg Confession when in fact they were not. A Lutheran church is not one which merely calls itself that, but actually confesses the Book of Concord in word and deed. This church draws the boundaries of church fellowship accordingly.

PRIESTHOOD AND MINISTRY

One of the very pivots of the whole Reformation was 1 Peter 2:9:

> But you are a chosen people, a royal priesthood, a holy nation, God's special possession, that you may declare the praises of him who called you out of darkness into his wonderful light.

In these golden phrases, rich in Old Testament background, the Reformation church rediscovered the God-given grandeur attending the spiritual priesthood of the whole people of God. The Middle Ages had made huge class distinctions in the church between the laity and the clergy or "spiritual estate." Then, too, there was the special race of monks and nuns, the "religious." They were thought to be keeping Christ's "evangelical counsels" of poverty, chastity, and obedience, while the common herd of Christians could occupy themselves at a much lower level with the mere Ten Commandments. Even Thomas Aquinas had permitted himself to speak of entrance into the monastic life as equal to baptism![12]

The Reformation made short shrift of such fantasies. Not that the genuine value of some earlier monastic services went unrecognised. "Formerly the monasteries had conducted schools of Holy Scripture and other branches of learning which are profitable to the Christian church, so that pastors and bishops were taken from monasteries."[13] Again: "Anthony, Bernard, Dominic, Francis, and other holy Fathers chose a certain kind of life for study or for other useful exercises."[14] Indeed, it may well be asked whether some modern missionary challenges, such as the drug- and

---

12. *Editor's note:* As noted in SA III xiv. See AE 17, 70 and AE 41, 199.
13. AC XXVII 15 (Tappert, 73).
14. Ap IV 211 (Tappert, 136).

crime-infested inner cities of the U.S.A. would not be served better by some form of ordered Christian community than by conventional clergy with vulnerable families.

What is objectionable about monastic life, as it finally turned out, is the two-fold idea that special humanly devised disciplines and exercises earn merit before God and thus put monks and nuns onto a higher plane than ordinary Christians. In fact, God wishes to be served and is pleased precisely by the faithful performance of ordinary duties in daily life. "To obey is better than sacrifice" (1 Sam. 15:22). Further, forbidding people to marry is a teaching promoted by demonic powers (1 Tim. 4:1–3).

Turning now to the relations between laity and clergy, the biblical picture of the royal family (Eph. 2:19) is a good starting point. There is only one holy family of God, and every baptized, believing Christian is equally a member of it. The Lord Himself says, "You are all brothers" (Matt. 23:8). This exalted royal family status or dignity belongs to all Christians without exception, whether they are illiterate peasants, learned scholars, pious housewives, faithful farmers, good pastors, or honest salesmen. The fact that some family members must give themselves, at the Father's direction, entirely to the work of the family's affairs and enterprises does not put them into a different class from the rest. All have equal royal and priestly standing, only some have one set of duties and some have another.

This Reformation truth needs to be applied again in our day. Some speak and act as though the big thing were to have some office in the church, while "mere membership" is humdrum. People even talk of getting others "interested" in the church by giving them some office, say, elder or treasurer. This is topsy-turvy, though. Nothing could be grander than to be a baptized child and priest of God, to be His heir by faith, to serve Him daily in true devotion according to one's calling in life, and to come together regularly with the rest of the family around the family table where the Lord Himself is our Food! Compared with such glorious royal family privileges, the differences in daily duties and offices are trifling indeed. Christians serve and please God just as well in any useful work. The point is to do something for which one is well-fitted. Better to be a good farmer or lawyer than a bad preacher!

What, then, is the ministry? We may begin by clearing up our language. The Greek words which, having passed through Latin, became *minister, to minister,* and *ministry* in English mean "servant," "to serve," and "service." In the New Testament this group of words has at least three levels of meaning. The first is the general meaning of serving or service, most often in connection with food (Luke 10:40; 12:37; 17:8; John 2:5; Acts 6:2, etc.). Secondly, the words refer specifically to the ministry (service) or ministers (servants) of the Word (Acts 6:4), of the New Testament (2 Cor. 3:6), of the Spirit (2 Cor. 3:8), of reconciliation (2 Cor. 5:18), or of the Gospel (Col. 1:23). Finally, in its most specific sense, the word *servant* means "deacon," as distinct from pastors or bishops (Phil. 1:1; 1 Tim. 3:8–12; see also Rom. 16:1).

It is the second of these meanings, that is, the ministry of Word and Sacraments, with which we are concerned here. Of this office, the Augsburg Confession says: "In order that we may obtain this [justifying] faith, the ministry of teaching the Gospel and administering the sacraments was instituted." [15] Unlike, for example, German, in English we do not string words together like railroad cars into compound word-trains. Since it is clumsy to keep repeating entire phrases like "the ministry of the Gospel," it became customary to speak simply of "the ministry," which served as shorthand for the longer phrase.

This sort of shorthand worked very well until it became fashionable to talk about all Christians having a "ministry," on the basis especially of Ephesians 4:12. Now it is perfectly true that all Christians are to serve— that is, be useful to—Christ and one another. Our word group is very occasionally used in this way in the New Testament (John 12:26; Phm. 13; 1 Pet. 4:10). Calling this general service "ministry," however, and talking about all Christians consequently being "ministers" blurs the distinction between this general "ministry" of all and the special ministry of some, namely, the ministry of Word and Sacraments.

Luther's usage was clear: all Christians are born by baptism into the priesthood, but some are called by the church into the ministry. Accordingly, in the rest of this chapter, "the ministry" shall mean not the generic service of all Christians but rather the public ministry of preaching the Gospel and administering the sacraments.

Christ chose twelve apostles (Matthias replaced Judas, Acts 1:12 ff.), and later a thirteenth, St. Paul (Gal. 1:1). Their office was that of the Word (Acts 6:2–4) and Sacraments (Matt. 28:19–20). These apostles were equipped with extraordinary miraculous gifts and powers (Acts 2:43; 8:18; 2 Cor. 12:12). Yet that miraculous aura surrounding them did not comprise the essence of their office. The essence, rather, was the faithful proclamation of the Gospel (including, of course, the sacraments). The twelve, once properly constituted with the addition of Matthias, were not replaced at

---

15. AC V 1 (Tappert, 31).

their deaths by new apostles. They were succeeded by "ordinary" ministers like Timothy, who in turn would entrust the saving truth to "faithful men, who shall be able to teach others also" (2 Tim. 2:2 KJV). The
Apostolate was the *extraordinary*, foundational (Eph. 2:20) form of the
one Gospel ministry, while today's ministry is its *ordinary* continuation.
Stewards or administrators of "the mysteries of God" (1 Cor. 4:1 KJV) is
what St. Paul called not only himself but also Apollos and therefore others ministers of the Gospel.

St. Paul also says: "For what we preach is not ourselves, but Jesus
Christ as Lord, and ourselves as your servants [literally, *slaves*] for Jesus'
sake" (2 Cor. 4:5). This text cuts two ways. On the one hand, far from
acting as lords over their flocks, entitled to impose their own whims on
the church (2 Cor. 1:24; 1 Pet. 5:3), Christ's ministers are to rule only with
the solemn evangelical authority given them by the Chief Shepherd, His
Gospel and sacraments. In the exercise of this sacred task they should
be obeyed with the obedience due Christ and His Word (Heb. 13:17).
On the other hand, they are not errand boys to carry out the whims of
popular or majority opinion, that is, to scratch itching ears (2 Tim. 4:3).
To be sure, they are servants, a status of which no follower of Jesus can be
ashamed (Matt. 20:28; John 13:14), yet they serve "for Jesus' sake." Therefore they serve the Lord and His church according to His revealed will.
Beyond this, neither ministers nor people have anything to impose on
each others' consciences. It is sacrilege to turn the Christian pilgrimage
in the ship of the church into a farcical "Love Boat" cruise, with the clergy as crew to provide drinks and diversions on demand to self-indulgent
passengers!

"All things are yours," writes St. Paul to the church at Corinth, with
special reference to the public ministry among them (1 Cor. 3:21). As
the Bride of Christ, who is one with Him, the church possesses all the
treasures of salvation He has entrusted to her (Eph. 4:11; 5:25–32; see
Gal. 4:24–31). The ministry of distributing these saving riches is naturally
part and parcel of the church's possessions. Clearly, therefore, the ministry is "His and hers." He has given the office to her, and she fills it according to His command. It is noteworthy that even the apostolic vacancy left
by the death of Judas was filled not by the apostles acting alone, but by the
whole embryonic church acting together (Acts 1:15, 26). No individual or
group in the church has a monopoly on the Keys of the heaven-opening
Gospel. These Keys were given three times in the New Testament: once
to Peter (Matt. 16:19), once to the whole church (Matt. 18:18), and once to
the apostles (John 20:23). By the gift of Christ, therefore, the Keys belong

originally to the church, the house-mother of Christendom.[16] They are committed by her to her "public service," the ministry, who are to exercise these Keys officially and publicly on behalf of Christ and His one holy church. The ministry is also accountable to the church (Col. 4:17) on the basis of God's Word.

Since the church "alone possesses the priesthood, [she] certainly has the right of electing and ordaining ministers."[17] The church, however, consists neither of the people by themselves, nor the ministers by themselves, but rather hearers and preachers together. Neither flocks nor shepherds may act without due regard for each other. On one hand, the ministry belongs to and is conferred by the church. The ministry has no powers other than those given by Christ to His church, for public exercise through His and her ministry. On the other hand, barring emergencies, the church acts publicly and officially through her ministry. In calling men to the ministerial office therefore, the churches act "with the participation of their pastors."[18] As the public teachers of the church, the pastors have the primary duty to examine the candidates in respect of their orthodoxy and of their ability to teach. (See 1 Tim. 3:2 and Tit. 1:9 together with 2 Tim. 2:2.) The qualifications for the public ministry are clearly set out in the New Testament, for instance, that the office cannot be committed to a woman (1 Cor. 14:34–35; 1 Tim. 2:12). A qualified candidate, having been chosen by the people, is publicly placed into his office by the church through the public ministry. The laying on of hands, although not a divinely commanded action, is a good custom dating back to the apostolic-era church (1 Tim. 4:14; 2 Tim. 1:6). This act is therefore a fitting part of the public inauguration into the office.[19]

While ministers are called to particular congregations or fields of service, they may later be called elsewhere. Therefore the whole church has a stake in who is admitted into the ministry. Congregations must take proper account of this legitimate interest of their sister-congregations. An orthodox minister in one place is recognised as such by the entire orthodox church everywhere. This double aspect of a ministry in one place, but recognized in all places, is reflected in our liturgical language. "Ordination" signals a man's entry into the ministry as a life-long work. It happens

---

16. *Editor's note:* See LC II 42.
17. Tr 69 (Tappert, 331).
18. "adhibitis suis pastoribus" in the Latin original of Tr 72. *Editor's note:* See Marquart, *The Church,* 147, note 7.
19. *Editor's note:* Marquart placed a footnote number into the text at this point, but what the note was to say is unknown.

only once. "Installation" or "investiture" places a minister into his particular charge. Of course, that may happen repeatedly.

The evangelical understanding of the ministry differs from both Roman Catholic *traditionalism* and Reformed *biblicism*. Rome holds that the traditional division of the ministry into bishops, presbyters, and deacons exists by divine command and institution. Eastern Orthodoxy and the Anglican communion largely share that view. The Reformed, for their part, hold that the New Testament prescribes a particular form of church structure or polity, although they differ among themselves about exactly what the form is. It is typical of the Reformed approach to see a number of different offices as divinely established in the New Testament, then to try to copy just these offices for today's church life. The Lutheran Reformation, by contrast, recognized that no uniform pattern of offices can be found in the New Testament, and that behind the variety of forms lies basically *one* office of the Gospel and sacraments. When the seven were chosen in Acts 6, for instance, this did not signal the creation of a new divinely prescribed office. Rather, the church acted in Christian liberty to make provision for very important practical needs, precisely in order that the one divinely established office of the Gospel might devote itself to "the ministry of the word of God" (Acts 6:2; see 6:4).

This is not to say that it is wrong to divide the one ministry of the Gospel into various ranks or grades, as circumstances may suggest. Several Lutheran churches have maintained or restored the threefold bishop-presbyter-deacon scheme. However, all such rankings are man-made and exist by human authority alone. They fall in the realm of Christian liberty, not of divine command. Further, no human scheme or authority can strip a minister of the Gospel of his responsibility to confess the truth, and if necessary to suffer for it. In the New Testament itself, *presbyters* (elders) and *bishops* (overseers) are not, initially, on different levels, but are, in fact, the same people (Acts 20:17, 28).

In short, as there is only one life-giving Gospel, about which everything in the church revolves (2 Cor. 2–5), so there is only one public ministry which dispenses these sacred "mysteries of God" (1 Cor. 4:1 KJV). Beyond that office, the church may establish as many auxiliary offices as in Christian liberty she may think wise.

Finally, it should be clear that there is no competition whatever between the priesthood of all and the public ministry of some. The proper work of a priest is to sacrifice. As God's holy loyal priesthood, Christians glorify God for His grace by offering *themselves*, yes, their "bodies" (Rom. 12:1; see 1 Pet. 2:5), not words, primarily, or things or actions. This sacrifice forms their sublime worship. Their self-offering takes place basically in the course of daily life and calling. Being a spiritual priest does not mean playing assistant pastor or exercising some sort of leadership role in public worship, although it does of course include a life of daily prayer. This entire priestly life revolves about the altar from which Jesus, the High Priest Himself, distributes until the end of time forgiveness, life, and salvation with His own very body and blood. Those priests who are also called as ministers simply serve their fellow-priests in faithfully and publicly proclaiming, transmitting, and distributing these divine riches.

CHURCH AND STATE

"You know that the rulers of the Gentiles lord it over them," says the Savior, "and their high officials exercise authority over them. Not so with you. Instead, whoever wants to become great among you must be your servant" (Matt. 20:25–26). The kingdom of Christ and the kingdoms of this world are totally different: "My kingdom is not of this world" (John 18:36).

It would be quite wrong to imagine, however, that God rules only the little patches marked "church," while having no effective control over the rest of the universe. God indeed rules the kingdoms of this world too, and in the interests of His church at that (Rom. 8:28–39), but by very different means. In the world generally God rules by His directive and permissive will, and with irresistible power. The instruments of His rule are the various created orders and authorities, such as nature, marriage, parents, teachers, police, judges, armies, and the like. Here lawful governments have a perfect right and duty to use "the sword" (Rom. 13:4) to enforce civil order and justice. This is the realm not of the Gospel but of the Law, indeed, of that natural law which is accessible to all men through conscience, common sense, and moral reflection (Rom. 2:14–15).

Christ's church has altogether different aims and methods. Here Christ rules with His grace, through His holy Gospel and sacraments. The church is the beach-head of heaven on earth (Gal. 4:26; Phil. 3:20). Her divinely given mission (Matt. 28:18 ff.) is the celebration and distribution to mankind of those riches of eternal life which God has given the world "in his Son" (1 Jn. 5:11). The New Testament, and therefore the church, has no political, social, or economic program for the world. Of course, the church's strictly spiritual life and work do have profound political, social, and economic effects within human history.

Significantly, when the Savior was asked to adjudicate a quarrel about an inheritance, He replied: "Man, who appointed me a judge or an arbiter between you?" (Luke 12:14). Instead of a lecture on social responsibility, He went on to give a warning against greed. If He, then, Who is the Judge of the living and of the dead, disclaims jurisdiction in this sort of dispute, by what right can His modern representatives claim the authority He refused?

Modern churches vie with the United Nations organization in making pronouncements about affairs all over the globe. The apostolic church's agenda in Acts 15 was rather more modest. Taking no notice at all of the grave problems besetting the vast Roman Empire, the Council of Jerusalem dealt only with questions which, though they may have seemed petty, impinged on the very nature of the Gospel. This concentration on the saving Gospel (see Gal. 1!) kept the apostolic church from the fallacy which seemed so self-evident to the World Council of Churches in Amsterdam in 1948, when in its report on "The Church and the Disorder of Society," it set "the responsible society" as "the goal for which the churches in all lands must work."[20]

When the Christian congregation at a given place comes together, this is not to promote general uplift, community service, or social crusades, but to worship the risen and present Savior (John 20:19–29; Acts 20:7–11; 1 Cor. 10:16–17; 11:17–34), and to receive, cherish, and transmit the saving power of His cross and resurrection. The church's solemn assemblies participate in the greatest mysteries in heaven and on earth, as "with angels and archangels and with all the company of heaven we laud and magnify" His glorious name. It is frivolous, even sacrilegious, to treat the awesome transactions between the Most Holy Trinity and His priestly people as useful publicity stunts for various worthy causes.

> Therefore, the two authorities, the spiritual and the temporal, are not to be mingled or confused, for the spiritual power has its commission to preach the Gospel and administer the sacraments. Hence it should not invade the function of the other, should not . . . make or prescribe to the temporal power laws concerning worldly matters. . . .
>
> Thus our teachers distinguish the two authorities and the functions of the two powers, directing that both be held in honor as the highest gifts of God on earth.[21]

What is set out here is Luther's so-called doctrine of the "Two Kingdoms." This teaching is better termed that of the "Two Governments," for

---

20. See Marquart, *The Church*, 190.
21. AC XXVIII 12–13, 18 (Tappert, 83).

it is one and the same King Who rules both. If one has understood the radical difference between Law and Gospel in the Bible, then one cannot avoid what this difference entails, namely a radical distinction between the spiritual and the civil or political realms.

Yet there are those who believe that this distinction is mischievous, indeed that it was "the greatest disaster in all the history of ethics," since it supposedly led from Luther ultimately to Hitler and his concentration camps.[22] The argument is that restricting the express rule of God's Word to the church, and letting the state be governed by reason alone, gives the state a false independence from moral accountability.

Such a colossal misreading of the real intent and import of the Two Kingdoms doctrine calls for comments along several lines. In the first place, it is surely worth noting that unlike his Roman Catholic and Reformed opponents, Luther in principle rejected religious persecution. The church, he held, could be defended only with spiritual weapons (2 Cor. 10:4), and no one could or should be compelled by force to profess this or that faith.

Second, by "reason" Luther did not mean simply calculating ability or I.Q., as modern readers are likely to assume. He meant rather a discipline of mind grounded in man's moral nature, which even after the Fall recognizes certain basic decencies implanted in creation (Rom. 2:14–15).

Third, a clear-cut distinction between something like a minimal public morality and the more comprehensive moral requirements of particular religions is in fact the only workable scheme in modern pluralistic societies. So abortion, for instance, ought to be outlawed not because it is a sin against God (which it is!), but because it is a crime against humanity. The principle is very clear when applied to acts like theft, robbery, or murder. All such acts are regarded as wrong by most religions. Yet it would be silly to argue that therefore governments may not treat these acts as crimes, lest the "religious freedom" of irreligious people be violated!

Fourth, separation of church and state does not mean separation of religion and politics. Christians, after all, live in both realms. They cannot leave their consciences behind when they enter the voting booth or exercise the duties of various political offices. Under modern democratic arrangements, citizens have a share in the authority described in Romans 13, and bear responsibility for how it is exercised. Christian citizens therefore have the clear obligation to use their political, economic, and social power

---

22. William Barclay, *Ethics in a Permissive Society* (London: Collins, 1971), 187.

for the well-being of their fellow human beings and not simply for their own advantage. This the church must teach. Exactly which public policies would best ensure the neighbour's welfare, though? This question must be settled in the public arena. Wisdom, historical understanding, prudential judgment, technical information, strategic analysis, and many other complex factors enter into such decisions. Here the church as church has neither competence nor warrant to pontificate.

Fifth, the most important reason for keeping the spiritual and the political realms strictly distinct is the overriding need to keep the Gospel, that one needful thing (see Luke 10:42), free and uncompromised in the church. Violent political passions are injected into the churches today, all in the name of world improvement. They do not belong there.[23] Political theology repeats the terrible cry for Barabbas (Matt. 27:21), the Liberation Front terrorist of his day. This man stood for something more practical and "relevant" than Jerusalem's Prince and King of Peace, Who offered "only" liberation from sin, Satan, and eternal death! The Jerusalem from above, our spiritual mother (Gal. 4:26), is the holy Bride of Christ, arrayed in the royal garments of salvation. It would be mockery to force upon her the uniform of a moral night watch-woman constantly out to police the state.

CHURCH GOVERNMENT

The Christian church is a constitutional monarchy, the King Himself having granted to His realm a gracious divine constitution in the Holy Scriptures (Eph. 2:20). Only God's Word may rule in the church, not human opinion or authority of any sort.

Even this principle, however, is not as unambiguous as it may at first appear. A question dividing the Lutheran from the Reformed churches is whether the Bible, the Word of God, is a book of divine regulations, or the book about Jesus Christ. Therefore, is the kingdom of God to be found where His Law is kept or where His Gospel treasures are distributed?

Of course Christians are to grow in the newness of life and obedience to God. Yet such growth comes through the Gospel, not the Law (Gal. 3:2). Christ rules His church, His kingdom of grace, not with the Law but with the Gospel. This is why the right decisions about doctrine, Gospel doctrine, stand out as so central in New Testament times (Acts 15; Gal. 1–2) and in all the truly great ages of the church. The unity and purity

---

23. *Editor's note:* Marquart placed a footnote number into the text at this point, but what the note was to say is unknown.

of the Gospel proclamation—that is the one over-riding task and concern of councils, synods, conferences, and conventions of Christ's church!

Christ is present with the smallest possible church. The "two or three" of St. Matthew 18:20 equals more than one. Even such a small church has as much spiritual authority as does a congregation of many thousands. What matters is not any human chain of command, but only the Saviour's own authority which is everywhere the same, mediated and manifested in and through His pure Gospel and Sacraments. Therefore wherever the church exists, she has the full authority to be and to act as Christ's church in that place. She need not procure a "franchise" from some larger church structure elsewhere. Local churches are not bound to any divinely prescribed administrative or supervising structures.

None of this means that congregations may stand proudly apart from one another, acting indifferent to the equal dignity, duties, and responsibilities of other orthodox congregations. (See 1 Cor. 14:36.) Rather, all orthodox churches are to cultivate the utmost regard for each other. They need to cooperate in their sacred work in and for their common Lord according to each church's circumstances. Orthodox churches owe each other mutual recognition, that is, church fellowship. Not external constitutions but joint orthodox confession of the pure Gospel and sacraments forms the true external bond of church unity and fellowship. This unity is expressed and exercised basically in altar and pulpit fellowship, which can in turn involve such things as joint mission work, maintenance of seminaries and publications, and the like. Such activities will usually require administrative structures, devised by the church in Christian liberty, for the sake of jointly pursuing the church's divinely assigned mission.

Unlike the Old Testament church, which had a detailed Ceremonial Law, the New Testament church has very few divinely established outward observances. First there is Baptism, the Sacrament of entrance into Christ and His church. Then there is preaching, including especially the absolution, and for this there is a divinely instituted public ministry. Finally there is the Holy Supper, as the focal point for the church's public life and worship (Acts 20:7 ff.; 1 Cor. 10:16–17; 11:17 ff.). All other arrangements in the church are made in Christian love and freedom, for the sake of good order (1 Cor. 14:40). It should be recalled, too, that a church consists neither of hearers only nor of preachers only, but of hearers and preachers together. (See, for example, Phil. 1:1.)

This very freedom of the church means that decisions must be made constantly about many details. In principle, two sorts of questions arise.

There are matters which are settled in the Word of God. Voting in such matters means not that the truth is being established by vote, but that consensus in and submission to the Word is thereby sought and expressed. There are also matters not decided by God's Word. Love is empress in these cases. Here neither majorities nor minorities have any right to bind one another's consciences, but everyone should stand ready to accommodate everyone else (Eph. 5:21). The more spiritually mature people are, the more they must "bear with the failings of the weak, and not . . . please" themselves (Rom. 15:1). While minorities can ordinarily be expected to accept majority decisions for the sake of peace and good order, majorities may sometimes have to yield to minority preferences for the sake of love and unity.

The assertion in the church of any authority counter to or beyond that of Christ Himself in His life-giving Gospel and sacraments introduces a counter-Christian impetus. This does violence to the holy Bride of Christ. We face here the spiritual horror of Anti-Christ. Be it noted that the Greek word *anti* means not only "against" but also "in place of." Subtle competition and displacement often prove more effective than open opposition. (Thus, Satan much prefers to masquerade as an angel of light rather than as a chimney-sweep reeking of brimstone. See 2 Cor. 11:14.) The counter-Christian spirit can and does exist in many different forms and degrees (e.g., St. Matt. 16:22–23; 26:51; St. Luke 9:33–41; Rom. 16:18; 1 Jn. 4:3), and also therefore in the flesh of orthodox Lutheran pastors when they, like Peter, seek to evade the cross with human wisdom or power!

Institutionally, however, this usurpation of power over Christian consciences has reached its climax in the Papacy. From small beginnings in apostolic times (2 Thes. 2:7) this spiritual tyranny has since 1870 (Vatican I) formally claimed divine infallibility for its own pronouncements on faith and morals. Still more, the Papacy in the name of Christ officially declares "anathema" (accursed) anyone who confesses the Gospel, that is, anyone who confesses "that justifying faith is nothing else than trust in divine mercy, which remits sins for Christ's sake, or that it is this trust alone by which we are justified."[24] The Reformation unmasked the Papacy as that "lawless one," sitting in the Temple, that is, the church of God, as if he were God (2 Thes. 2:1 ff.). Revelation 17 supports Carlyle's famous judgment that the Papacy is "the ghost of the Roman Empire sitting crowned upon the grave thereof."

---

24. Quoted in *Examination* I, 460.

THE CHURCH IN GLORY

St. Paul wrote: "For to me, to live is Christ and to die is gain," and "I desire to depart and be with Christ, which is better by far" (Phil. 1:21, 23). He was not thinking, in the modern manner, of a basically private "going to heaven." The true biblical hope of heaven has nothing to do with this bloodless sort of "passing on." To be sure, the souls of believers go to heaven at death (St. Luke 23:43; Acts 7:59, etc.). Yet this transition is not our ultimate hope. Rather, that hope springs from the resurrection of the body and the life everlasting, not as isolated individuals but in the blessed company of the whole church (Phil. 3:20–21; 1 Thes. 4:13–18), to feast forever in the new heaven and the new earth (2 Pet. 3:13) at the cosmic wedding banquet of the Lamb and His Bride (Rev. 21).

The church in heaven and the church on earth are already one. (See Heb. 12:22–24.) We confess this reality especially in the Communion Preface, when we unite "with angels and archangels and with all the company of heaven" to chant the Saviour's praises. An old Scandinavian custom makes the point well: the altar rail is always at least slightly curved, because it is only a small visible foreground of a larger, unseen circle (2 Cor. 4:18) to which we here belong.

This confident expectation of everlasting life has from the beginning given great strength and courage to Christians in the face of suffering and death. The venerable Bishop Polycarp, a student of the apostle St. John, was arrested in 167 AD and told that he could save his life by cursing Jesus. He calmly replied: "Eighty-six years have I served him, and he never did me any wrong. How can I blaspheme my King who saved me?" Threatened with fire, the bishop said: "The fire you threaten burns but an hour and is quenched after a little; for you do not know the fire of the coming judgment and everlasting punishment, that is laid up for the impious."[25] And so Polycarp was burnt alive, praising God like Stephen as he was being killed. (See Acts 7:54–60.) Similar scenes have been enacted throughout the church's history, also in our time under the fearful persecutions of modern pagan regimes.

In our Western world, where pleasure and luxury beckon on every hand, we modern believers need to recover the old Christian sense of the reality and nearness of heaven. What often spoils it for us moderns is the vague suspicion that heaven will be a boring eternal choir practice! Such a dismal

---

25. "Martyrdom of Polycarp," *Early Christian Fathers*, trans. and ed. Cyril C. Richardson, The Library of Christian Classics, vol. 1 (Philadelphia, PA: Westminster, 1953), 152, 153.

prospect almost seems to impose upon us a duty to have as much fun as possible now, before it's all over. But this vision of heaven as loss and impoverishment actually turns out to be the same unfaith that drove Adam and Eve out of Paradise. It amounts to sheer distrust of God to think that He somehow begrudges us true happiness and withholds it from us so that we must reach for it ourselves, even against His warning Word. Yet even when the mirages of sin conjure up contrary appearances in which deserts look like oases and bleaching bones seem to hold luscious refreshment, faith trusts God to look out for our true interests and well-being.

Scripture tells us very little about what eternal life will be like. None of those raised from the dead by our Lord (Jairus's daughter, the young man of Nain, Lazarus) gave interviews about what they had experienced. St. Paul, who was "caught up" into heaven and paradise, reported only that he "heard inexpressible things, things that no one is permitted to tell" (2 Cor. 12:4). Really, should we expect anything else? Our language, derived from earthly experience, simply lacks the capacity to express the grandeur of the world to come. Scripture therefore describes it only in pictures and images, like the vivid scenery in the Book of Revelation. We have to do the same sort of thing when trying to explain, say, marriage to a three-year-old, or nuclear physics to members of an illiterate bush tribe.

Luther showed the way when he wrote his little four-year-old Hans about a beautiful garden, with children in golden frocks gathering up rosy apples, pears, cherries, and plums, and playing with ponies that had golden bridles and silver saddles.[26] From childhood, Christians need to learn that we will find eternal life infinitely more satisfying and exciting than the most intense pleasures that this dull, sin-sick earth can offer. In cinematic terms, the resurrection life in the new heaven and the new earth will resemble a multi-dimensional technicolour extravaganza, as compared with the silent and flitting black-and-white shadows of our present existence.

Delivered from the faithless spectre of a funless heaven, we shall be convinced with St. Paul "that our present sufferings are not worth comparing with the glory that will be revealed in us" (Rom. 8:18). Here also modern Christians find the strength and the courage to sacrifice all else for the pearl of great price (Matt. 13:45–46), and to hold in contempt the gaudy allurements of the world, the devil, and the flesh. The more genuinely we believe this, the more our church-services, too, will reflect eternity's disturbing grandeur instead of the cozy clubbiness that accompanies secular self-indulgence.

---

26. AE 49, 323–324.

For eternity, taken seriously, is of course disturbing. What an awesome weight of responsibility rests upon our earthly life if this single, unrepeatable stretch of existence within space and time leads necessarily to one of only two possible outcomes: either the eternal enjoyment of God, or else deprivation and punishment without end! Yet that is precisely our situation (Matt. 25).

Today there are cheap substitutes or alternatives to the sober and sobering teaching of Holy Scripture. Especially popular among these loom the various forms of occultism. For instance, there is the idea of re-incarnation, which reduces the value of each life by inventing truly inflationary numbers of still more lives to come. If one or more of these many lives become spoilt, in such thinking, no permanent harm is done. One may always catch up in the next few rounds. This fantasy makes a farce of the biblical truth that people die once and face judgment afterward (Heb. 9:27).

Occult religiosity studiously avoids the terrible reality of sin. Instead, it chatters cheerfully about wholeness, harmony with nature, and unity with the universe. This happy balance is putatively to be achieved by means of physical and psychological techniques, not through repentance. Without Fall, sin, or final judgment, no one needs a Savior. Not from beyond but from within ourselves comes whatever "salvation" there is, as we discover and use our own inner powers and mend our neglected links with nature. There are, of course, no means of grace. What counts is not self-denial, but cultivation of healthy biorhythms and the like. Religion is to be sought and found in direct personal experience and emotional fulfillment rather than in "cold" authoritative externals like God-given doctrine and sacraments.[27] At the end lies no resurrection, no last judgment, and no ultimate watershed between heaven and hell. Instead, there is a gentle, gradual transition to various other levels or "planes" of existence. With these "higher levels" one may be in touch even now through psychic experiences or spiritist seances, depending on one's occultist preferences. The destructive results of such delusions may be studied in the dreadful twentieth-century case of Bishop James Pike, who turned to spiritism as a substitute religion.[28]

The fact is that God "has set a day when he will judge the world with justice" (Acts 17:31).

---

27. *Editor's note*: Marquart placed a footnote number into the text at this point, but what the note was to say is unknown.
28. *Editor's note*: Marquart placed a footnote number into the text at this point, but what the note was to say is unknown.

> Then fright shall banish idle mirth,
> And hungry flames shall ravage earth,
> As Scripture long has warned us.[29]

The smug nineteenth-century world view tended to scoff at this whole prospect, since it was thought that matter could be neither created nor destroyed. Texts like 2 Peter 3:12 were considered quaintly amusing: "That day will bring about the destruction of the heavens by fire, and the elements will melt in the heat." After Hiroshima the amusement has abated noticeably, bringing to mind again the question from the previous verse: "Since everything will be destroyed in this way, what kind of people ought you to be?"

Nor will physical destruction be the worst of it. When sea and grave shall have given up their dead (Rev. 20:11–15), the King will judge all mankind and will assign each person to one of two destinations, eternal life or eternal punishment (Matt. 25:31–46). Those who will inherit eternal life, solely and alone by faith in the Son of God (John 5:24), will then rejoice forever in God's own happiness, in the new Jerusalem of the new heaven and the new earth (Rev. 21:1 ff.).

If some say too little about this eternal life, others say far too much—that is, more than Scripture really teaches. The idea of a so-called "millennium" has made for a distraction from the true Christian hope about the "last things" (*eschatology*). *Millennium* means "one thousand years," thought to be a literal thousand-year period before or after the last judgment during which the church will allegedly rule the world. This notion is based on a vision in Revelation 20 that includes a thousand years—one thousand, the cubic number 10^3, symbolising completeness or perfection—along with picturesque expressions that no one takes literally such as "key," "chain," and "serpent."

There are two basic versions of this millennial belief. According to one, Christ's second coming will occur before the "millennium." This is called "pre-millennialism." The other view, termed "post-millennialism," holds that Christ will return after the thousand year period of the church's triumph. The latter view is, it seems, in the minority at the moment. This is the "optimistic," utopian version of millennialism. It sees Christianity as winning out all over the globe with the accompaniment of unparalleled social, economic, and political uplift, issuing finally in the golden age. Pre-millenialism displays more pessimism, believing that things will go from

---

29. *Editor's note:* See *LSB* 508:1; *TLH* 611:1.

bad to worse until Christ intervenes in Person and by force to establish His earthly reign (occupation?), with headquarters in Jerusalem.

The Augsburg Confession roundly rejects all such ideas, that is, "Jewish opinions to the effect that before the resurrection of the dead the godly will take possession of the kingdom of the world, the ungodly being suppressed everywhere."[30] Here we have what has been called "a-millennialism," the teaching that no literal thousand-year earthly reign is to be expected either before or after the Lord's return. With Scripture, amillennialists hold that His return will occur suddenly and in the absence of warning. Without further ado, this return will initiate the Last Judgment (Matt. 24:30–50; 1 Cor. 15:52; 1 Thes. 4:13–5:3).

By far the most popular form of millennialism today is the version of pre-millennialism known as "dispensationalism." This view was promoted by the very influential *Scofield Reference Bible*, which divides God's dealings with men into seven distinct ages or "dispensations." In practical terms, the main idea of this scheme is that the Old Testament prophecies about Israel still await fulfillment in a Jewish national state. In this view, the church embraces only a part of God's plan. Indeed, the church really amounts to a sort of consolation prize. For it is taught that Christ had truly wished to restore the Davidic kingdom in Jerusalem. Since He did not find the right response in about the year 30, He founded the church as a sort of interim measure. Once the "age of the church" is over, though, Christ will return and convert the Jews as a body, assume the royal throne of David in Jerusalem, then rule the world from there for one thousand years until Judgment Day.

This shocking demotion of the church to a stop-gap measure, overshadowed by a Jewish national state as "the real thing," rests on a topsy-turvy system of biblical interpretation. Instead of interpreting the "shadowy" Old Testament types and predictions in the clear light of their New Testament fulfillments (Col. 2:17; see John 1:17), dispensationalism reinterprets and devalues the New Testament realities to fit a rigidly literalistic reading of Old Testament texts. What the New Testament presents as the surpassingly glorious, final, and permanent arrangement (2 Cor. 3–5) is turned in this way into something temporary and preliminary after all. To dispensationalists, the political/millennial "Israel" will be still greater!

We might note the way a few particulars are explained. Although St. Peter clearly says that Joel 2:28–32 was fulfilled then and there at Pen-

---

30. AC XVII 5 (Tappert, 38–39).

tecost, as the culmination of Jesus' cross and resurrection (Acts. 2:16 ff.), the *Scofield Reference Bible* claims that this is only a preliminary fulfillment, relating to the church. It still remains to be fulfilled as related to Israel. Hair-splitting and arbitrary distinctions are invented in support. Contrary to the clear thrust of Acts 2:30–36, the "throne" of verse 30 is supposed to be David's and Christ's own, but different from God's throne on which Christ is meanwhile sitting (Rev. 3:21) until the "Israel" plan can be put into effect! Again, "Kingdom of God" and "Kingdom of Heaven" are supposed to differ in no fewer than five respects. Yet it is perfectly clear that both expressions mean exactly the same thing. (Compare Matt. 5:3 with Luke 6:20, and Matt. 13:31 with Mark 4:30 and Luke 13:18.) Worst of all, the *Scofield Reference Bible*'s comment on Revelation 19:7 insists that the Lamb's wife, or the church, is different from Israel, or Jehovah's wife (Is. 54:1–10; Hos. 2:1–17), presently adulterous and "yet to be restored"! Is God then a bigamist?[31]

These forced artificialities and fantasies about a political Israel maintain the very misunderstandings of Old Testament prophecies expressly corrected by the resurrected Savior. The two disciples on the road to Emmaus had told their unrecognized Companion how "we had hoped that he was the one who was going to redeem Israel" (Luke 24:21). The Stranger then responded:

> How foolish you are, and how slow of heart to believe all that the prophets have spoken! Did not the Christ have to suffer these things and then enter his glory? [Luke 24:25–26, author's translation]

St. Luke adds that "beginning with Moses and all the Prophets, he explained to them what was said in all the Scriptures concerning himself" (Luke 24:27). Notice that not a word appears here about any political Israel, allegedly the main content of the "Davidic covenant"!

A few verses later we read:

> "This is what I told you while I was still with you: Everything must be fulfilled that is written about me in the Law of Moses, the Prophets and the Psalms."

And what sort of thing is this "everything"? The Gospel continues:

---

31. *The Scofield Reference Bible*, ed. C. I. Scofield (New York: Oxford University Press, 1917), 1003, 1150–1151, 1334, 1348.

Then he opened their minds so they could understand the Scriptures. He told them, "This is what is written: The Messiah will suffer and rise from the dead on the third day, and repentance for the forgiveness of sins will be preached in his name to all nations, beginning at Jerusalem." (Luke 24:44–47)

In other words, the scriptural predictions about Christ are properly understood when they are referred to His life, death, and resurrection. This, and not a millennium, is to be preached to all nations. To introduce here the utterly irrelevant anti-climax of a great political destiny for the nation of Israel is to falsify the Saviour's teaching. He would hardly have failed to mention such a notion had He meant to teach it, let alone emphasize it.

St. Paul also makes it very clear that those who believe in Christ constitute the true spiritual Israel. The church thus consists of Abraham's spiritual, not physical, descendants (Rom. 2:28–29; 9:6–8). Theirs and theirs alone are the glorious promises of God, and whether they happen to be Jews or Gentiles makes not a scrap of difference (Gal. 3:28).

Christ's kingdom of grace, or his church, will remain under the cross until the end of time (St. Luke 18:8; 2 Tim. 3:1ff.; 2 Pet. 3:3). Earthly glory and dazzling success hold out false hopes. Nor should Christians be distracted from their heavenly pilgrimage and expectations by useless preoccupations with Middle Eastern politics, as if these had any special theological significance. In a way it is understandable that when the Gospel and sacraments have been spiritualised down to mere pictures and illustrations, while at the same time the symbolical visions of Revelation are taken literally, people should grope for something tangible to hold on to. It is not surprising that such substitute sacraments take the form of holy real estate in Palestine or of breathless guessing games about the next twist in the cosmic soap opera of "The Late Great Planet Earth."[32]

God's Word calls Christians away from all such false, arid superstitious hopes and distractions. For the Lord calls us to sobriety and preparedness (Matt. 25; 1 Thes. 5:4–11; 1 Pet. 4:7) and to a cheerful pursuit on earth of the path of duty and devotion.

> And when the strife is fierce, the warfare long,
> Steals on the ear the distant triumph song,
> And hearts are brave again, and arms are strong.
> Alleluia! Alleluia![33]

---

32. *Editor's note:* See the title of Hal Lindsey with C. C. Carlson, *The Late Great Planet Earth* (Grand Rapids, MI: Zondervan, 1970).
33. See *TLH* 463:5; *LSB* 677:5.

Chapter Nine

WHY CHRISTIANITY?
FAITH, FACTS, AND REASON

Editor's note: In his seminary apologetics course, Marquart mentioned that as a parish pastor he used to start adult instruction classes with a lesson on apologetics. He had initially planned to begin his doctrine book for laypeople in a similar way, with this chapter. However, in a 1987 letter concerning the book, then in progress, he wrote that this lengthy treatment of the question "Why Christianity?" might, "in view of formidable footnotes and complexities untypical of other chapters, perhaps appear as an apologetic appendix, rather than as an intimidating first chapter." He attached to his letter a revised outline of the projected book that listed "Why Christianity?" as the ninth and final chapter. We have kept it in just this place.

WHAT IS AT STAKE?

Is there a God? Or did the universe just pop up by itself? The answers to these questions have been hotly disputed in the marketplace of ideas. Why does this discussion seem to yield so much more heat than light, though? The reason is, no doubt, that what lies at stake are not remote academic pedantries but rather matters of the deepest and most practical import for every human being.

It would not be difficult to multiply complaints like Maxine Schnall's: "Where did we go wrong? I hear that question from everyone these days, as if we are all victims of a massive shipwreck. Awash in the debris of our cultural values, the survivors struggle to keep from drowning in a limitless sea of options."[1] Yet the real reason why our culture has come unhinged is rarely faced. The tendency is to chatter about all sorts of parochial details, especially those of the personal or psychological sort, but to miss the global picture. And that big picture is this: *Western civilisation minus God equals nihilism!* One cannot juggle away the underpinnings, and expect the elaborate structure they supported to remain standing as if nothing has happened.

Those who deny God have good reason to downplay the importance of what they are doing. Take the erstwhile tour-guide of the cosmos, Carl

---

1. Maxine Schnall, *Limits: A Search for New Values* (New York: Potter, 1981), 3.

Sagan. As viewers of his television spectaculars were dazzled by vistas of galaxies and supernovas, of vast radio-telescopes and tiny viruses, this evangelist of secular humanism relentlessly drove home the point: The universe made itself, God and creation are but ancient superstitions, and we ourselves no more than atoms whirling together briefly in a meaningless dance until the suns die and all is nothing again. "But is this all?" beams Sagan. "Is there nothing in here but molecules? Some people find this idea somehow demeaning to human dignity. For myself, I find it elevating that our universe permits the evolution of molecular machines as intricate and subtle as we."[2]

Minus the Madison Avenue mask, the picture is considerably less cheery:

> That Man is the product of causes which had no prevision of the end they were achieving; that his origin, his growth, his hopes and fears, his loves and his beliefs, are but the outcome of accidental collocations of atoms; that no fire, no heroism, no intensity of thought and feeling, can preserve an individual life beyond the grave; that all the labour of the ages, all the devotion, all the inspiration, all the noon-day brightness of human genius, are destined to extinction in the vast death of the solar system, and that the whole temple of Man's achievements must inevitably be buried beneath the debris of a universe in ruins—all these things, if not quite beyond dispute, are yet so nearly certain, that no philosophy which rejects them can hope to stand. Only within the scaffolding of these truths, only on the firm foundation of unyielding despair, can the soul's habitation henceforth be safely built.

So wrote Bertrand Russell, one of the twentieth century's leading minds.[3] His bleak vision is at least honest and realistic.

Already in the nineteenth century there were those who did not share the optimistic view that Christian ethics could be preserved after Christian dogma had been given up. "We are living on the perfume of an empty vase," said the famous French infidel, Renan.[4] Dostoyevsky and Nietzsche had seen with equal clarity, though from opposite poles, that with the rejection of God morality was doomed as well. Dancing, as he fancied,

---

2. "A Gift for Vividness," *Time*, 20 October 1980, 68.

3. Bertrand Russell, "A Free Man's Worship," quoted in *Objections To Humanism*, ed. H. J. Blackham (London: Constable, 1969), 18.

4. Quoted in Arnold Lunn and Garth Lean, *Christian Counter-Attack* (New Rochelle, NY: Arlington, 1969), 18.

on the grave of God, Nietzsche sneered: "Naiveté: as if morality could survive when the God who sanctions it is missing!"[5]

With God and His antiquated morality out of the way, Nietzsche expected the morally unfettered Superman to arise, and to perform heroic feats "beyond good and evil." The twentieth century has fulfilled this hope more terribly than even Nietzsche could have imagined. It has been a century of Hitlers and Stalins and their imitators, down to the squalid little aspiring supermen who terrorise modern schools, subways, and neighbourhoods. The liberation from traditional "shackles" has brought in its wake wholesale butcheries of human beings, born and unborn, on an unprecedented scale. "We are teaching savagery and are naively appalled at the success of our instruction." This grim judgment had in view not communist hordes but our own Western public's education and entertainment. The verdict was rendered by Professor Duncan Williams, in his aptly titled *Trousered Apes*.[6]

As a matter of plain common sense, if there is no intelligent Creator before whom we are responsible, then ethics is no more than personal whim. If man is simply a freak of nature, then all of his cultural imaginings amount to a cosmic joke. He has no more dignity or significance than cats or cactuses—less, in fact, for cats and cactuses are blissfully unaware of their absurdity. Disposing of unwanted humans in that case is the same as exterminating roaches or bacteria. Indeed, statements like "murder is evil" or "you shall not steal" then belong to the same logical class as "I hate asparagus" or "Please pass the mayonnaise."[7] It is all simply a matter of taste or preference, unless of course some lovers of asparagus or haters of mayonnaise should manage to seize the power to enforce their own irrational choices. In that case prudence may dictate compliance, but certainly not ethics. It is hardly surprising that the one great certainty com-

---

5. Friedrich Nietzsche, *The Will To Power*, trans. Walter Kaufmann and R. J. Hollingdale (New York: Random House, 1967), 147.

6. Duncan Williams, *Trousered Apes* (New Rochelle, NY: Arlington, 1972), 29. It is worth quoting Malcolm Muggeridge's commendation of this book as "a cogently argued, highly intelligent and devastatingly effective anatomisation of what passes for culture today, showing that it is nihilistic in purpose, ethically and spiritually vacuous, and Gadarene in destination." *Editor's Note:* I have not located the source for the Muggeridge quote.

7. A. J. Ayer, *Language, Truth, and Logic* (New York: Dover [1952]), 108: "And we have seen that sentences which simply express moral judgments do not say anything. They are pure expressions of feeling and as such do not come under the category of truth and falsehood."

municated by modern education is that everything is relative, and that good and evil reside in the eye of the beholder.[8]

A great deal rides on the question of God's existence! If there is a God, then an objective moral order makes sense. If not, man is up against cosmic chaos. It's everyone for himself. As Stephen Crane put it:

> A man said to the universe:
>> "Sir, I exist."
>> "However," replied the universe,
>> "The fact has not created in me
>> A sense of obligation."[9]

ATHEISM WITH GUSTO

For common sense, the manifest order of the universe has always served as evidence for the existence of an intelligent Creator. This order reaches its dramatic peak in the world of living organisms. Let a modern biologist give us an expert glimpse into this enchanted realm:

> Fifty years ago naturalists were content with the observation that bats catch moths. Then came the discovery that bats produce sounds inaudible to the human ear and use echoes to locate their prey. Now it appears that not only do moths have soundproofing, but that they have ears specifically designed to listen in to an approaching enemy transmitter. To counter this advance, bats developed an irregular flight path, which confused the moths until they in turn came up with an ultrasonic jamming device. But bats still catch moths, and it can only be a matter of time before research discovers the next development in this escalating drama of nature.[10]

Such marvels of "bio-engineering" confront us everywhere in living nature. It seems obvious that if machines cannot throw themselves together

---

8. "There is one thing a professor can be absolutely certain of: almost every student entering the university believes, or says he believes, that truth is relative" (Allan Bloom, *The Closing of the American Mind* [New York: Simon and Schuster, 1987], 25). Or: "This century's totalitarianism, trampling the human personality and all its rights, rhinocerouslike, underfoot, is only the application of this theory to life, or humanism put into *practice*" (Vadim Borisov in A. Solzhenitsyn, ed., *From Under the Rubble* [Boston, Toronto: Little, Brown, 1975], 201).

9. Quoted in James W. Sire, *The Universe Next Door* (Downers Grove, IL: InterVarsity Press, 1979), 13.

10. Lyall Watson, *Supernature* (London: Hodder Paperbacks, 1974), ix–x.

by chance, then neither can plants and animals, any and all of which are vastly more complex than any and all machines.

William Paley famously made this very point with his analogy of the watch. Unlike a stone, he argued, a timepiece like a watch cannot be dismissed as having always been there. Nor did it come about by way of natural processes. The watch is too obviously "contrived," that is, structured by some purposive intelligence. A watchmaker must therefore be assumed, even if none can be seen in the vicinity. Plants and animals are even more obviously the result of deliberate design. Organs such as eyes exhibit an incomparably greater degree of complexity and precision than their crude mechanical counterparts like telescopes. Here was the essence of Paley's argument in his classic *Natural Theology*, which quickly captured the imagination of the educated public, and remained influential for much of the nineteenth century.[11] This book no doubt helped to inoculate public opinion in the English-speaking world against the anti-Christian furies unleashed by the French Revolution.

The great appeal of Paley's work lay in his having harnessed the immense prestige of science. Philosophy, notably in the person of David Hume, had begun to dissolve all established certainties in a flood of systematic doubt. Christian truth and even the very existence of God were not to be exempt from the rising tide of skepticism. The waves were already lapping at the foundations and the grand old house seemed ready to topple into the swollen stream when Archdeacon Paley arose and drove back the waters. Moreover, and to our present point, Paley for his feat employed not the cumbersome old machinery of Dogma but the bright new magic of Science itself. Theology, after all, could have been dismissed with a sneer. Before Science, however, even Philosophy had to bow, however grumblingly. The vital question of God's existence seemed settled now once and for all, and by means of solid scientific evidence. This was Paley's memorable achievement.

"Then," as one professor intoned, not without relish, "with a suddenness only less surprising than its completeness the end came; the fountains of this great deep were broken up by the power of one man, and never in the history of thought has a change been effected of a comparable order

---

11. Henry, Lord Brougham and Sir Charles Bell, eds., *Paley's Natural Theology* (London: G. Cox, 1853). See D. L. LeMaheiu, *The Mind of William Paley* (Lincoln, NE: University of Nebraska Press, 1976).
12. Cited in R. E. D. Clark, *Darwin: Before and After* (Exeter, NH: Paternoster, 1966), 87.

of magnitude."[12] Charles Darwin's *Origin of Species* burst like a bombshell upon the mid-Victorian scene in 1859.

The idea of evolution itself should not have struck anyone as new. It went back, in fact, to the crude speculations of the atheistic, materialistic philosophers of ancient Greece prior to Socrates. Darwin's grandfather, Erasmus Darwin, and others had offered evolutionary schemes in more modern garb, but without convincing evidence. It was Charles Darwin's great distinction to provide a plausible account of how evolution might have occurred.

His main explanation was "Natural Selection."[13] The *Origin* illustrated the workings of this process with an impressive wealth of detail. There were two steps. First, the offspring of biological organisms always differ at least a little from the parents and from each other. Second, some of these variations will fit in better with the environment than others. Thus the organisms with the most advantageous features will tend to win out in the struggle for food and life over organisms less well-adapted to their surroundings. So by a gradual accumulation of tiny changes, selected because of the difference they made in the struggle for survival, nature has produced all the wide variety of living organisms known today. Their uncannily complex parts and organs and their marvelous adaptation to their environment indeed give the impression of an intelligent plan or design. This impression is an illusion, though, according to Darwin. Blind Natural Selection by itself, unaided, did it all—simply by relentlessly eliminating nature's failures over millions of years.

Now, why should all this be rehearsed here? Why should a book about God even mention Darwin? This is just the point: Darwin's proposal, it was at once realized, had broad cultural implications far beyond biology or even science itself. If Darwin was right, he had successfully gotten rid of any intellectual necessity for God.

Apart from divine revelation itself, Paley's argument from design back to Designer had seemed the one respectable support left for the public acknowledgement of the Creator. Darwin's Natural Selection effectively undid Paley's sort of argument. This knocked the props from under the public, social status of the supremacy of God. Thomas Huxley, one of Darwin's earliest and most influential converts, celebrated the triumph of irreligion in the sonorous rumble of his Victorian eloquence:

---

13. Actually, Darwin's idea of Natural Selection was not original. See Loren Eiseley, *Darwin and the Mysterious Mr. X* (New York: Dutton, 1979) and A. C. Brackman, *A Delicate Arrangement*, (New York: Times Books, 1980).

The oldest of all philosophies, that of Evolution, was bound hand and foot and cast into utter darkness during the millennium of theological scholasticism. But Darwin poured new lifeblood into the ancient frame; the bonds burst, and the revivified thought of ancient Greece has proved itself to be a more adequate expression of the universal order of things than any of the schemes which have been accepted by the credulity and welcomed by the superstition of seventy later generations of men.[14]

Others have agreed. Michael Ruse, a modern apologist for Darwin and Darwinism, also portrays Western Civilisation as a sort of blind alley which had for two thousand years interrupted and arrested the noble progress of evolutionary thought. The ancient Greek atheists had been well on their way, complains Ruse, when "all speculation pointing toward a genuine evolutionism was abruptly stopped by two things: first, by the metaphysical systems of Plato and Aristotle . . . and, second, by the rise and spread of Christianity, bringing with it what Carlyle contemptuously referred to as 'Hebrew old clothes.'"[15] Neal Gillespie's respected study, *Charles Darwin and the Problem of Creation*, expressly argues that Darwin's own achievement was more philosophical than scientific. What Darwin had managed to do was to shift the whole of biology from a theistic ("creationist") into a non-theistic ("positive") frame of reference. This shift, says Gillespie, "eventually took God out of nature (if not out of reality) as effectively as atheism."[16]

Despite lingering scientific doubts and even objections, Darwinism won the day, particularly in the Anglo-Saxon world. This was largely on the strength of Darwinism's cultural appeal. It was an idea whose time had come. The alluring scent of liberation from traditional religious constraints was in the air. Darwin was seen as having driven the last nail into the coffin of God. Natural selection had finished off natural theology. On this great certainty the modern cult of Secular Humanism had staked the claims of its Cultural Revolution. These are pressed in detail by the movement's various sects and denominations, among which Marxism and Freudianism have carried the most potent virus-strains. Sir Julian Huxley,

---

14. Quoted by L. Harrison Matthews, F.R.S., in his Introduction to Charles Darwin, *The Origin of Species* (London: Dent & Sons, 1971), xiii.

15. Michael Ruse, *The Darwinian Revolution* (Chicago, IL: University of Chicago Press, 1974), 3. One detects in such utterances something more akin to the passions of philosophy and even religion than to the cool objectivity of science.

16. Neal C. Gillespie, *Charles Darwin and the Problem of Creation* (Chicago, IL: University of Chicago Press, 1979), 153.

grandson of Thomas, spoke for them all when he declared final victory in connection with the 1959 Darwin centenary celebrations in Chicago:

> Darwinism removed the whole idea of God as the creator of organisms from the sphere of rational discussion. Before Darwin, people like Paley with his famous *Evidences* could point to the human hand or eye and say: "This organ is beautifully adapted; it has obviously been designed for its purpose; design means a designer; and therefore there must have been a supernatural designer." Darwin pointed out that no supernatural designer was needed; since natural selection could account for any known form of life, there was no room for a supernatural agency in its evolution.[17]

ATHEISM WITH A WHIMPER

Beneath the fulsome centenary rouge, however, the body of Darwinian doctrine was doomed to decay. For the whole scientific landscape had changed abruptly since Darwin's day. Gone was the old view of the universe as a clattering machine made up of indestructible little particles of matter. Einstein's famous equation had shown matter and energy to be interchangeable. Our seemingly solid world had turned out to be a pudding of congealed light, with black hole currents beckoning from afar.

The cosmos had in fact become strangely mental. Sir James Jeans wrote that "the universe appears to have been designed by a pure mathematician," and that it could be best pictured "as consisting of pure thought, the thought of what, for want of a better word, we must describe as a mathematical thinker."[18] Even Soviet scientists, trained in the rigidities of dialectical materialism, could not quite escape the impact of divine design in matter-energy.[19] One leading Soviet nuclear physicist, B. P. Dotsenko, defected in Canada in 1966, and explained that physics had convinced him of the existence of God.[20]

---

17. Sol Tax, ed., *Evolution After Darwin: The University of Chicago Centennial Discussions* (Chicago, IL: University of Chicago Press, 1960), vol. 3, *Issues in Evolution*, ed. Sol Tax and Charles Callender, 45–46. *Editor's Note:* The source is a November 21, 1959 WBBM-TV broadcast previewing the Darwin Centennial Celebration in Chicago. Newspaper columnist Irv Kupcinet and former Illinois governor Adlai Stevenson interviewed Huxley and other panelists.
18. James Jeans, *The Mysterious Universe* (New York: Macmillan, 1930), 146.
19. David V. Benson, *Christianity, Communism, and Survival* (Glendale, CA: Regal Books, 1971), 21 ff.
20. B. P. Dotsenko, "From Communism to Christianity" (interview), *Christianity Today*, 5 January 1973, 4–12.

This came as a far cry from the stereotypical scenario of science-on-one-side, God-on-the-other. In the West it actually happened that distinguished physicists rebuked trendy, miracle-denying theologians like Rudolf Bultmann for their obsolete notions of physics![21] On the other hand, the popular Big Bang theory of the origin of the universe has been criticised for not admitting openly that the scheme implies a Creator who, as it were, presses the button to set off the big bang atomic bomb.[22]

The revolution in physics also upset the old view of science as a growing reservoir of infallible truths, guaranteed by logic and objective observation.[23] Professor Sir Karl Popper in particular became known as a pioneer of a more modest and realistic philosophy of science which stressed the role of reason, imagination, and creativity.[24] A good scientific theory, in his view, is not one which safely restates the obvious. Rather, a good theory risks refutation by capturing as large a chunk of the world as possible and making predictions about it which can then be tested and possibly falsified. Nothing can be verified or proved true once and for all, but many things can be falsified and so ruled out. In this way science makes progress. A theory which cannot possibly be disproved, no matter what the state of evidence, does not constitute science but dogma. The respected Cambridge University philosopher of science Mary Hesse argues convincingly that all scientific theories are "underdetermined" by the factual evidence, cosmological theories especially so. We can never know in advance which present day scientific theories will be proven wrong in the future, and our most general, wide-ranging theories about the universe "are almost certainly false."[25]

Turning squarely to the fate of modern Darwinism, it cannot be our purpose here to recite all the woes that have befallen it.[26] The central and

21. Werner Schaafs, *Theology, Physics, and Miracles*, trans. Richard L. Renfield (Washington DC: Canon Press, 1974), 25.

22. Hannes Alfvén, "Cosmology: Myth or Science," in *Cosmology, History, and Theology*, ed. Wolfgang Yourgau and Allen D. Breck (New York: Plenum Press, 1977), 1–14.

23. For a comprehensive account, see F. Suppe, *The Structure of Scientific Theories* (University of Illinois Press, 1977).

24. See especially Karl Popper, *Conjectures and Refutations* (New York: Harper Torchbooks, 1965); and *Objective Knowledge* (Oxford: Clarendon Press, 1979).

25. Mary Hesse, *Revolutions and Reconstructions in the Philosophy of Science* (Bloomington, IN: Indiana University Press, 1980), 78, 147–148, 241–242.

26. See for example M. Denton, *Evolution: A Theory in Crisis* (New York: Adler & Adler, 1985); W. R. Fix, *The Bone Peddlers* (New York: Macmillan, 1984);

most devastating development in this saga needs to be considered, however, as a surprising sequel to the whole Paley/Darwin episode.

That nature is highly predictable has of course been known for some time. If nature acted now this way and now that, without any apparent pattern, science as we know it would be impossible. Yet in fact stones fall down and not up, heated water boils instead of freezing, and the earth goes 'round the sun in a year, not a week. Nature's processes, then, move along certain definite pathways in preference to others. Is it possible to discern in all this flux an overall direction? Yes! Everything tends towards chaos and dissolution.

Consider some obvious examples. Piles of rubble do not tend to turn themselves into cathedrals or spacecraft. On the other hand, cathedrals and spacecraft, left to themselves, do gradually turn into piles of rubble. Bombs dropped on houses produce heaps of bricks, but bombs dropped on heaps of bricks never produce houses. A cup of tea will not organise itself into a hot half and a cold half, but the tea will quickly be mixed to a uniform temperature even if hot water had been poured in on one side of the cup and cold water on the other.

Nature, then, is a one-way street on which the traffic moves from order to disorder. Its basic traffic law is the famous Second Law of Thermodynamics, also known as the Entropy Law. In its original form this law said that some of the heat used, say, to perform mechanical work in a steam engine is always lost to the system and thus unavailable for further work. This increase of unavailable energy is called "entropy." Later the law was broadened to say that a closed system—that is, one cut off from further energy supplies—will increase not in order but in disorder. Left to itself, order will be dissipated into disorder. A statistically unlikely pattern will decay into a statistically probable randomness.

Evolution, if true, needs to run in precisely the opposite direction. Evolutionist Joseph Needham claimed this expressly: "The law of evolution is a kind of converse of the Second Law of Thermodynamics, equally irreversible but contrary in tendency."[27]

P.-P. Grassé, *Evolution of Living Organisms* (New York, London: Academic Press, 1977); M.-W. Ho and P. T. Saunders, eds., *Beyond Neo-Darwinism* (London, New York: Academic Press, 1984); N. Macbeth, *Darwin Retried* (Boston, MA: Gambit, 1971); and L. Sunderland, *Darwin's Enigma* (San Diego, CA: Master Books, 1984).

27. Quoted in Jagjit Singh, *Great Ideas in Information Theory, Language and Cybernetics* (New York: Dover, 1966), 80.

How is evolution supposed to defy the second law of thermodynamics? The standard answer to this dilemma is that living organisms are not isolated systems but lie open to constant supplies of energy, ultimately from the sun. This energy enables them to overcome the downward pull of the Second Law and to upgrade themselves instead to ever-higher levels of complexity. Julian Huxley, for instance, cheerfully admitted that evolution "is an anti-entropic process, running counter to the second law of thermodynamics with its degradation of energy and its tendency to uniformity." Huxley saw nothing wrong with this, since the sun is always more than able to cover any energy overdrafts incurred by evolution. "With the aid of the sun's energy," he wrote, "biological evolution marches uphill, producing increasing variety and higher degrees of organisation."[28]

This supposed solution is much too glib and easy, however. The trouble lies deeper. If the letters SOS or HELP appeared on a sandy beach, or if a bowl of alphabet soup spelt out strings of "HAPPY BIRTHDAY," no one would imagine that long ages of sunshine and tidal action in sea or soup were responsible for these effects.

The missing factor here is *information*, of course, and no amount of raw energy can supply information. Some sort of intelligent programming is required. Norbert Wiener may well have hit upon the most important lesson of our whole computer age when he wrote that "Information is information, not matter or energy. No materialism which does not admit this can survive at the present day."[29]

Modern information theory arose largely out of the needs of military communications technology during World War II.[30] The theory describes the (statistical) nature and behaviour of that mysterious commodity, "information," which is now coded and flashed about the globe and beyond in myriads of signals by various electronic communications systems.

It turns out that information behaves strictly according to the Second Law of Thermodynamics. Random signals ("noise") do not upgrade coded messages but destroy them. It takes care and wit to keep noise from nibbling away at information, as even the *New York Times* amply confirmed when it apologised for calling someone a "defective," and explained that the man was really a "detective on the police farce." Large numbers of ran-

---

28. Julian Huxley, introduction to *The Phenomenon of Man*, by P. Teilhard de Chardin, trans. Bernard Wall (New York: Harper and Row, 1965), 27.
29. Norbert Wiener, *Cybernetics, or Control and Communication in the Animal and the Machine* (Cambridge, MA: MIT Press, 1948), 132.
30. See the readable account in Jeremy Campbell, *Grammatical Man* (New York: Simon and Schuster, 1982).

dom signals only make matters worse. Electrical interference will show up as "snow" on TV screens. It cannot create even the shortest commercial. Nor could a bolt of lightning, though possessed of energy aplenty, upgrade a commercial into, say, *War and Peace!*

Put more technically, this means that we have here a special case of the second law. It can be stated thus: "any processing of information from already existing sources may decrease, but not increase, the numerical measure of this information." [31] Jacques Monod, an arch-materialist who thought that life was an impossibly lucky number that "just came up," as at Monte Carlo, clearly recognised as "one of the fundamental statements of information theory . . . that the transmission of a message is necessarily accompanied by a certain dissipation of the information it contains," and that this is "the theoretical equivalent of the second law of thermodynamics."[32]

In the flurry of excitement over the first "electronic brains," as they were called, many thought that these devices would soon explain the riddles of the human brain. However, the distinguished physicist Walter Heitler pointed out the true lesson of the brain/computer analogy:

> What the comparison does show us, if we take it seriously, is just about the opposite of what the constructors of these animated mechanisms . . . think they are showing. If the nervous system is comparable with an electronic brain, then it has certainly not arisen by chance mutation. . . . And it also follows that the nervous system clearly derives from a constructor or constructors who must have had at least the same amount of intelligence as the totality of the brain workers (from Newton on) who have made the construction of the electronic brain possible.[33]

The argument is all the more telling when one remembers how the human brain, with a neo-cortex of some ten thousand million neurons, vastly outclasses man-made computers:

> We can only dimly imagine what is happening in the human cortex or indeed in the cortices of the higher mammals, but it is at a level of complex-

31. P. Masani, ed., *Norbert Wiener: Collected Works with Commentaries* (Cambridge, MA: The MIT Press, 1976–1985), vol. 4, *Cybernetics, Science, and Society: Ethics, Aesthetics, and Literary Criticism; Book Reviews and Obituaries*, 816.
32. Jacques Monod, *Chance and Necessity* (New York: Vintage, 1972), 198–199.
33. Walter Heitler, *Man and Science* (Edinburgh and London: Oliver and Boyd, 1963), 71.

ity, of dynamic complexity, immeasurably greater than anything else that has ever been discovered elsewhere in the universe or created in computer technology.[34]

So said a world-renowned neurophysiologist, Sir John Eccles, in his 1977/1978 Gifford Lectures. (Together with his friend Popper, Eccles has also vigorously attacked the popular materialistic notion that mind and brain-functioning are the same thing.[35]) In these Gifford Lectures Eccles confessed that although he had tried to follow the materialist version of origins as far as he could, he had "grave misgivings. As an act of faith, scientific faith, it demands so much. The great French novelist François Mauriac whimsically said that it demanded an act of faith greater than for 'what we poor Christians believe.'"[36]

The nervous system, however, presents only a special case of a much more fundamental difficulty. That computers mimic brains in some ways is obvious. What is not so obvious is that immensely sophisticated forms of information-processing underlie life itself. This is the import of the Nobel Prize-winning discovery, by Crick, Watson, and Wilkins in 1953, of the now famous double helix as the structure of DNA. This "Golden Molecule" of life functions as a bio-computer tape, containing the genetic "program" for each cell, each organ, and each organism. The language of these instructions has four basic "letters" (A, T, C, and G), which the living cell "reads" in units of three, so that the recipes for all the spectacular complexities of living organisms are "spelt out" in various combinations and re-combinations of the $4^3=64$ basic units.

The updated Darwinian ("neo-Darwinian") theory, which Julian Huxley and the others had celebrated so fervently in 1959, held that random gene mutations supplied the minor changes upon which Natural Selection then acted its wonders to perform. But if mutations are simply "typing mistakes" in the copying of the DNA code, then we are faced with the absurdity of a primitive, amoeba-like cell—and where had *it* come from?—accidentally stenciling its way up Darwin's family tree by means of copying errors! At a notable symposium Murray Eden of the Massachusetts Institute of Technology put the hopelessness of the neo-Darwinian recipe like this:

34. John Eccles, *The Human Mystery* (Berlin, Heidelberg: Springer International, 1979), 160.
35. John Eccles and Karl Popper, *The Self and Its Brain* (Berlin, Heidelberg, 1977).
36. John Eccles, *The Human Mystery*, 235.

The chance of emergence of man is like the probability of typing at random a meaningful library of one thousand volumes using the following procedure: Begin with a meaningful phrase, retype it with a few mistakes, make it longer by adding letters, and rearrange subsequences in the string of letters; then examine the result to see if the new phrase is meaningful. Repeat this process until the library is complete.[37]

In 1981 one of the world's leading physicists and cosmologists, Sir Fred Hoyle, gave the number $10^{40,000}$ (1 followed by 40,000 zeroes) as a minimal starting point for estimating the information content of man and the higher mammals. Hoyle went on to say that the chance that organisms of such information content might have emerged by evolutionary processes during the relatively short time of our universe's existence was comparable with the chance that "a tornado sweeping through a junkyard might assemble a Boeing 747 from the materials therein."[38] These odds are even more awesome in light of a simple thought-experiment described by Jagjit Singh: Given a machine equipped with the English alphabet, and allowing it one million tries per second, how soon can the machine be expected to come up, by chance, with the 31-letter line from Shakespeare's *Twelfth Night*, "O mistress mine, where are you roaming"? According to Singh, standard probability calculations show that it would take the machine "some three hundred million times the putative age of the cosmos to run through the" $(26)^{31}$ possibilities.[39] The information content of our little ditty from Shakespeare is of course vanishingly small compared with that of the humblest louse in Shakespeare's wig!

In refuting Jacques Monod's twin gods of Time and Chance, the French mathematician Georges Salet insisted that only one conclusion was possible, namely that Intelligence must have existed before life. To the objection that this was philosophy and not science, Salet replied that he would not quibble about words but that the conclusion itself "flows from observation and rigorous analysis of the facts."[40] The facts are that DNA is a vast self-processing information system, and that, as a measure of improbabil-

---

37. Paul S. Moorhead and Martin M. Kaplan, eds., *Mathematical Challenges To the Neo-Darwinian Interpretation of Evolution* (Philadelphia, PA: Wistar Institute Press, 1967), 110.

38. "Hoyle on Evolution," *Nature* 294 (12 November 1981), 105. See also Fred Hoyle, *The Intelligent Universe* (New York: Holt, Rinehart & Winston, 1983), 19.

39. Jagjit Singh, *Great Ideas*, 209.

40. Georges Salet, *Hasard et Certitude* (Paris: Éditions Scientifiques Saint-Edme, 1972), 332.

ity, information is the very opposite of randomness or "the law of higgledy piggledy" (as Sir J. F. W. Herschel called Natural Selection). Therefore there is no escaping the verdict of Ludwig von Bertalanffy, the founder of the general systems theory:

> Considered thermodynamically, the problem of neo-Darwinism is the production of order by random events. . . . In the absence of . . . organizing forces, the second principle of thermodynamics and its equivalent in information theory (Shannon's Tenth Theorem stating that information can be converted into noise but not vice versa) will prevail.[41]

If this sort of argumentation is anywhere near the mark, then we may well call modern information theory "Paley's Revenge." For this body of facts and ideas has quite unexpectedly given Paley's rusty old watch a new, computerized—and thus much more formidable—form. In this new form, the "watch argument" haunts all stubborn conceits about a self-creating universe. Thanks to the informationist approach which led to the discovery of the DNA code, neo-Darwinism at any rate is finished. And since neo-Darwinism is by far the most prestigious and representative version of evolution, that theory itself is now in disarray. Its flagship torpedoed and sinking, evolution's smaller vessels and lifeboats are scurrying away in all directions to avoid being dragged down too.

Yet we do well to remember that, as Hoyle and Wickramasinghe observe shrewdly, although the numbers disprove the received evolutionism, "it is possible, in the fashion of a grand master with a lost game of chess, to wriggle ingeniously for a while."[42] This wriggling seems most evident in attempts to squirm out of the second law's iron grip. Those who want to believe that cosmic order does arise out of chaos after all, conjure impressively with the name of Nobel laureate Ilya Prigogine.[43] Some go so far as to say that the second law simply does not apply in biology.[44]

---

41. Ludwig von Bertalanffy, "Chance or Law," in *Beyond Reductionism* [The Alpbach Symposium 1968], eds. Arthur Koestler and John R. Smythies (New York: Macmillan, 1970), 73.

42. Fred Hoyle and N. C. Wickramasinghe, *Evolution from Space* (London: J. M. Dent & Sons, 1981), 24.

43. Ilya Prigogine and Isabelle Stengers, *Order Out of Chaos* (New York: Bantam, 1984).

44. As one claim put it, the conflict between evolution and the second law "is genuine and is best solved by rejecting the dogma that the second law is universally valid" (Joseph Wayne Smith, *Reason, Science, and Paradox* [London: Croom Helm, 1986], 29). Prof. Benjamin Gal-Or of the Israel Institute of

It is impossible for non-scientists like the present writer to track and assess the validity of the host of technical details involved in various current proposals. As we have seen, the history of science and philosophy should warn us not to expect in this realm fixed truths, settled forever. Until there is something more solid than assumption and speculation to the contrary, though, the safest bet by far is that if anything in our current picture must go, it will not be the second law of thermodynamics. Present attempts to wriggle 'round it and save a collapsing evolutionism look rather like the earlier rescue operations in behalf of that imaginary counter-oxygen, "phlogiston," after it had run up against gravity.[45] Today gravity remains, however reinterpreted, while phlogiston has long since been discarded.

Evolution made its big splash by appearing to prove God intellectually unnecessary, in the name of science. Thanks to an improved science, it is ending up seeming more and more like voodoo.[46]

ESCAPE INTO MUSH

If bio-information makes such a telling point against atheism, why then are not more people convinced by it? The short answer is that the emotional case for atheism simply swamps the intellectual case against it!

There is a strong belief today, shared by both Christians and non-Christians, that the existence of God cannot be proved because it is a

---

Technology finds the implications of information theory so unpalatable that he rails against cybernetics as an unscientific pseudo-theology, in which information "becomes a 'ghost,' a 'soul,' a sort of modern 'Holy Spirit'"[!] (Benjamin Gal-Or, *Cosmology, Physics, and Philosophy* [New York: Springer, 1981], 375).

45. "In fact, phlogiston never inspired much experimental work. Its service was rather the characteristic service of 'principles,' from Aristotle onwards: the intellectual one of enabling us to arrange our thoughts and give them some sort of unity" (H. T. Pledge, *Science Since 1500* [London: Her Majesty's Stationery Office, 1966], 112).

46. The Nobel laureate Francis Crick, of DNA-fame, suggests that life may have been sent to earth by some super-civilisation via spacecraft! See his *Life Itself* (New York: Simon and Schuster, 1981). Clearly no scientist would think of resorting to flying saucers as an explanation of life's origins unless the situation were desperate.

There is said to be "general acceptance" in the West of the approach promoted by a Soviet scientist, A. Oparin. See John Farley, *The Spontaneous Generation Controversy from Descartes to Oparin* (Johns Hopkins University Press, 1977), 187. Farley does not mention, however, Oparin's own professed dependence on Marxist dialectical materialism and its pseudo-scientific 19th-century prophet, F. Engels. See A. I. Oparin, *The Origin of Life on the Earth* (London: Oliver & Boyd, 1957), xi–xii, 92, 230, passim.

matter of faith, and faith rests on things other than facts or proof. This scheme amounts to a sort of amiable no-fault divorce between believers and unbelievers. Believers are free to indulge their itch to believe without worrying about intellectual attacks upon it, while unbelievers can cheerfully ignore religion as an emotional refuge for the tender-minded. Best of all, both parties can continue happily in the same lodges, country-clubs, and PTAs without unseemly bouts of "divisiveness."

Convenient as this arrangement no doubt is, intellectually it makes for a muddle. First, and contrary to a silly judicial doctrine, philosophical argument about God and religious faith in Him are two quite different things. Second, faith needs stronger foundations than the probabilities of science, not weaker ones. Third, in the realm of probable, statistical argument the existence of God is not a matter of "faith" but of proof. This is what Mortimer Adler meant by his insistence on a purely "pagan" or philosophical way of thinking and talking about God.[47] A good argument for God, said Adler, is logically just like an argument for the existence of sub-atomic particles, which also are known not by direct observation but from "traces" or effects.[48] It should be noted, too, that while this chapter has concentrated only on one single line of argument for the existence of God, such arguments may be framed quite apart from the whole Paley/Darwin business. In fact, this is what most modern framers of such arguments do.[49]

We now come to the emotional attraction of atheism. Not long ago two physicists were interviewed over a Chicago radio station. They gave fascinating accounts of the intricate structure of matter and of the universe. The host then asked the physicists whether in view of all this seemingly purposeful order, they believed in God. "No," replied one of them, "because if we did, we should have to live very different lives." How refreshingly honest! Aldous Huxley put it like this: "I had motives for not wanting the world to have a meaning; consequently assumed that it had none. . . . For myself the philosophy of meaninglessness was essentially an instrument of liberation, sexual and political."[50]

The tragic figure of Nietzsche is typical here. He lost his clergyman father at a tender age. His dismal childhood then cramped his mind,

47. Mortimer J. Adler, *How To Think About God* (New York: Macmillan, 1980), 9.
48. Mortimer J. Adler, *The Angels and Us* (New York: Macmillan, 1982), 56.
49. Adler, *How To Think About God*; J. Smith, *Reason, Science, and Paradox*; Richard Swinburne, *The Coherence of Theism* (Oxford: Clarendon, 1977) and *The Existence of God* (Oxford: Clarendon, 1979).
50. Aldous Huxley, *Ends and Means* (New York: Harper, 1937), 270 ff.

beneath the veneer of philosophy, into a lifelong tantrum against God. In one revealing passage Nietzsche insists that the "question of the mere 'truth' of Christianity" is "secondary." It is Christian morality which must be fought tooth and nail as a "capital crime against life."[51] Also, Nietzsche bitterly blamed Luther, "this calamity of a monk," for having "restored the church and, what is a thousand times worse, Christianity, at the very moment *when it was vanquished*," defeated, that is, by the noble paganism of the Renaissance, which "had triumphed at the seat of the opposite values—*even in the very instincts of those who were sitting there*."[52]

Sartre, too, clenching his little fist against God, was moved by something other than a syllogism.[53] Marx, Lenin,[54] and Stalin[55] all were delighted to find in Darwin's *Origin of Species* a scientific excuse for their atheism.

The real emotional appeal of atheism, however, lies at a still deeper level. To quote Nietzsche again: "I abhor Christianity with a deadly hatred, because it created sublime words and gestures to throw over a horrible reality the cloak of justice, virtue, and divinity."[56] Perhaps no one has put the matter more poignantly, from a Christian point of view, than John Henry Newman. While admitting the intellectual force of the arguments for God's existence, Newman remarked: ". . . but these do not warm me or enlighten me; they do not take away the winter of my desolation. . . . The sight of the world is nothing else than the prophet's scroll, full of 'lamentations, and mourning, and woe.'" His description is worth citing in full:

> To consider the world in its length and breadth, its various history, the many races of man, their starts, their fortunes, their mutual alienation,

---

51. Nietzsche, *Will to Power*, 152.
52. Walter Kaufmann, trans. and ed., *Basic Writings of Nietzsche* (New York: Modern Library, 1968), 776 (italics original).
53. Jean-Paul Sartre, *Words* (London: Penguin, 1967), 62–65, cited in Colin Chapman, *Christianity on Trial*, vol. 2, *Questions of God, Man, and the Universe* (Berkhamsted, Hertfordshire: Lion, 1974), 31.
54. Alain Besancon, *The Rise of the Gulag: Intellectual Origins of Leninism* (New York: Continuum, 1981), 8, 207–208.
55. E. Yoarslavsky, *Landmarks in the Life of Stalin* (Moscow: Foreign Languages Publishing House, 1940), 8–9: "G. Glurdjidze, a boyhood friend of Stalin, relates [an early conversation he had with Stalin]: . . . 'I'll lend you a book to read; it will show you that the world and all living things are quite different from what you imagine, and all this talk about God is sheer nonsense,' Joseph said. 'What book is that?' I enquired. 'Darwin. You must read it.'"
56. Nietzsche, *Will to Power*, 364.

their conflicts; and then their ways, habits, governments, forms of worship; their enterprises, their aimless courses, their random achievements and acquirements, the impotent conclusion of long-standing facts, the tokens so faint and broken of a superintending design, the blind evolution of what turn out to be great powers or truths, the progress of things, as if from unreasoning elements, not towards final causes, the greatness and littleness of man, his far-reaching aims, his short duration, the curtain hung over his futurity, the disappointments of life, the defeat of good, the success of evil, physical pain, mental anguish, the prevalence and intensity of sin, the pervading idolatries, the corruptions, the dreary hopeless irreligion, that condition of the whole race, so fearfully yet exactly described in the Apostle's words, "having no hope and without God in the world,"—all this is a vision to dizzy and appal; and inflicts upon the mind the sense of a profound mystery, which is absolutely beyond human solution.

We come face to face here with the "heart-piercing, reason-bewildering" problem of evil. Looking at the teeming, bustling vitality of our world and finding there no reflexion of its Creator, says Newman, is like looking into a mirror and not seeing one's face. Something is very wrong. "I can only answer," says Newman, "that either there is no Creator, or this living society of men is in a true sense discarded from His presence." Therefore:

> *if* there be a God, *since* there is a God, the human race is implicated in some terrible aboriginal calamity. It is out of joint with the purposes of its Creator. This is a fact, a fact as true as the fact of its existence; and thus the doctrine of what is theologically called original sin becomes to me almost as certain as that the world exists, and as the existence of God.[57]

This baffling problem of evil was of course recognised long before Newman. Psalms 37 and 73, for instance, already address it. Luther saw that common sense is up against the radical dilemma

> either that there is no God or that God is unjust. As [Ovid] says: "Oft I am moved to think there are no gods!" For look at the prosperity the wicked enjoy and the adversity the good endure, and note how both proverbs and that parent of proverbs, experience, testify that the bigger the scoundrel the greater his luck.[58]

---

57. J. H. Newman, *Apologia Pro Vita Sua*, ed. David J. deLaura (New York: Norton, 1968), 186–187 (italics original).
58. AE 33, 291.

All the furies of modern unbelief are matched—and check-mated!—in Luther's terrible pronouncement that in our sort of world, "before [God] can be God he must first appear to be the Devil."[59]

Luther saw more clearly here than Paley. Paley wanted nature to show not only that God exists, but also that He is good and kind. This linking of two quite different questions later proved fateful.

When the Victorian optimism that "God's in His heaven, all's right with the world" (Browning) collapsed amid the horrors of World War I, many people thought atheism the only honest alternative left. What they did not see, and perhaps could not, was that the god who perished in the flames of Europe's self-destruction was not the living God of the prophets and apostles. No, this "deity" had been a sentimental fraud made up by two centuries of liberal German theology. Malcolm Muggeridge once called this god an empty skin stuffed with Freudian entrails. This cosmic Santa Claus was incapable of judgment, wrath, or punishment. His chief duty was the maintenance of decent levels of jollity for all. The Great War proved this god's incompetence or his gross dereliction of duty, and so he was dismissed by a dissatisfied electorate.

Many, then, were done with a Christianity which they thought had failed. Others were moved by the same events in an opposite direction. They came to see that what had been smashed was only a sentimental veneer that had falsely represented itself as the real thing. D. R. Davies, for instance, left us a moving account of this sort of pilgrimage.[60] He showed how the events of our century shattered his optimistic Enlightenment faith in the innate goodness of man and drove him back to a sober Christian realism about sin and grace, divine judgment and mercy. Evil turned out to be not some feature of the social system, but a deep-seated cancer inoperably lodged in the very vitals of human nature. That of course was just what Christianity had said—until the 18th century Enlightenment came along with its flattering fables about a human race "come of age."

The fact of God and the fact of evil stand out as two quite different issues. Mixing them up can prove very misleading.[61] "God exists," as a truth of philosophy or common sense, is not the same thing at all as the Christian conviction that "God loves us." Actual cruelty in the world falsifies neither of these propositions, but for different reasons.

---

59. Quoted in Roland H. Bainton, *Here I Stand* (New York: Mentor, 1950), 169.

60. D. R. Davies, *On to Orthodoxy* (New York: Macmillan, 1949).

61. For a classic example see Antony Flew, "Theology and Falsification," in M. L. Diamond and T. V. Litzenburg, eds., *The Logic of God* (Indianapolis, IN: Bobbs-Merrill, 1975), 257 ff.

That "some sort of God exists" is, as we have seen, a highly probable inference from the nature of the world in general and of bio-information in particular. The odds against randomness, and therefore in favour of a creative Intelligence, or "some sort of God," are simply overwhelming. To reject this conclusion just because one does not like the sight of a nature "red in tooth and claw" is to abandon reason for emotion. The disturbing reality of evil cannot logically undo the reasonable conclusion that an information-rich nature must have been "programmed" by a superior Intelligence.

Yet Christians do not hold that "God loves us" because of statistics, including numbers comparing the relative incidence of good or ill fortune in an average population. Nor is the conviction that "God loves us" at all a mushy optimism about life in general. Rather, this belief rests squarely on specific words and promises anchored in the cross and resurrection of Jesus Christ.

Can such a belief be falsified? In principle, yes. The Christian content of "God loves us" stands or falls with the integrity of the New Testament portrait of Jesus as God Incarnate. Disprove that, and "God loves us" becomes a chimera. If the New Testament picture of God is true, though, then it is also true that *He* loves *us*. All the world's ghastliness can only highlight this fact.

Luther's famous Heidelberg Disputation of 1518 makes these matters very clear. He writes there that a person who merely makes inferences about God from nature "does not deserve to be called a theologian."[62] Such a person is engaging simply in natural theology. So-called "natural theology" is not theology at all, however, but philosophy. Luther was very far from denying either the validity (Rom. 1:20) or the social and cultural value (Rom. 2:14–15) of a "natural" or philosophical knowledge about God.

Only when this philosophy pretends to be theology does trouble begin, for it then makes of itself more than it can possibly be. Such philosophy-theology, in which medieval scholastics took some pride, having thought itself very clever to have sniffed out God's tracks in nature, goes on to imagine its divine Prey available on reasonable human terms. This conceit confuses a modest inference of "some sort of God" with a personal knowledge of Him. That is like presuming an intimate acquaintance with someone on the basis of a few foot-prints seen on the beach.

---

62. Heidelberg Disputation, Thesis 19 (AE 31, 40). Thesis 19, it should be noted, is badly mistranslated in this edition. The reference to Rom. 1:20 makes it perfectly clear that Luther means "things which *have been made*," not "which have actually happened." Luther was not disparaging the facts of God's saving work as proclaimed in Holy Scripture!

None of this will do, of course. A real knowledge of God comes not from philosophical detective work, however brilliant, but only from God's own self-disclosure. He is to be found only where He chooses to make himself available, not where we may find it sensible or convenient to locate Him.

Who then is a real theologian? Luther replies: only he "who comprehends the visible and manifest things of God seen through suffering and the cross."[63] The allusion here is to Exodus 33:23, where Moses is allowed to see the "back" of God. We meet God not in haughty flights of fancy or feats of intelligence, but under the humble "masks" in which He gives Himself: the Baby in Bethlehem, the Man on the Cross, baptismal water, life-giving words, consecrated bread and wine.

This is Luther's great "theology of the cross."[64] Its opposite is an arrogant "theology of glory," which thinks it has trapped and domesticated God but is really only talking to itself.

"Natural theology" of the sort found in the American Declaration of Independence, which appeals to "the laws of nature and of nature's God," seemed bold and liberating in the days of Thomas Jefferson. It did not bind one, after all, to the revealed Christian mysteries and miracles. Then came Darwin, who, in the words of Sir Arthur Keith, did more than anyone else to lift "the pall of superstition" from mankind. Now, for an emancipated contemporary intelligentsia spoilt on Darwin, even the old natural theology seems much too constraining. The implication that the universe has a built-in moral order enrages those addicted to the drug of unbridled moral and cultural relativism.

And with Darwinian props crumbling, what will happen to our leading cultural hallucinations? They will hardly fade away meekly in favour of a large-scale return to natural theology. The likely direction of post-Darwinian drift may be gauged from Hoyle's and Wickramasinghe's odd speculations about hierarchies of extra-terrestrial "intelligences."[65] The New Age mix of occultism, Eastern mysticism, and California hype is well able to supply whatever cosmic "intelligences" are needed to keep the Darwinian corpse twitching and lurching in a parody of life.

"Psychic phenomena" lend sufficient scientific credibility to this natural theology substitute. Marilyn Ferguson's *The Aquarian Conspiracy*

63. Heidelberg Disputation, Thesis 20 (AE 31, 40).
64. For a classic treatment see H. Sasse, "The Theology of the Cross," in *We Confess Jesus Christ* (St. Louis, MO: Concordia Publishing House, 1984), 36–54.
65. Hoyle and Wickramsinghe, *Evolution from Space*, 129–145.

documents in detail the enormous cultural appeal of the trendy Mystical Mush. Feeling, intuition, and direct experience are its guides, not doctrines, authority, or sacraments. Even a prominent physicist is persuaded, apparently, that the universe is pulsating in a cosmic "Dance of Shiva," the Hindu god of death.[66] In our Western world a pseudo-Hindu occultism was popularised by theosophy and anthroposophy. For a striking example of how this form of occultism can be used to save evolution from the quicksands of randomness and Natural Selection, the reader is referred to *The Loom of Creation*, by British academics Dennis Milner and Edward Smart. Their book is sub-titled suggestively, "a study of the purpose and the forces that weave the pattern of existence."[67]

Occultism and mysticism allow our self-indulgent "public opinion" to enjoy the best of both worlds. On the one hand, there is no cramping moral order, like that of the old natural theology. The mushy normlessness of "self-realisation" leaves one free to fornicate, abort, and divorce at will, and to vibrate all the closer for it to the inner harmonies of the cosmos! On the other hand, mysticism fills up the yawning void of a meaningless universe. In a sense, it is true that the coarsest "third world" witchcraft is closer to the mark than the Western university superstition that everything came from nothing by itself. Animism at least knows that there's more to the universe than meets the eye.

The fundamental flaw of mysticism or "enthusiasm" ("God within") is simply, to quote G. K. Chesterton, that it is the worst possible of all false religions. "That Jones shall worship the god within him turns out ultimately to mean that Jones shall worship Jones."[68] Or, as Ronald Knox famously quipped: "Fanaticism feels it knows not what. Faith knows what it does not feel." The instinctive preference for a shapeless mysticism over the discipline of intellectual and moral order is no doubt related to man's tendency, observed by Kipling, to fudge and to compromise, so that

> Very rarely will he squarely push the logic of a fact
> To its ultimate conclusion in unmitigated act.[69]

---

66. Marilyn Ferguson, *The Aquarian Conspiracy* (Los Angeles, CA: Tarcher, 1980), 374.
67. D. Milner and E. Smart, *The Loom of Creation* (New York: Harper & Row, 1976), 234–282. This book includes a valuable annotated bibliography.
68. Gilbert K. Chesterton, *Orthodoxy* (New York: Dodd, Mead, and Company, 1959), 138.
69. Rudyard Kipling in *The Oxford Dictionary of Quotations* (Oxford University Press, 1979), 299.

WHY THEN CHRISTIANITY?

The existence of God, some sort of God, does not the end the discussion but simply begins it. Only at this point do things really get interesting. For the question then arises quite inevitably: Which God?

This is the point where many simply throw up their hands and say: with all the many religions in the world, each one claiming to be the only truth, on what possible grounds should one of these religions be preferred to all the others? The trouble is that people generally have become accustomed to a shallow alphabetical-table treatment of religions which makes them all look more or less the same. The reality is very different.

Actually, the world's major religions may be numbered on one's fingers: Hinduism, Confucianism, Taoism, Buddhism, Judaism, Christianity, and Islam. Apart from these one finds mainly animism and local cults like Shintoism. The Eastern religions at their best do not claim to be divine revelations at all. Rather, they present themselves as the accumulated wisdom of great sages. They tend to pessimism and scepticism to the point of atheism, as in original Buddhism.[70] As for the great historical religions, they diverge from common roots. Judaism and Christianity differ over whether Jesus is or is not the real culmination and fulfillment of the Old Testament. Islam is but a flamboyant adaptation of Christianity to Mohammed's claim that he was "the" ultimate prophet.

The modern tendency is to fob off the various religions with the *Alice in Wonderland* maxim that "all have won and all must have prizes." The whole notion of "religious language" may be said to have been invented for this very purpose. In "religious language" things are supposed to be "true" in some sense other than the "ordinary" meaning of truth. Stripped of scholarly jargon, the basic idea is that in religion any lot of nonsense can be "true" if only somebody is sincere about it.

Prof. J. N. D. (Sir Norman) Anderson, then at the Institute of Advanced Legal Studies in the University of London, was told once by a Muslim colleague that what mattered in religion was not so much the truth or falsity of the basic facts, but whether the religion in question made a person happier and more helpful. Anderson's response to this widespread pragmatism is worth noting:

> I replied—somewhat flippantly, I fear—that when I was a boy at school we played a football match against what was then called a lunatic asylum.

---

70. J. N. D. Anderson, ed., *The World's Religions* (Grand Rapids, MI: Eerdmans, 1972), 99 ff. See also, by the same scholar, *Christianity and Comparative Religion* (London: Tyndale, 1970).

(I vividly remember being locked in while we changed our clothes, so that we should not get mixed up with the other lunatics!) And we were told that one of the patients in that institution firmly believed that he was a poached egg, and went about every day asking for a piece of toast to sit on. If he was given this, he at once became contented and amenable, while if it was withheld he remained unhappy and fractious. But I could hardly believe that my Muslim friend would regard that as an adequate religion![71]

This issue arose already at the beginning of the Christian era. The Roman Empire was quite sophisticated about religion. All sorts of exotic new cults were regularly brought to Rome by its victorious armies from the remote outposts of the empire. Rome would gladly have accommodated the Christian religion too, had it not been for the latter's exclusive claims. The insistence of Christians that Jesus alone is the Way, the Truth, and the Life—not Jupiter and Venus, Isis and Osiris, Mithra, Cybele, and the rest—infuriated tolerant Romans. Christians were perceived as arrogant and subversive atheists.

Yet the Christians' grating insistence on truth and fact also had to be respected. The other religions all had "once-upon-a-time" stories to tell, of course. There were no historical particulars, though, and certainly no eye-witnesses. It proved enormously impressive when Christianity came along and calmly described the most extraordinary events which had happened in datable time and in real space: beginning in Bethlehem, under Caesar Augustus, when Quirinius was governor of Syria, and culminating at a cross and an empty tomb after a public trial and mob scenes before Pontius Pilate.

These reports, furthermore, had not come from scheming scholars, overwrought aesthetes, or religious visionaries. They came from down-to-earth folk like fishermen and tax-officials, people full of a very normal reluctance to believe (Luke 24:25; John 20:24–29). How then was this unlikely crew brought to its later unshakable convictions? Certainly not with breathing exercises and meditations in vision-prone grottoes! No, the Lord simply made the apostles trot along with Him for three years, in the broad light of day, with their eyes and ears open and their minds fully engaged. In the end He rose from the dead, as He had said He would, knowing full well that anyone determined to reject the claims of God would "not be convinced even if someone rises from the dead" (Luke 16:31).

---

71. J. N. D. Anderson, *Christianity: The Witness of History* (London: Tyndale, 1969), 8.

Everything all hinges on the truth of the resurrexion. When the modern Bible translator J. B. Phillips came to the fifteenth chapter of First Corinthians, he was struck by the impact of this matter-of-fact account: "Quite suddenly I realised that *no man had ever written such words before.* As I pressed on with the task of translation I came to feel utterly convinced of the truth of the resurrexion. Something of literally life-and-death importance had happened in mortal history, and I was reading the actual words of people who had seen Christ after his resurrexion."[72] In a broadcast discussion with another translator of the Gospels, Dr. E. V. Rieu, Phillips asked: "Did you get the feeling that the whole material is extraordinarily alive?" Rieu replied: "It . . . changed me; my work changed me. And I came to the conclusion that these words bear the seal of . . . the Son of Man and God."[73] In a similar vein, the exquisite wordsmith Malcolm Muggeridge wrote: "Is it not extraordinary to the point of being a miracle, that so loose and ill-constructed a narrative in an antique translation of a dubious text should after so many centuries still have power to quell and dominate a restless, opinionated, over-exercised and under-nourished twentieth-century mind?"[74]

The "dubious" nature of the text is actually more rhetoric than reality. Oft-quoted is the verdict of Sir Frederic G. Kenyon, a former Director and Principal Librarian of the British Museum: "The interval then between the dates of original composition and the earliest extant evidence becomes so small as to be in fact negligible . . . Both the *authenticity* and the *general integrity* of the books of the New Testament may be regarded as finally established."[75]

As for the idea that the New Testament offers camp-fire stories and legends, Prof. Schadewald, the distinguished "graecist" of Tuebingen University, replies that if the New Testament with its conscientious interest in the facts is legend, "then no scholarly study of ancient history exists at all."[76] The Oxford classicist A. N. Sherwin-White likewise finds it "astonishing."

72. J. B. Phillips, *Ring of Truth* (London: Hodder & Stoughton, 1967), 26–27.
73. Phillips, *Ring of Truth*, 56.
74. Malcolm Muggeridge, *Jesus Rediscovered* (London: Fontana Books, 1969), 37.
75. Quoted in John Warwick Montgomery, *Where Is History Going?: Essays in Support of the Historical Truth of the Christian Revelation* (Grand Rapids, MI: Zondervan, 1969), 45 (italics original).
76. Reported in W. Kuenneth, "Die Grundlagenkrisis der Theologie Heute." Essay read to the Council of the European Evangelical Alliance, London, September, 1968, 11.

that while Graeco-Roman historians have been growing in confidence, the twentieth-century study of the Gospel narratives, starting from no less promising material, has taken so gloomy a turn in the development of form criticism that the more advanced exponents of it apparently maintain—so far as an amateur can understand the matter—that the historical Christ is unknowable and the history of his mission cannot be written.[77]

The point here is not the inspiration and inerrancy of the sacred text, which is an article of faith. The present point is simply the New Testament's historical integrity. In this sense Sherwin-White says that to reject the "basic historicity" of the Book of Acts, for instance, "even in matters of detail must now appear absurd. Roman historians have long taken it for granted."[78]

We may conclude with a literary judgment and a legal one. C. S. Lewis wrote:

> I have been reading poems, romances, vision-literature, legends, myths all my life. I know what they are like. I know that not one of them is like this. Of this text there are only two possible views. Either this is reportage—though it may no doubt contain errors—pretty close up to the facts; nearly as close as Boswell. Or else, some unknown writer in the second century, without known predecessors or successors, suddenly anticipated the whole technique of modern, novelistic, realistic narrative. If it is untrue, it must be narrative of that kind. The reader who doesn't see this has simply not learned to read.

Sir Norman Anderson, who cites the above from C. S. Lewis,[79] records his own considered judgment in a study styled as, "A lawyer sifts the evidence for the life, death, and resurrexion of Jesus Christ":

> The idea that these stories might have been legends rather than lies seems at first sight somewhat more plausible. Had it been possible to date the records a century or two after the event—and repeated attempts to do precisely this have been made by a series of brilliant scholars—the suggestion might have been feasible. But the attempt has decisively failed, crushed under a weight of contrary evidence; and there can be no reason-

77. A. N. Sherwin-White, *Roman Society and Roman Law in the New Testament* (Grand Rapids, MI: Baker, 1978), 187.
78. Sherwin-White, 189.
79. J. N. D. Anderson, *A Lawyer Among the Theologians* (London: Hodder & Stoughton, 1973), 11.

able doubt that the testimony to the resurrexion can be traced back to the very first decade after the event. It seems meaningless, therefore, to speak of legend when we are dealing, not with stories handed down from generation to generation, but accounts given by the eyewitnesses themselves or attributed to them while they were still present to confirm or deny them.[80]

From the very beginning, Christianity wished either to be accepted at face value or not at all. It is more honest to stone Jesus for blasphemy than to mutter vaguely about His "great ethical teaching" while rejecting His claim to be God. Faith in Him is certainly more than belief in facts, but it is not less. Sages and illiterates, housewives and presidents, reformers and harlots, all are leveled before Him in their common need, which only He can supply.

---

80. Anderson, *Christianity: The Witness of History*, 90–91.

INDICES

SACRED SCRIPTURE INDEX

LUTHERAN CONFESSIONS INDEX

FC Solid Declaration

NAME AND SUBJECT INDEX

AE 40, 214 • 83
AE 41, 137–138 • 16
AE 41, 199 • 134n
AE 43, 200 • 71
AE 45, 70 • 133n
AE 49, 323–324 • 147
AE 53 • 89n
AE 54, 476 • 10, 66
AE 97 • 89n
AE 107 • 89n

M

Marquart • ix–xv
Marx • 170
Marxist, Marxism • 19, 64, 159, 168n
Mary, Mother of God • 44, 53
Means of Grace • 69, 97
Methodism • 116
millenialism • 149–150
Millennium • 149, 152
Milner, Dennis • 175
Modernists • 48
Monod, Jacques • 164, 166
Muggeridge, Malcolm • 155n, 172, 178

N

Nagel, Norman • x, 119n
Needham, Joseph • 162
Newman, John Henry • 170–171
Newton, Sir Isaac • 21, 164
Nietzsche, Friedrich • 154–155, 170

O

Oesch, Wilhelm • x

P

Packer, James • 8–9
Paley, William • 157–158, 160, 162, 167, 169, 172
papacy • 18, 127, 130, 145
Pelagius • 133
Pentecost • 7, 80–81, 99, 100, 124,

Pentecostal, Pentecostalism • 79, 98–99, 116
Pieper, Franz • ix, xii, 60n
Plato • 159
Poe, Edgar Allen • 24
pope • 14–15, 19–20, 103, 130
Pope, Alexander • 21
Popper, Sir Karl • 161, 165
Preus, J. A. O. • x
Preus, Robert D. • xi, xii, xiii, xv, 33
Prince William of Bavaria • 14

R

rationalism • 22
Real Presence • 101–104, 107, 108
Renan (French infidel) • 154
Roman Catholic • 16, 25, 30, 102, 110, 127, 132, 139, 142
Ruse, Michael • 159
Russell, Bertrand • 154

S

Sacrament • 22, 84, 87–88, 96, 117, 144
Sacrament of the Altar (see also Lord's Supper) • 85, 101, 103, 108–119, 123–124
Sacramental union • 107
Sagan • 154
Salet, Georges • 166
sanctification • 47–48, 55–58, 63, 66–67
Sartre • 170
Sasse, Herman • x, 102n, 174n
Schadewald, Prof. • 178
Schleiermacher, F. • 22
Scripture • 3–18, 20–24, 26–28, 31, 33–46, 48, 53, 56–57, 70–71, 75, 77, 133–134, 143, 147–152
Shape of the Liturgy, The • 112
Sherwin-White, A. N. • 178–179
Smart, Edward • 175
Socinians • 48